The
American
Revolution

THE
AMERICAN
REVOLUTION
★ *A Global War* ★

R. Ernest Dupuy
Gay Hammerman
Grace P. Hayes

David McKay Company, Inc.
NEW YORK

MAP CREDITS: *pp. 83 and 238 from* Geography and Map Division, Library of Congress; *pp. 85, 105, 185, 205 and 224 from* Trevor Nevitt Dupuy and Grace Person Hayes, THE MILITARY HISTORY OF THE REVOLUTIONARY WAR NAVAL BATTLES. Copyright © 1970 by Franklin Watts, Inc. Reprinted by permission; *p. 143 from* U.S. Naval History Division, Department of the Navy. THE AMERICAN REVOLUTION, 1775-1783; AN ATLAS OF 18th CENTURY MAPS AND CHARTS: THEATERS OF OPERATIONS. Washington: U.S. Government Printing Office, 1972; *p. 202 from* E. B. Potter and Chester W. Nimitz, Eds., SEA POWER: A NAVAL HISTORY. Copyright © 1960. Reprinted by permission of Prentice-Hall, Inc., Englewood Cliffs, New Jersey.

Library of Congress Cataloging in Publication Data

Dupuy, Richard Ernest, 1887-1975.
    The American Revolution, a global war.

    Bibliography: p.
    Includes index.
        1.   United States—History—Revolution, 1775-1783—
Foreign participation.   2.   United States—Foreign relations—Revolution, 1775-1783.   3.   United States—
Foreign relations—Europe.   4.   Europe—Foreign relations—United States.   I.   Hammerman, Gay M., joint
author.   II.   Hayes, Grace P., jount author.   III.   Title.
E269.F67D86   973.3   76-13151
ISBN 0-679-50648-9

Contents

Preface

Not surprisingly, Americans have always viewed the War of the American Revolution as an entirely American conflict. We fought for our independence. The French who fought here came "to help us." And that was that.

The typical American view of the Revolutionary War has also largely limited it to the events that took place along the eastern seaboard of the thirteen states, and perhaps the fight between the *Bonhomme Richard* and the *Serapis*.

Probably few Americans know that the Spanish and Dutch were also in the war, or that the French and British fought naval battles off the coast of India as part of the war, or that eight islands in the Caribbean were captured by the French or British during the course of the war. Most naval histories of the American Revolution by Americans do not even mention such famous naval battles as that of the Saints, where Rodney broke eighteenth-century naval doctrine as dramatically as he broke through the French line. Even a resounding British defeat in what is now the United States, like the capture of Pensacola by the Spanish governor of Louisiana, is generally forgotten. As for the complicated European power struggles that lay behind the battles, the secret agents traveling back and forth across Europe with plans for sending supplies to the American rebels or peace feelers from one foreign minister to another, or Empress Catherine the Great's league of neutral nations, only historians are likely to associate them with the War for American Independence.

The idea of telling the story of the Revolutionary War as the world war it was, the first world war in which the United States fought, was that of R. Ernest Dupuy, Colonel, U.S.A., retired.

Colonel Dupuy, author and coauthor of numerous books on
military history, brought to this task a unique background that
fitted it well. As a working newspaperman in his youth and a
popular writer all his life, he loved a good story. As a professional soldier and student of military history, he himself knew
well all the worldwide events of the Revolutionary War that are
strange to most Americans. And as the son of a French father
who always maintained his family ties in France, he had a special
feeling for the French and European involvement in the war.

From the beginning, it was agreed that the three of us would
work together on the book. Colonel Dupuy would write the
chapters dealing with land forces. Grace Hayes, a former naval
officer and coauthor of an earlier book on Revolutionary War
naval battles, would deal with the naval war, which forms an
important part of the international conflict. Gay Hammerman,
whose academic training is in modern European history,
although she has worked in military history for twenty years,
would handle the diplomatic parts of the book. And we would all
read and revise each other's work to achieve a unified whole.

Colonel Dupuy became ill in January 1975 and died in April of
that year. He left notes on his extensive research, and draft
chapters on the French forces in North America and on Bernardo de Gálvez. We have incorporated his work and have
redivided responsibility for the book, with Gay Hammerman
taking on most of Colonel Dupuy's remaining chapters and the
story of the war in the Caribbean, while Grace Hayes took on the
fighting in India. We have read and revised each other's work
thoroughly, and the book is in reality a joint product.

We are especially grateful to Colonel Dupuy's son, Trevor N.
Dupuy, for reading the manuscript and giving us helpful suggestions, indispensable corrections, and welcome support.

Knowing Colonel Dupuy as we did, we have been constantly
aware as we worked of the approach he would have taken to the
material—scrupulously honest, but always lively. We have tried
to be guided by it.

Gay Hammerman
Grace P. Hayes

I

WHAT WENT BEFORE

1

The Global Framework

Most Americans think of the Revolutionary War as a series of land battles in New England, New York, Pennsylvania, and the Carolinas, culminating in General Cornwallis's surrender at Yorktown, Virginia. But the war in North America was in fact the hub of a much larger war, a war that extended around the earth to the shores of India, fought by men speaking many languages and owing their primary allegiance not to the cause of freedom for thirteen colonies but to kings and potentates far from the shores of the western Atlantic. The war of 1775-1783 was, in fact, a global war.

In this war, Frenchmen fought Englishmen on the Atlantic and Indian oceans while polyglot armies battled from New England to Georgia, Spaniards fought Englishmen on the shores of the Mississippi, amphibious forces seized Caribbean islands, British troops captured a Dutch trading base in Ceylon, and Britain's own home islands were raided by an American naval hero whom the British described as "the Scotch renegade Paul Jones." A new nation was born, helped into the world by men who cared little for the cause of the United States of America.

Not only was the American Revolution a global war, it was in part a rekindling of a global war that had preceded it by a dozen years, a war in which the North American colonies of Great Britain had played a peripheral but by no means insignificant role. This was the Seven Years' War, known in America as the French and Indian War, called by Winston Churchill "the first world war," and named by a growing group of Anglo-American historians the Great War for the Empire. It was because the American Revolution offered a chance to redress their losses in this Great War for the Empire that France and Spain entered the new war that started at Lexington and Concord, thus extending that fight for freedom into a worldwide conflict.

3

Colonies and Power in the Eighteenth Century

Trade was power in the eighteenth century, and a country's wealth and power depended upon its moving its goods to the markets of the world by sea, and protecting its commerce upon the ocean's paths. Empire was not sought for splotches of territory on a map, or even for masses of people, although it was generally believed that large populations were desirable. Empire was sought first for gold and silver, and then for contributions to trade warfare. Nations could buy goods for export from their colonies at moderate prices. Rice, tobacco, sugar, cotton, dried fish, hemp for rope, and the dye-yielding indigo plant—all of these came from Europe's colonies. Some went to manufacturers in the home country. Others were re-exported just as they arrived. All contributed to the wealth and power of the empires.

The colonies, in turn, served as markets for goods manufactured in the mother country. In North America, for example, the colonies bought from England such luxuries as silver, china, fine furniture, and sparkling flint glasses—and more essential things, like cotton and linen fabrics, warm woolen cloth, and guns. A system of taxation—in the British Empire it was embodied in the Navigation Acts—encouraged colonists to buy goods manufactured in the home country and to ship their raw materials to home-country ports.

Thus to the great powers of Europe in the eighteenth century colonies were important, and the merchant ships that plied the seas between the colonies and the home ports were vital. They had to be protected, particularly during periods of war. Hence, to the maritime powers a powerful navy was essential. Nations would go to war in order to gain and to protect colonies and trade.

The French and Indian War

The Seven Years' War started in America in 1754 in a small frontier incident. To forestall a move by the French from Canada, young Lieutenant Colonel George Washington was sent by the British royal governor of Virginia to fortify the strategic spot at the confluence of the Monongahela and Allegheny rivers that commanded the head of the Ohio River. When Washington and his men reached the place where Pittsburgh now stands, he found that the French had arrived before him. So he hastily built his own little fort—appropriately named Fort Necessity—some distance away on unfavorable terrain. He soon had to surrender it to a French attack.

When word of this reached King George II and his minister, the duke of Newcastle, they decided to respond to the French move into Pennsylvania. They sent Major General Edward Braddock to Virginia to take command of British and colonial forces and oust the French. Braddock conferred with the governors of six colonies, and they planned attacks on four key French strongholds—Fort Beauséjour on Nova Scotia's Bay of Fundy, Fort Duquesne at the Pittsburgh site, Crown Point on Lake Champlain, and Fort Niagara between Lake Erie and Lake Ontario. All of these commanded important waterways. Without them, movement into the interior of the continent was limited. Seizing them would prevent the French from achieving their apparent purpose of encircling and constricting the British colonists, of keeping them permanently locked between the ocean and the Allegheny Mountains.

The attack on Fort Beauséjour was successful. The British also defeated the French in the Battle of Lake George, part way to Crown Point, although they never tried to take Crown Point itself. The Niagara expedition left Albany, got halfway to its objective, and then turned back when news of French reinforcements made the project seem foolhardy.

Braddock himself led the expedition to Fort Duquesne. It was carefully prepared, but his reconnaissance forces were inadequate. He needed Indian scouts to tell him what his enemy was up to, and he had not provided himself with any. Moreover, he had no screening arm to protect the front and flanks of his main force from surprise. His column of marching redcoats was ambushed by the French and their Indian allies just short of Duquesne. Unable to regroup his scattered troops to meet the French and Indian attack effectively, Braddock went to his death along with half his command. His rear guard—with Washington as one of its officers—was able to withdraw successfully.

Braddock's defeat in this Battle of the Monongahela caused the British army to adopt more flexible tactics and led to the creation of "light" companies. Despite American folklore about the foolish rigidity of the redcoats during the American Revolution, the British learned much from Braddock's defeat, and from their other experiences in this novel frontier conflict.

The Seven Years' War

The outbreak of the Seven Years' War in Europe was unrelated to the war in America. It grew out of a shift in the pattern of alliances called the Diplomatic Revolution of 1756—a series of ally swappings that left Frederick II, the Great, of Prussia, threatened by alliances of hostile powers and rulers, and supported only by a defensive alliance with Great Britain. Frederick was a great military strategist, tactician, and organizer, but he was far from great in diplomatic judgment. Expecting attack from Austria, France, Russia, Sweden, and Saxony, he struck first, invading Saxony; he succeeded only in solidifying the coalition against him. The war was on between Prussia and England on one side and the powers of the anti-Prussian coalition on the other. England and France, already fighting in North America, declared war on each other.

Britain then had to decide whether to concentrate on the war overseas or the war in Europe, and how to distribute its men and weapons. The great William Pitt, at the height of his powers, became leader of the government in 1757. He decided that there would be an all-out war against France for the empire in North America and India, and that there would also be effective help to Prussia in the European war. By remarkable feats of organization and superb choices of commanders, Pitt was able to bring it all off—although the support to Prussia did not meet Frederick's expectations.

The War in America

As the war in North America began in earnest in 1756, the British were faced with a new French commander, the able Marquis Louis Joseph de Montcalm de Saint-Véran. No sooner had he arrived to take command of the French forces in Canada than he crossed Lake Ontario to capture and destroy the British settlement at Oswego. The next year he forced the British to abandon an attack on Louisburg, the strategic French post guarding the ocean entrance to the Gulf of St. Lawrence. Then Montcalm moved down from Fort Ticonderoga, his base south of Crown Point, and captured Fort William Henry, at the southern tip of Lake George. Pitt countered by sending two excellent British generals to lead the struggling British and colonial force.

In 1758 General Jeffrey Amherst and young Brigadier General James Wolfe, with effective help from the British navy, succeeded in taking Louisburg after hard fighting, gaining for the British the key to the St. Lawrence River and thus to Canada.

Ticonderoga held against a determined British attack, but Fort Duquesne, where the war had started, was taken by British troops and renamed Fort Pitt. Fort Frontenac, across Lake Ontario from Oswego, also fell to the British, and Pitt made plans to crush the French in 1759.

After taking Ticonderoga and Crown Point in July 1759, British soldiers headed for Quebec. For two months, Wolfe, who commanded the British attackers, looked in vain for a way to attack the city, which stands atop daunting cliffs, high above the St. Lawrence River. Wolfe managed to occupy high ground across the river from Quebec and, with his guns sited there, to pound much of the city to ruins. But he could not touch its defenses or its defenders, and his men could not scale its heights in the face of determined French opposition.

Finally, in a desperate venture, Wolfe landed men at night just upriver from Quebec, and sent a few volunteers scrambling up the steep heights. They surprised the French guard post and gained a foothold. Then they cleared defensive obstacles from an old footpath up the cliffs that Wolfe himself had spotted earlier with his telescope from across the river. The waiting British army followed the path up to the Plains of Abraham, just west of the French city.

The French fought well and bravely, but they had no artillery with which to drive off the swarming British. They lost. At the battle's end, Montcalm, who was forty-seven, lay dying; and Wolfe, at thirty-two, was dead. Quebec itself fell to the British five days later. Montreal was taken the following year, and Canada surrendered. French power in North America was broken.

The War in India

Meanwhile, another young English commander, Robert Clive, was destroying French military power in India. He recaptured the British town of Calcutta, which had been seized earlier by the Indian ruler of Bengal, took Chandernagore from the French, and defeated a French-aided Bengali force fifteen times

the size of his own at Plassey in June 1757. French reinforcements arrived in India, but the British continued to win battles,
with Pondicherry, the center of French trade in India, falling
early in 1761. When the neutral Dutch grew restless over British
seizures of their shipping, and launched a naval expedition in
1759, the British defeated the Dutch fleet in a naval battle and
captured the Dutch port of Chinsura. Britain was the dominant
European power in India.

And on the Seas

The naval actions of the Great War for the Empire were
fought on the Atlantic Ocean, the Indian Ocean, the Mediterranean Sea, and the Caribbean Sea. Before war was formally
declared, Admiral John Byng was sent to protect two strategic
British possessions in the Mediterranean: Gibraltar and
Minorca. The French had already landed in force on Minorca
when Byng arrived off that island. Unable to engage the French
squadron defending Minorca, Byng abandoned the effort and
sailed back to Gibraltar. For this failure, he was court-martialed
and executed. Voltaire used the incident in *Candide* as an example of the absurd horrors prevalent in the world, remarking that
the English had shot an admiral "pour encourager les autres."
Once war was declared and Pitt was in control, Britain used its
naval power most aggressively, for Pitt understood well the
importance of seapower. One after another, British victories
were won at sea: in the Bay of Bengal (1758); near Gibraltar
(1759) in the Battle of Lagos; off the coast of India, decisively, in
the naval battle of Pondicherry (1759); and off the coast of
Brittany in the Battle of Quiberon Bay (1759), which ended
French naval power for the rest of the war. French privateers
captured or sank many English merchant ships, but, once there
was no longer a French fleet to protect French commerce, British privateers and naval vessels almost completely removed
France's merchant vessels from the high seas.
In the Caribbean, British forces captured two French islands
valuable for their sugar, Guadeloupe and Martinique, territories
considered by many more crucial to the French Empire than all
of vast, vacant Canada. They also took Grenada, St. Lucia, St.
Vincent, and Dominica.
Pitt even sent British forces to attack the French posts on the

west coast of Africa. Gorée, a rocky island near modern Dakar, where the great western bulge of Africa pushes closest to the Western Hemisphere, was France's chief slave-trading center. The British seized it in 1758.

Spain: Entrance and Exit

While the fighting went on, the French foreign minister, the duc de Choiseul, was delicately maneuvering Spain into the war. As a result of his work, in August 1761 a Family Compact—the ruling houses of Spain and France were different branches of the Bourbon family—was signed. King Charles III of Spain promised to enter the war against England by May 1762 if peace had not been made before that time. In return, France promised to give Minorca to Spain and agreed to make Spanish demands on England, including the cession of Gibraltar, part of its negotiating terms.

Pitt, learning of the Family Compact, was eager to preempt Spain's action by declaring war immediately and seizing the annual Spanish treasure fleet, then on its way home from Mexico. Young King George III, who had just been crowned, disapproved Pitt's plan, and Pitt resigned.

As Pitt stepped off the stage, he left behind him plans for dealing with Spain once war was declared. When Spain did declare war, in January 1762, the British Navy was prepared. Most of the French islands in the Caribbean had been captured by the end of June, and the British were ready to start on Spain's possessions. Havana was taken in August, and with it a dozen Spanish ships of the line and huge amounts of money and goods. Before the end of the year, Manila and the Philippines had fallen, and treasure ships carrying millions of dollars in silver and other treasure had been seized by British sailors. It had been an expensive half year for Spain, and Charles III was eager to come to terms.

The Salvation of Frederick

Meanwhile, Frederick the Great was hard-pressed by the coalition of nations surrounding his, in spite of financial help from Britain and supportive British attacks on French ports, in spite of his enemies' many errors and hesitations, and in spite of his own superior organizational and tactical skill. He had simply taken on too many opponents at once. The Austrians occupied Berlin, his capital, in 1757; the Russians occupied it again in 1760 and burned most of it. By the end of 1761 his situation appeared hopeless. Completely encircled by enemies, and with Pitt's resignation in October throwing doubt on any further aid from Britain, Frederick believed that only fortune could save him.

Fortune did. Empress Elizabeth of Russia, perhaps his most implacable enemy, died in January 1762, when everything looked blackest for Frederick. Her throne was taken by her nephew Peter III, weak and immature, who idolized Frederick and had no love for either France or Austria. He gave back to Frederick all the territory Russia had conquered from him, and made peace. If Peter could have had his way, in fact, he would have signed an alliance with Frederick and gone to his aid.

It seemed a miracle, one that would give false hope to Adolf Hitler, under comparable circumstances, 180 years later. The coalition against Frederick began to fall apart as soon as Peter's Russia withdrew from the war, and the way was open for a general peace.

Unfinished Business

Just as the Seven Years' War had really been two wars—one with national and dynastic aims fought in Europe, and the other, aimed at securing world empire, fought overseas by France and England—so there were two peaces. The peace that ended the war in Europe was simple enough. Russia and Sweden had already left the war. Austria and Prussia made peace on the terms *status quo ante bellum*. Nothing in Europe had been changed by the long and bloody war.

Much had been changed, however, by the great war on the oceans and beyond them. For England, the peace that ended that war was a great success. By the Treaty of Paris, signed in February 1763, France handed over to England all of Canada, keeping only fishing rights off Newfoundland and two tiny islands there to serve as bases for the fishermen. The French also renounced all claims to land east of the Mississippi River, the claims that had actually started the war when Frenchmen built fortresses and attacked British colonists living near the frontier. New Orleans and the great Louisiana territory were to remain French under the treaty (although the French had already made other arrangements for them), but Britain was guaranteed navigation rights on the Mississippi.

Of great importance in the war that was to follow, Britain returned to France the Caribbean islands of Martinique and Guadeloupe, which British troops had captured during the war. Pitt bitterly protested giving back any territory. Had he still been leader of the government nothing at all would have been returned. In fact the war would probably have continued until every French colony was captured. Leaving the French with the remnants of an empire was also leaving them with the beginnings of one, Pitt believed, and many agreed with him. There were others in England who favored giving back Canada and keeping sugar-rich Guadeloupe and Martinique. But the decision was made otherwise. Some concessions seemed necessary in order to help Britain's ally Frederick keep most of his territory on the Continent, and to achieve an immediate settlement. There were cynics, too, who suggested that the British sugar planters in the West Indies lobbied for the return of Guadeloupe and Martinique to France lest they become part of the empire trading system and compete in British markets. In any case, big, cold, largely unpeopled Canada, its bulk no longer a threat to the British colonies in North America, was chosen over the tropical islands.

This was not all. Although Pondicherry, Chandernagore, and France's smaller posts were returned, France lost most of the prestige and influence in India won earlier in the century. The important slave-trading centers of Senegal and Gorée on the African coast went under English control. And in a separate, secret treaty, France gave up its holdings west of the Mississippi, and New Orleans, to Spain, as compensation for Spanish losses.

Actually, Spain did not lose very much from its humiliating year of war. East and West Florida, which included a strip along the Gulf Coast west to the Mississippi, went to Britain in exchange for the return to Spain of Cuba. The Philippines were also returned to Spain. Minorca went back to England, but of course Spain had not had Minorca before the war. Spain's net loss, even before it received the Louisiana territory, thus amounted only to the Floridas—and at least $11 million in treasure ships and ransom.

France's power in India was ended; France's power on the North American continent was ended; and France's position as the dominant power on the European continent was ended. At court ceremonies in the capitals of Europe, British diplomats now took precedence over French diplomats. It was a stunning defeat, but not so complete as Pitt had wanted. To Americans, viewing Europe's history through eyes focused on events in North America, France's defeat has seemed complete because it removed France from American history—except as a kindly helper who came with Lafayette during the Revolutionary War. To William Pitt, France's defeat was far too tentative and the peace terms disgracefully moderate. France still challenged the supremacy of Britain.

The Powers of Europe in the Sixties and Seventies

As the Seven Years' War ended and events moved toward revolution in America, Great Britain was the strongest nation in Europe, and was growing stronger. Its healthy flow of exports had increased, according to estimates, by 90 percent between 1720 and 1763. Improvements in manufacturing techniques had given Britain strong weapons in the never-ending trade war of the eighteenth century. Coal was replacing wood as an industrial fuel and was making manufacturing more efficient. Many small changes in products added up to more marketable goods —more iron implements fully shaped and ready to use, linens and cottons with printed designs, paper and glass of better quality. Britain's strong navy and appropriately placed naval bases protected its important trade with the North American and Caribbean colonies. But the British government, confident in its mastery of the world's waterways, decided to pay off debts accumulated during the war by economizing on naval expenditures. As a result the navy was in a slack period as the American Revolutionary War approached. It was also rent by jealousies and animosity among its senior officers, and these were reflected in the efficiency of the British fleets in battle.

France, still Britain's principal rival, had by no means been permanently banished from the seas. French ships continued to sail to the Far East and to the Caribbean islands, and in spite of British navigation laws there was some secret direct trade between France and North America. And, of particular importance, while Britain was resting on its laurels France and its great minister Choiseul were determinedly rebuilding the shattered French navy. By the late 1770s French and English seamen agreed that the new French ships were faster and easier to handle than British ships of the same size, and that they were bigger and stronger than British ships carrying the same number of guns.

The Netherlands (the United Provinces) was still a significant power. It had been the leading trading, shipping, and banking nation of the world in the mid-seventeenth century. But the Dutch had lost out to France and Britain in the competition for trade and colonies because their small land territory lacked defensible frontiers and because they lacked a strong enough navy and adequate naval bases to protect their fine merchant fleet. England, superior in naval tactics and naval commanders in the seventeenth century, had fought three naval wars against the Dutch between 1650 and 1675, and these Anglo-Dutch wars had left the Netherlands weakened as a naval power. Nevertheless its trade was still strong, and its banking services—loans, credit, and insurance—were depended on by other trading nations. Much earlier the Dutch had been pushed out of North America, but they still had the islands of St. Eustatia (now St. Eustatius) and Curaçao in the Caribbean. And they had the rich Netherlands Antilles in the Far East, the archipelago that is now Indonesia. To protect their position the Dutch strove for neutrality in European waters and adopted the slogan "free ships, free goods"; that is, ships of neutral nations should be able to carry goods of all kinds freely to fighting nations in wartime.

Spain's power had plummetted from its sixteenth-century predominance, but it clung to a considerable empire, which was still used largely as a source of gold and silver. Its economy had slowly recovered from its nadir at the beginning of the eighteenth century. The new ruling dynasty, the Bourbons, had brought the nation out of bankruptcy by mid-century, and a series of brilliant ministers had revitalized agriculture and industry and greatly strengthened Spain's international position. Although its brief participation in the Seven Years' War brought humiliation and some losses, Spain remained a significant power.

Of the other nations of Europe, only Russia was striving to become an overseas imperial power. Peter I had finally ended Sweden's dominance in the Baltic Sea early in the eighteenth

century and had created a navy for Russia. Catherine II, vigorous and intelligent, had wrested power from her inept husband,
Peter III, soon after his accession. She had ambitious plans for
driving the Turks out of Europe and seizing the Black Sea coast,
as Peter I had longed to do before her. British and British-
trained officers had strengthened the Russian navy. Russian
trade was growing, and a strategic product, pig iron, had become
a leading export. Trees for masts and other naval stores were
important to the seafaring nations of western Europe.

Thus in 1775 Great Britain was the strongest nation in
Europe, but there were many rivals eager to displace the mighty
British. A worldwide competitive game was being played with
exportable goods, colonies, merchant ships, and fighting navies.
The struggle for supremacy framed the war for independence
of thirteen British colonies in North America.

2

The Revolution That Made the War

John Adams felt strongly that Americans tended to confuse the American Revolution with the Revolutionary War. The war, he wrote to Thomas Jefferson, "was no part of the Revolution. It was only an effect and consequence of it." Adams, well aware that he was presenting an unconventional view, went on to state that the Revolution had taken place in the minds of the people from 1760 to 1775, "before a drop of blood was spilled at Lexington."

The revolution that made the war began in the aftermath of the Seven Years' War. It was an internal struggle within the colonies and between the colonies and England, with the other powers of Europe acting only as onlookers. But they were concerned onlookers, partly because trade with North America was involved, and partly because any trouble within the British Empire could make Britain vulnerable to revenge for the losses France and Spain had suffered during the Seven Years' War. French secret agents clipped newspapers in North America and listened carefully to tavern talk in colonial capitals.

The Seven Years' War had cost England a great deal of money, and the British government believed that the North American colonists should pay what it considered their fair share of it. And the best and easiest way to exact payments was through taxes. For a dozen years after 1763 there was a pattern of thrust and parry, parry and thrust, as ministers, Parliament, and king imposed taxes and asserted their right to impose taxes, while intellectual colonial leaders responded with constitutional objections, and popular colonial leaders organized street protests.

A secondary theme during the same years was the British determination to set a western boundary line to white settle-

15

ment, so as to maintain fair and peaceful relations with the Indians, and an opposing determination by colonists in frontier areas to move west freely and to be protected in their new homes. Britain had replaced France as the country across the sea that held dominion over the great forests west of the Alleghenies. It had at the same time naturally become to some extent the ally and protector of the Indians against encroaching settlement and settlers. And when this happened, another wedge was driven between the North American colonists and the government in London.

The Small Revolution of 1764-1766

Although there had been earlier constitutional rumblings not connected with the expenses of the Seven Years' War, the trouble really began with the Stamp Act of 1765, passed to help pay for that war. Protest began a year before the act was passed, when the Grenville ministry announced its plans to impose this tax on legal documents, books, newspapers and pamphlets, playing cards, and several other items. This was not an evil new tax contrived especially for the colonies, but a tax long levied in England. It would have worked some hardship, however, and colonial spokesmen immediately began attacking it on constitutional grounds: Parliament had no right to tax the colonists, since they were not represented in Parliament; tariffs on imported goods, long collected, were proper, since they were intended to channel trade between parts of the empire, but "internal" taxation for revenue purposes not levied by Americans—never! James Otis and Daniel Dulany wrote eloquent pamphlets, Patrick Henry spoke of Caesar and Brutus, and violence broke out in Massachusetts and Rhode Island. Houses of public officials were razed, books and furnishings were looted or burned, and the officials themselves were hanged in effigy. Mobs rioted in the cities of other colonies, and one colonial assembly after another passed resolutions condemning the Stamp Act.

The act was never enforced, and Parliament finally had to repeal it in an effort to restore order. At the same time it passed a law proclaiming that it had the power to make laws for the colonies without any exceptions; it simply had decided not to exercise the prerogative in this particular case.

The Townshend Acts

Having learned nothing useful from the Stamp Act crisis, the British government, with Chancellor of the Exchequer Charles Townshend taking the lead, pushed through Parliament a series of acts in 1767, the most important of which imposed import taxes on certain much-needed commodities brought into the colonies from Great Britain. The government's attitude seemed to be, "Very well, if they don't care for internal taxes, we'll give them external taxes with a vengeance." Although technically the taxes were "external," being on imports, they were in complete contradiction of the spirit of the Navigation Acts, which imposed tariffs on foreign manufactured goods so as to encourage trade between Great Britain and the North American colonies. These Townshend tariffs were taxes on articles from Britain itself, and their clear purpose was to raise money. So again, colonial leaders saw them as a way of bypassing the legislative bodies of the colonies. Responses of the colonies to the Townshend Acts included John Dickinson's *Letters from a Farmer in Pennsylvania*, and a circular letter of protest from the Massachusetts House of Representatives, which was resoundingly reaffirmed after the British Secretary of State for America asked that it be rescinded. The "anti-rescinders" were toasted up and down the colonies. Nonimportation agreements—boycotts of British goods—were passed by most of the colonial legislatures in protest against the Townshend Acts. Riots and inflammatory newspaper articles in Boston led the British to station troops there.

New York saw repeated altercations at this time over a revolutionary symbol, the Liberty Pole, which sprouted overnight in streets and squares. British troops chopped down the poles and the popular-activist Sons of Liberty set them up again, over and over. In January 1770, several men were wounded when Sons of Liberty fought British soldiers.

Then, as a direct result of the stationing of British troops in Boston, came the so-called Boston Massacre of March 1770. In all the turmoil of protest and efforts to maintain order and British control, the "massacre" was probably the first incident in which lives were lost.

Lord North, who had just become prime minister, moved for the repeal of the Townshend Acts, with the exception of the tax on imported tea, on the very day of the Boston Massacre. By this time, however, the momentum of revolution was becoming irresistible. The protesting colonists had a body of theory, developed by men like James Otis, Patrick Henry, and John Dickinson, a theory of rights and freedom based on ancient Greek and Roman thought, more recent European writers, and English constitutional law. They had martyrs, symbols, and a growing distrust of the British government's good faith. Soon a note of suspicion of conspiracy began to appear in the writings of colonial leaders—British actions were perceived as a deliberate attempt to "enslave" the colonists, to take away their traditional English constitutional rights, to subdue them. From 1770 every anniversary of the Boston Massacre was the occasion for a stirring, sometimes inflammatory, memorial oration. The protest movement was sweeping toward independence.

Many of the cooler-headed, more thoughtful leaders—John Adams, Thomas Jefferson, and the rest—were making their own decisions for independence. From 1770 on, the concept of natural law as the basis for just government began to be emphasized in their speeches and writings, broadening the principle of the colonists' rights as Englishmen under the British constitution. The way was being prepared—partly consciously, partly unconsciously—for a declaration that the North American colonies were not a necessary, permanent part of the British Empire, but rather connected to the empire only by an implicit contract between the colonists as a people and the British sovereign. Their rights as Englishmen derived from their rights as men.

Tea

Parliament's efforts to help the financially pressed British East India Company began the denouement. So that the East India Company might undersell all other sources of tea, by the Tea Act of May 1773 the company was relieved of paying regular duties in England and of selling its tea at auction. The tea would be shipped directly to America and sold there on commission by specially appointed agents. These agents' jobs were snapped up by British-oriented colonists who did not realize what troubles awaited them. The colonists would still have to pay the tax on tea. It was the only survivor of the Townshend Acts, and a symbol for both Britons and Americans of Parliament's power to tax the colonists. Even with the tax, the East India Company tea would be a bargain for the American consumer, cheaper even than the smuggled Dutch tea they had been buying more cheaply than British tea since 1770. But symbols now had far more power than did a few coins.

The colonies were already near the explosion point. The revenue schooner *Gaspée*, burned as she lay aground off Providence in June 1772, was one of several British vessels thus treated by Americans. The angry British response to the *Gaspée* incident raised the fear that Americans might be taken to England to be tried for treason. Resolutions protesting the unconstitutionality of denying local trial to those accused were passed in colonial assemblies and town meetings all through the colonies. Committees of Correspondence by this time were binding the colonies together and bringing a response from all colonies if one was threatened. Belief in a deliberate campaign to enslave the colonies grew stronger, and the Tea Act was seen as part of this campaign.

Everyone knows what happened to the tea shipped to Boston. Nor was any landed in New York, where Governor William Tryon wrote that tea could be landed only "under the protection of the point of the bayonet, and muzzle of the cannon." The Philadelphia tea agents were forced to resign, and the tea ships that put in there promptly departed for England without unloading. Nowhere was the tea landed without vigorous protest.

Intolerable Acts

Parliament, the king, and the ministry responded to the dumping of tea in Boston Harbor by pushing through four acts that the colonists named the Coercive, or the Intolerable, Acts. All were aimed at Boston and Massachusetts. They closed the port of Boston, unilaterally changed Massachusetts' chartered form of government to give the British authorities tighter control, provided that government officials should be tried in England — not America — for capital crimes committed in suppressing disorder, and provided for quartering British troops in privately owned houses and barns, whenever barracks were not available.

There was a great rush of protest throughout the colonies. Resolutions were passed by scores of counties and towns. Support for Boston came from elected bodies and mass meetings from New England to South Carolina. A Continental Congress was called for September 1774.

Delegates from twelve of the thirteen colonies met in Philadelphia. In the evenings they drank toasts to the king, the perpetual union of the colonies, and the hope that "British swords never be drawn in defense of tyranny." During the days, they drafted and passed a declaration of rights and grievances that founded American rights on the British constitution, the charters of the several colonies, and also—a victory for the more radical-minded—on natural law. Most important, they approved a document that was called the Association and was referred to as "the Grand American Association" by some of the local groups that enforced it. The Association pledged the delegates and the colonies they represented not to import or consume British goods and—with some reservations—not to export colonial goods to Great Britain. It started a movement up and down the colonies for self-sufficiency and local industries; it also inevitably led to expanded trade with non-British nations.

Fighting Begins

The confrontation now began inexorably moving toward open warfare. The British government refused to take notice of any of the declarations and petitions sent to it by the Congress. The Association was seen as treasonous. Colonial activists, realizing their physical helplessness if hostilities broke out, began seizing stores of gunpowder; the smuggling in arms and powder through ports in the West Indies increased. In February 1775 Parliament asked the king to declare Massachusetts in a state of rebellion, a clear preface to putting down the insurgents by force. The king ordered reinforcements to Boston. The British government had chosen a course certain to lead to war as the only way to correct what seemed to be an intolerable situation. When the British general in Boston, Thomas Gage, sent a force to seize a cache of Patriot arms and supplies at Concord, the fighting began with the small but bloody encounter on Lexington Green.

Protesters Become Rebels

Immediately after the fighting at Lexington and Concord, a militia Patriot army began gathering around Boston, besieging the British there. Ethan Allen and his Vermonter Green Mountain Boys took Fort Ticonderoga, strategically poised between Lake George (and the Hudson) and Lake Champlain (and the St. Lawrence). The Second Continental Congress convened the same day (May 10), and a few days later the Green Mountain Boys took Crown Point. By the end of the month Benedict Arnold had captured the little British post at St. Johns, Canada. At almost the same time, British reinforcements, including three major generals, had arrived in Boston. Several colonial royal governors fled to nearby British warships, provincial congresses took over the reins of government from colonial assemblies, and a hill outside Boston, erroneously known to history as Bunker Hill, was fortified by Patriot militiamen. Congress chose George Washington as commander in chief of the Continental Army it had just authorized; the same day (June 17), the British attacked "Bunker Hill" (Breed's Hill), and the Americans stood them off long enough, and inflicted enough casualties, to make the battle a thoroughly Pyrrhic British victory.

From New England and New York, Pennsylvania and Virginia, regiments marched to join the besiegers of Boston. On August 23, George III formally declared the colonies in open rebellion. In October Benedict Arnold set out with 1,100 volunteers to invade Canada.

Beginnings of Foreign Relations

The resisting colonists were still officially, by their own words, loyal British subjects. Yet when the king declared them in rebellion in August 1775, and when Parliament voted a complete naval blockade in November, it looked very much as though the colonial leaders would have to prepare to fight a long war for independence. With the realization that a successful war would require money and support beyond their own means, they naturally began to seek foreign assistance. But they were not yet ready to declare for independence, and preparations for a long war and approaches to foreign nations had to remain a secret.

On September 18, 1775, Congress set up a committee to obtain desperately needed war matériel, calling it simply the Secret Committee. It was made up of businessmen and merchants with experience in foreign trade, including Benjamin Franklin, Silas Deane, Robert R. Livingston, John Alsop, Robert Morris, Thomas Willing, and John Dickinson. Morris, who was a business partner of Willing's in Philadelphia, dominated the committee. Franklin, while he was representing colonies in England during the years immediately preceding 1775, had shrewdly foreseen the coming war and had established contacts with friends in France and with ship captains visiting London; through them he had helped in getting gunpowder and other war stores smuggled to the colonies. He was thus an obvious choice for the Secret Committee, whose basic purpose was to intensify these smuggling efforts. Gunpowder was something the colonies did not manufacture in large quantities. In fact, they had almost none. It was small wonder that so many of the incidents that prefaced the Revolutionary War involved powder and arms seizures by either Patriot or British forces. The little stores the Patriots captured could not last long. Nitrates and sulfur were now infinitely precious, absolutely essential to the Patriot cause's survival.

A second secret committee appointed by Congress was called the Committee of Secret Correspondence and was the embryo of a foreign ministry (or Department of State). Set up in November 1775, it was dominated by Franklin and included John Dickinson, John Jay of New York, Benjamin Harrison of Virginia, and Thomas Johnson of Maryland, all able men. It immediately began tentative, discreet efforts to secure help for the colonies from the leaders of Europe, who had much cause for rejoicing in the crisis shaking the British Empire.

Rebels Become a Nation

Fourteen months after the fighting at Lexington, the American cause had made some progress. Montreal had been captured, although Quebec had not, and the retreating American army was leaving Canada with no lasting gains. The British had evacuated Boston on March 17, earning Washington a gold medal from a grateful Congress and giving Irish Americans of subsequent generations in Boston a local holiday on St. Patrick's Day. North Carolina militiamen had defeated Scottish loyalists at Moore's Creek Bridge in a battle that has been called "The Lexington and Concord of the South." Several colonies had set up navies for their own protection, and Congress had voted the beginnings of a Continental Navy. Esek Hopkins had carried the war to the Bahamas and captured the island of New Providence

(Nassau). Americans and British were at war; there was no hope of reconciliation until it was over. The revolution in men's minds had brought about a war, and now that war was making necessary a declaration of national independence.

On April 15 Congress recommended that all the colonies reject royal authority and form independent governments. It was the good fortune and the glory of the American Revolution that this was an easy thing to do. The basic institutions existed. There had been elected legislative assemblies in all the colonies, and at the consummation of the Revolution these became independent state legislatures. If an assembly was officially dissolved by a royal governor, another similarly elected group, or even the same group under a new name, was waiting to take its place. There were to be long debates over the exact form state governments would finally take, but the Revolutionary Americans never had to try to create a new world, as their French counterparts did. They had only to take command of, and responsibility for, the world they already possessed.

In Congress on June 7, Richard Henry Lee of Virginia moved a resolution for national independence. A committee to draft a statement explaining to the world the reasons for declaring independence was appointed on June 11. The statement was drafted by Thomas Jefferson, with the help of a number of useful suggestions from John Adams and Benjamin Franklin. Congress voted to declare independence on July 2 and approved the Declaration two days later.

The Americans had their new nation, founded on what they asserted was the natural right of men to form governments by contract, and to disown a government if it broke the contract. This was not a novel idea to intellectuals of the period, but it seems at first glance a somewhat strange idea with which to approach the powerful men of continental Europe, men without whose help the new nation had little chance for survival.

It was to these very men, however, that the Declaration was largely directed. One of the strong arguments for declaring independence was that it would enable the Americans to form alliances and obtain military aid from abroad. And one of the reasons for couching the Declaration in terms of natural right rather than the colonists' rights as Englishmen was to make it clear that this was no internal quarrel but a war between two sovereign nations.

II

SOLDIERS FROM EUROPE

3

Foreign Volunteers in the Continental Army

The first men who came from Europe to help the embattled Americans were not sent by their governments. They came one by one, or in handfuls, and they gave the officer corps of the American Continental Army a decidedly international flavor.

When fighting broke out in America, there had been peace in Europe for twelve years. This was a long time for a soldier to wait for promotion, and promotions were rare or nonexistent in peacetime. Perhaps one or two of the volunteers who flocked to America were inspired by republicanism or the natural rights doctrine; the overwhelming majority were simply ambitious professional fighters looking for a war. Fortunately a number of them were very competent military men.

It is hard to know how many foreigners there were in the Continental Army. Six out of the twenty-seven major generals in the army were volunteers from Europe, but the percentage was much higher at this rank than at any other; one hundred foreign officers is probably as good a guess as any. Of enlisted men there were very few, for only an officer could afford to transport himself across the Atlantic.

The Europeans who came varied in birth from wealthy aristocrat to impoverished commoner; most were honorable, some were scheming rascals, some were unfailingly gallant, while others were difficult in the extreme. Without exception, however, they were ambitious, forceful, self-starting men. Not one was dull. A handful stand out from all the rest.

27

The Boy General

Marie Joseph Paul Yves Roch Gilbert du Motier, marquis de Lafayette, was nineteen years old when he came to the United States. It was his time of testing, the adventure that was to prove his manhood. The fact that he was wealthy, married, and a father—and was a major general almost from his arrival in America—did not make the trial any less real for him.

Young Gilbert—who used that name alone and later joked that it was not his fault that he had been "baptized like a Spaniard" in honor of a host of saints—had grown up as a lonely little boy in a household of women. He had been a marquis for as long as he could remember; when he was two years old his father was killed fighting the British at Minden in the Seven Years' War.

When Gilbert was eleven, his mother took him to Paris, and there he assumed a strangely anomalous position as an important person who was nevertheless something of an outsider. There was a paucity of heirs in his family, and as one relative after another died his wealth increased. By the time he was thirteen, he could look forward to having at his disposal when he reached twenty-one an annual income of 120,000 livres. This has been estimated as approximately equal to $432,000 a year in 1976 buying power; it was, of course, untaxed.*

Yet the young marquis de Lafayette did not feel very comfortable among the aristocracy gathered at the royal court in Versailles. He was a *nouveau riche*—the title had been held by a member of his family for only three generations. A social inferior, he was patronized.

He was also physically unprepossessing—slight of build, not at all handsome, and quite awkward. Not especially good at riding or dancing, nor very successful at any physical sport, he was constantly teased about his inadequacies.

When he was sixteen, Lafayette was married to a girl of fourteen, Adrienne de Noailles, daughter of the duc d'Ayen. Just as Lafayette was one of the richest men in France, his bride's family was one of the most aristocratic and powerful; hence the suitability of the match. The Noailles family became almost Lafayette's only family, as both his parents and most of his other relatives

*Adjusted by use of the Department of Labor conversion factor from the 1965 figure in Louis Gottschalk, *Lafayette Comes to America*, pp. 11n, 22.

were by then dead. He had for all practical purposes become a Noailles, but not a warmly accepted one. His father-in-law did not think the quiet, shy boy showed much promise and was the more determined to push his career for that very reason. The duc's efforts made Lafayette increasingly and uncomfortably indebted to him.

The marquis's career was to be a military one. He had joined his grandfather's regiment when he was thirteen, but when he became engaged to Adrienne his future father-in-law saw to it that he transferred to his new family regiment, the Noailles Dragoons. The duc d'Ayen got him promotions there, so that he was the captain of a company on his eighteenth birthday.

It was through the commander of the army to which the Noailles Dragoons were attached that Lafayette became involved in the American Revolution. The comte de Broglie was a veteran intriguer who had headed Louis XV's secret diplomacy network, and he was also an experienced commander. He immediately saw the possibilities of the American Revolution for France, and also thought he saw some possibilities for himself. While conspiring to have France help the colonies, he schemed to have himself become commander in chief of the American forces and eventually an elected ruler—or stadholder, on the Dutch model—of the new nation.

Just at the time Broglie was gathering some volunteers for America, and Silas Deane, American commissioner in Paris, was enlisting them, Lafayette's personal frustrations made him especially eager to leave France for a stirring adventure. Although fond of the wife he had married as a child, the marquis had recently fallen in love with a very beautiful lady of the court, and had been rejected by her. His military career, into which he had poured all his hopes for self-fulfillment, was at least temporarily stalled by a new minister of war, whose reform policies placed many young and inexperienced officers, including Lafayette, on inactive status.

To get to America Lafayette had to defy his father-in-law and the king himself. The duc d'Ayen did not believe his ugly-duckling ward was ready for such an undertaking, and he obtained royal orders forbidding it. Lafayette could have been imprisoned indefinitely under a *lettre de cachet* for disobeying. After many hesitations and false starts—and prodded by Broglie, to whom he turned repeatedly during the months of preparation—Lafayette sailed for America on his own ship, bought

for the purpose, the *Victoire*. With him were Brigadier General
Jean de Kalb, a sturdy and distinguished soldier in his mid-
fifties, and thirteen other French officer volunteers.

Lafayette did not know that de Kalb and another of his com-
panions, the vicomte de Mauroy, were involved in Broglie's
plans to take military command and political control in the
United States; he did not even know of Broglie's plans.
However, after the men landed on the South Carolina coast
(June 1777) and made their way overland to Philadelphia,
Lafayette learned that Congress had received word of Broglie's
offer to supplant Washington. It also became clear that Silas
Deane was in disfavor with much of Congress for what appeared
to be lavish and indiscriminate recruitment of foreign officers at
ranks that gave them seniority over Americans. There were
reasons for Deane's behavior that seemed sound enough in
Paris, but Congress was in no mood to recognize the contracts
Lafayette and his companions had signed with Deane.

Lafayette's commission was saved by his title and his money—
he offered to serve without pay. Congress made him a major
general on condition that he accept seniority from the time his
commission was granted by Congress, not from the time Deane
issued it.

The commander in chief invited his new major general to
dinner at Philadelphia's City Tavern, and a warm relationship
was immediately formed between these two men from opposite
sides of the Atlantic, men whose physical resemblance was noted
by their contemporaries. Although Lafayette wanted command
of a division, and Washington would not give it to him, Washington invited the young Frenchman to become a member of his
family of aides, thus giving him the opportunity to observe and
participate in the war at the highest level. Washington also, at
their second meeting, told Lafayette that he would be pleased to
have his confidence as a "father and friend." Lafayette never
forgot these words.

In the midst of the all-consuming work of war leadership,
Washington had unexpectedly and in a real sense found a son;
the eager and untried Lafayette had in turn found a father.
Washington had no children of his own, and although he was a
doting stepfather, he was a discouraged one. He must have felt
keenly the contrast between lazy, pleasure-loving, overindulged
Jackie Custis and this Frenchman, who, at nineteen, had the
initiative to get himself across the ocean and the ambition and

daring to seek battlefield command. When Washington half apologized for the appearance of his troops on the drill field, thinking they would look ill trained indeed to a French officer, Lafayette politely replied that he had come to learn, not to teach.

Lafayette, for his part, had no father except the stern, deprecating duc d'Ayen, so that Washington's kindness, coming just as Lafayette was beginning to play a man's role in the world himself, moved him deeply.

Lafayette immediately began to attend Washington's war councils and soon had a chance to see action. He was with Washington at the Brandywine in September 1777, when the commander in chief, poorly served by several subordinates and not watching carefully enough for a possible envelopment, was struck in the right flank by Lieutenant General Sir William Howe, narrowly avoiding disaster. When it became clear that most of the battle's action would be on the American right, with Major General John Sullivan, Lafayette rode off to join the fight there. He worked vigorously to rally the faltering troops and was wounded by a musketball that passed through his leg.

Ardent in his search for military glory, Lafayette took every opportunity to experience combat. Conducting a vigorous reconnaissance in New Jersey in November 1777, he skirmished with a larger force of Hessians and came out the victor. Not content with his staff job, he continually begged Washington for the command of a division and finally won him over. Leading his division in the spring of 1778, he coolly escaped a British trap at Barren Hill as the American army was emerging from Valley Forge; he failed, however, to distinguish himself in Major General Charles Lee's near-debacle at Monmouth Courthouse and was keenly disappointed.

Lafayette had grandiose dreams of conquest. He wanted to command an expedition that would attack British territories in both the West Indies and India. He also yearned to lead an invasion of Canada, and was actually given command of such an expedition, planned for 1778, but the project was aborted.

Without understanding what was going on, Lafayette almost became part of the efforts of Brigadier General Thomas Conway, whose military skill he admired, to have Washington replaced by Major General Horatio Gates. Once he grasped the meaning of the Conway Cabal, however, Lafayette supported Washington with a vehemence that won affectionate thanks from the usually undemonstrative commander in chief.

When the French alliance became fact, a jubilant Lafayette welcomed Admiral d'Estaing when he arrived at Newport as visible evidence of French support. When d'Estaing subsequently failed to carry out his part of a joint attack with Sullivan's troops on the British position at Newport, Lafayette shared with both the French and the Americans the bitterness and mutual recrimination engendered by the resulting fiasco.

Deciding that the time had come to go to France and explore opportunities to serve as a Frenchman in the war, and believing also that he could lobby effectively for more French aid for the Americans, Lafayette sailed for home in January 1779.

The gawky adolescent who had left France was hailed as a hero on his return. The king and his father-in-law both forgave him, he was applauded when he appeared in public, his devoted wife greeted him joyfully, and he had little trouble in winning the favors of the beautiful Comtesse de Hunolstein, the woman whose rejection had helped drive him to America.

Lafayette's role in the war was not noticeably altered by his visit to France, although he was given part in a proposed invasion of England, and at one time was involved with John Paul Jones in the planning of an amphibious operation at Liverpool, in which he would have commanded the landing force. The most important outcome of his visit was the supplies and money, and, above all, the men he convinced the government to provide for America. He had not gone with a request from Washington for men, and there was by no means universal agreement that they were needed or indeed that they would be welcomed and could perform effectively in coordination with the Continental Army. Apparently Franklin had never requested men, feeling more strongly the need for money and supplies. But Lafayette was convinced that a French force was important, and he was not alone. His pleadings helped convince the French government to send to America some of the troops and ships made available for use elsewhere when the plan to invade England was abandoned. Lafayette yearned to command the French troops, but he recognized the wisdom of the choice of Rochambeau and returned to America still a Continental Army officer.

Back in Massachusetts in April 1780, Lafayette was again greeted as a hero. He had yet to do anything spectacular militarily, but his youth and charm, his intimacy with Washington, and his early commitment to the American cause had already won him a place as a Revolutionary hero that in some sections was second only to Washington's.*

Then came the climax of Lafayette's military career in America. Washington sent him, in February 1781, to command 1,200 light infantry troops in an effort to catch the traitor Benedict Arnold, who had been put to work by the British, raiding Virginia freely from a base at Portsmouth. Lafayette would have loved the glory of capturing Arnold, and he and Major General Friedrich von Steuben seemed to have him bottled up at Portsmouth, but the French squadron sailing to close the trap was driven off by a British fleet, and Arnold was reinforced by sea.

Washington then ordered Lafayette to help Major General Nathanael Greene in his masterful withdrawal in North Carolina before General Lord Cornwallis's eventually self-defeating advance. Lafayette created an effective diversion in Virginia, saving Richmond from Major General William Phillips, and was delighted to be fighting, in Phillips, the very officer who, as he had known from childhood, had ordered the artillery barrage that killed Lafayette's father at Minden.

Soon Cornwallis was in Virginia, Greene was fighting in South Carolina, and Lafayette was left commanding his few Americans against British forces more than twice the size of his command.

In Virginia, where Lafayette had feared that he would be out of the main action, he was in fact able to develop and exhibit all his military talents. He organized and improvised supply arrangements with astonishing energy and ingenuity under the most difficult circumstances, managed to keep his men clothed and fed, and skillfully maneuvered out of Cornwallis's way, while pursuing every effort to get reinforcements. He fell back from Richmond toward Fredericksburg to meet Brigadier General Anthony Wayne, who was marching to reinforce him. With British forces threatening his flank and rear, he nevertheless kept to his north-northwest axis of withdrawal, felling trees, burning bridges, and hiding boats behind him.

Then, when the meeting of Lafayette and Wayne seemed sure, Cornwallis decided further pursuit was useless. He turned

---

*For an example of the survival and growth of the Lafayette legend, see Lucy Larcom, *A New England Girlhood* (New Haven, Conn., 1961). See also Gottschalk, *Lafayette Comes to America*, Ch. 13, "The Rise of a Legend."

and tried to destroy the main American supply depot near Charlottesville, but Lafayette outmaneuvered him. Cornwallis then withdrew to Williamsburg to regroup his forces and await further orders from General Sir Henry Clinton in New York. Lafayette followed him as closely as he dared.

The only battle of the British withdrawal was at Jamestown Ford (Green Spring), where Lafayette's van, under Wayne, fell into a British trap and suffered heavy casualties. Lafayette kept watch on the situation, tried to warn Wayne in time, and worked vigorously and with reckless courage to steady the overwhelmed Americans and withdraw them in good order. These were by far the worst casualties Lafayette had ever sustained, but Cornwallis continued his withdrawal, and Lafayette was able to see and present Green Spring as a victory. Soon Cornwallis was established at Yorktown and Gloucester Point, Lafayette was standing guard nearby, and Washington and Rochambeau were on their way, not to New York, as originally planned, but to Virginia.

Lafayette was ill, probably with malaria, when Washington arrived at Williamsburg, but he immediately left his bed, jumped on his horse and rode to meet the commander in chief, whom he greeted with an open-armed Gallic warmth that astonished American observers.

Then came the siege of Yorktown. Lafayette begged Washington for command of all the American forces before Yorktown, but accepted Washington's refusal philosophically. The commander in chief put him in command of a division on the far right. Many of the men under Lafayette had been with him throughout his Virginia campaign, and when the time came to assault Redoubt 10, he wanted to give the honor of commanding the attack to Lieutenant Colonel Jean-Joseph Gimat, a veteran of the campaign. Alexander Hamilton, however, won command by appeal to Washington. This little episode dramatized the international quality of the Continental Army's officer corps: a Frenchman commanding an American division nominated a Frenchman under his command to represent America in the assault on Yorktown. As it happened, the storming by the French army contingent of its assigned redoubt at Yorktown also had an international flavor. It was an officer of the German-speaking Deux-Ponts Regiment who represented the French army in the corresponding assault. And the challenge he heard as his men approached the British redoubt was the "Wer da?" of a Hessian sentry.

Lafayette had by this time truly proved himself, both in reputation and in military fact. He returned to France in 1781, a greater hero than ever, and was helpful to American Minister Thomas Jefferson in many economic and political matters.

The marquis's star was bright in the early days of the French Revolution, and the day he sent the key to the Bastille prison to Washington was a proud one. His position as a reformist aristocrat became impossible as the Revolution swept forward, however, and he was lampooned in the press as "M. Moitié," a pun on his family name that scorned his "halfway" commitment to the Revolution and apparent indecision. Although he remained a devoted worker for freedom and humanitarian reform until his death in the 1830s, his greatest glory was achieved as a young man in the cause of American independence.

Gallant Saber, Headstrong Rider

Another noble European in the Continental Army was Casimir Pulaski. Born about 1748, the eldest son of a Polish count, he began military life as a boy, in the service of the duke of Courland, in Latvia. Then, when he was about twenty, events in Poland called him home.

Poland in the eighteenth century was an aristocratic republic, with a king who ruled not by right of heredity but by election. The Catholic nobles ran the country, rather ineffectively, and chose the king. They were hard-pressed by Russia, Austria, and newly powerful Prussia, all seeking domination over all or part of Poland. Catherine the Great of Russia at this time found a novel method for extending Russian control over Poland, a method based on the half-million Eastern Orthodox and half-million Protestants living in Catholic Poland without any political representation or many religious rights. (The rights of the Jews in Poland—over half the Jewish population of the world at the time—do not seem to have been considered.) Catherine demanded equal rights for the Protestants and the Orthodox, and also insisted that the traditional, ineffectual constitution of Poland continue as it was, a measure that would quash the efforts of Polish reformers to modernize their government.

To fight Catherine and the Russians, young Pulaski's father formed the Confederation of Bar (named for the town where it was organized), and Casimir came home to fight the Russians and the Polish government that had given in to them. Fight he did, heroically, for four years and with considerable success. But, despite help to the rebels from Turkey, the Russians crushed the confederation, the Pulaski estates were confiscated, and Casimir fled to Turkey. After working in vain for four years to get Turkey to attack Russia again, an impoverished Pulaski moved on to Paris.

There he met the wily foreign minister, Charles Gravier, comte de Vergennes, who had helped bring Turkey into the Polish civil war against Russia and was then, in 1776, engineering aid for the rebellious American colonies—all in the interests of France, of course. Vergennes urged Pulaski to go to America, and sent him to American representatives Silas Deane and Benjamin Franklin.

Pulaski at this time was twenty-eight years old, a Polish patriot, certainly, but hardly a liberal or believer in natural rights. The Confederation of Bar had stood firmly against anyone but Catholics having political rights as Polish citizens. Pulaski went to America simply because there was a war there and he was a soldier by profession. He had no financial resources except his saber arm and his military reputation.

The young Pole was a cavalryman and eager to command cavalry, but he first fought with the infantry at Brandywine and Germantown. Then he was given command of the new Continental cavalry under Brigadier General Anthony Wayne at Valley Forge. He scouted for supplies that hard winter of 1777-1778, but did not get along well with Wayne and resigned his command in March 1778.

Wayne was later called mad, but not for bad temper or mental instability. It was his extraordinary daring at Stony Point that won him the sobriquet. The personality problem seems to have been Pulaski's. Pulaski was also bitterly hostile to Stephen Moylan, a jovial, ambitious Irish-American who was given the cavalry command Pulaski resigned.

Congress next gave Pulaski what he most wanted, authority to form an independent legion under his own command.* Pulaski's Legion was sent to protect American supplies at Egg Harbor, New Jersey. There, on October 14-15, 1778, Captain Patrick

---

*A legion was a unit composed of both dragoons (soldiers armed, equipped, and trained to fight either mounted or on foot) and light infantry.

Ferguson fell on Pulaski's troops in a surprise night attack; the legion took heavy casualties in this inauspicious beginning of its career. Sent next to the upper Delaware to guard against Indian attacks, Pulaski complained that there were only bears to shoot at there. He wanted action.

Then, in early 1779, he was ordered to the support of Major General Benjamin Lincoln at Charleston, South Carolina. Arriving at Charleston on May 8, he learned that a British force was approaching the city, and rushed out to attack the advance guard. He was soundly defeated.

Bitter and disappointed about his American service, Pulaski nevertheless moved on with Lincoln to the siege of Savannah. That trouble-beset siege reached its climax on October 9, when French and American forces under Admiral d'Estaing and General Lincoln prematurely attacked the British fortifications. On a day when wrong-headed courage was rampant, Pulaski demonstrated a supreme amount of it by leading his cavalry in a charge against the British abatis. The sharpened tree branches impaled many horses, holding their riders firmly in the line of British fire. Pulaski was severely wounded and died on board ship two days later.

Although he did not win one battle in America, was apparently not an apostle of liberty, and was a hard man to get along with, it can truthfully be said, as it often is, that Pulaski was a Polish patriot, a valiant soldier, and a fighter for American independence. His soldier's death gilded anew the reputation that he had seemed doomed to lose in America.

Giant at Camden

Johann Kalb, for whom so many American streets and counties were to be named, was no nobleman by birth. Born into a peasant family of a little village called Hüttendorf, in Germany, he worked as a waiter until he left home at the age of sixteen. At this point there is a gap in what is known of Kalb's life. Apparently he decided that a military career was the way to fortune and self-respect, but he soon learned that without an aristocratic name he could be nothing but a common soldier—a mean and degrading life in most eighteenth-century armies. Since he had not been born with a title, he decided to give himself one.

Thus the name of Lieutenant Jean de Kalb appears on the

rolls of a French regiment six years after young Johann left
home, and Baron de Kalb he was from that time on.

De Kalb fought in the War of the Austrian Succession, studied
mathematics and languages, and polished his knowledge of
troop organization. He quickly showed his gifts for strategic
thinking and detailed planning, and in 1754, before the Seven
Years' War broke out, he worked out a plan for developing
forces for amphibious attacks on England and the British colonies. As often happened in his career, his bogus barony and
authentic talents were not enough to get him a hearing at the
centers of power, Versailles in this case. He served with distinction as a major in the war, but was disappointed in his hopes for a
promotion at its end. He married a wealthy woman, to whom he
seems to have been devoted, and retired from active life at the
age of forty-three.

In April 1767, however, de Kalb eagerly accepted the request
of the foreign minister, the duc de Choiseul, that he go to North
America as a secret agent for France, observing and reporting
on the state of public discontent following the Stamp Act crisis,
and on the possibilities of France's reaping the benefits of colonial dissatisfaction. De Kalb proved a good reporter, observant
and objective. He wrote Choiseul that, although there was much
discontent, if war should break out between England and France
the colonists would quickly rally to the mother country. If a
French army should invade the British colonies, it could look for
no help from the inhabitants, but rather for vigorous armed
resistance. Choiseul was not so well pleased with de Kalb's realistic views as with the reports of more optimistic agents; in any
case, some of de Kalb's reports were intercepted, and he had to
be recalled.

The accession of Louis XVI brought back to power the comte
de Broglie, who had earlier been de Kalb's patron. His military
career renewed, de Kalb became a brigadier general in late 1776.
Broglie saw in him an ideal agent to prepare the way for Broglie's planned assumption of leadership in the American Revolution. When Silas Deane promised him the rank of major general,
de Kalb decided to join Washington's forces.

De Kalb exerted much influence on Lafayette as that young
man made his own decision to go to America. The two sailed on
Lafayette's ship, *Victoire*, in April 1777 and stepped ashore
together on the South Carolina coast in June. With their thirteen
fellow volunteers, they made their way to Philadelphia. When

they found Congress unwilling to honor Silas Deane's commissions, de Kalb had the humiliating experience of seeing the delegates make an exception for Lafayette, giving a major general's sash to the boy who had never seen a battle, while excluding the distinguished fifty-six-year-old veteran, a general officer in his own right in France. De Kalb does not seem to have been bitter toward Lafayette, but he reasonably pointed out to Congress that although it was very generous of Lafayette to pay his own expenses and serve without salary, it was also very easy for Lafayette and impossible for de Kalb.

Just as the frustrated German was preparing to sail back to France, Congress voted him a newly created major generalcy. He promptly accepted.

Serving first near Philadelphia in late 1777, de Kalb spent the winter at Valley Forge. Recognizing Washington's greatness, and learning something of American attitudes, he realized the absurdity of Broglie's aspirations and continued serving the United States as his own man, not Broglie's. De Kalb had no chance to distinguish himself until April 1780, when, in command of a small Continental division of Maryland and Delaware men, among the best in the army, he was ordered to the relief of Charleston. The city was surrendered before de Kalb's division reached the Carolinas, and he moved on to the Deep River, in North Carolina. There he was joined by Major General Horatio Gates, who had taken command of the Southern Theater on Congress's orders and against Washington's wishes. By the time he approached battle, Gates would have with him not only de Kalb's fine division (about 1,000 men fit for combat) but also the 120 survivors of Pulaski's Legion and about 1,900 rather shaky Virginia and North Carolina militia.

As they marched through the Carolinas, de Kalb repeatedly gave Gates good advice, which Gates repeatedly ignored. De Kalb had reconnoitered the area before Gates arrived, and he recommended a roundabout but relatively safe route toward Camden. But Gates chose the short route, through pine barrens whose few inhabitants were mostly Tory and whose soil yielded poor rations—mostly green corn and green peaches. When a sizable British force was reported on high ground ahead, de Kalb urged a night march to turn their flank, but Gates dallied. After inexcusably dividing his forces, Gates finally moved to the attack. During a night march, Gates's ill-fed, dysentery-exhausted troops unexpectedly ran into the British, and de Kalb counseled withdrawal. Instead, Gates awaited the British attack.

It came the next morning, August 16. General Lord Cornwallis detected confusion among the Virginia militia on the American left and struck there. The militia broke and ran, and Gates's center, North Carolina militia, gave way, too, taking Gates with them. Only the right, de Kalb's Maryland and Delaware Continentals, held, and they held to the end. De Kalb repeatedly rallied his troops and continued fighting, although he was wounded when his horse was shot from under him. He was a huge man, and, even *in extremis*, his commanding presence held his men. When he finally fell, in the fiercest hand-to-hand fighting of the war, he bore eleven wounds; he died a few hours later.

Gates, after leaving the battlefield with the militia, rode straight to Charlotte, 60 miles away, arriving the same night. He covered another 120 miles in the next three days without pausing to file a report. This accomplishment may place him with Paul Revere and Israel Bissel as one of the noteworthy riders of the Revolution—not an enviable distinction for a defeated general.

Poland's Finest

What European could be more ripe for service in the American Revolution than a young soldier with engineering training—something the American Patriots badly needed—and also the spirit of adventure and a broken heart? With borrowed money, Tadeusz Kosciuszko (pronounced, roughly, Kos-tsu-shko) arrived in Philadelphia in August of 1776.

Kosciuszko was born in 1746, the son of an impoverished family of Polish gentry. He was a thoughtful boy, deeply inspired by reading Plutarch's lives of the great men of ancient Greece and Rome. He had Jesuit schooling—as did most boys educated in Poland then—and went on to the royal military academy, graduating as a captain in 1769. Kosciuszko missed the war of the Confederation of Bar; he was studying engineering and artillery doctrine in Paris on a government scholarship. When he did return to Poland he became involved in a love affair with a young girl he was tutoring, and it ended sadly; he was wounded by one of her father's retainers as the couple tried to elope. He fled to Paris.

When Kosciuszko landed in America, he had no general's

commission from Silas Deane, who probably had not arrived in Paris at the time Kosciuszko left. He looked about for a place to work, and was hired by the Pennsylvania Committee of Defense to work on plans for fortifying the Delaware River. He did a good job and soon won a commission as colonel of engineers in the Continental Army.

In the spring of 1777, the young Pole joined General Gates at Ticonderoga. He rebuilt the fortifications of Fort Independence, and he advised fortifying Sugar Loaf. It was not fortified, and Ticonderoga was lost to Burgoyne. Kosciuszko stayed with Gates, whose personal friend he had become, helped choose the battlefield for Saratoga, and directed the building of the fortifications. Engineers seldom get the credit that is given commanders, or even individual sharpshooters; Kosciuszko contributed significantly to the key victory of Saratoga.

In the spring of 1778, Kosciuszko was put in charge of the fortifications at West Point, where he performed with energy and skill. Gates asked him to join him in the south as his engineer officer, but before he arrived Gates had left the field at Camden in disgrace, his military career ended. Kosciuszko stayed to work for Nathanael Greene, and had the crucial job of managing Greene's transportation during his long withdrawal in 1781, a job he carried out with great success. As the war neared its end, Kosciuszko served as a cavalry officer in the south. He was one of the first American officers into Charleston when that city was recaptured in 1782.

The American Revolution was over, but Kosciuszko's career was only beginning. Thirty-eight years old when he returned to Poland, he became a major general in the Polish army in 1789, and rejoiced three years later in the new constitution that gave Poland a limited hereditary monarchy, a more workable government with ministerial responsibility and such reforms as religious toleration and the abolition of many class privileges. Not all Poles rejoiced, and some aristocrats who hated the new order conspired with the Russian government to destroy the constitution. Kosciuszko was a leader and a hero in the efforts of the little Polish army against Russia. When the Russians finally crushed resistance, and the Polish king gave in, Kosciuszko fled the country and became the leader of a group of exiles who dreamed and worked to redeem the Polish nation from outside control and to give its people more individual freedom. Naïvely sure that the leaders of the French Revolutionary government would help his cause like brothers, Kosciuszko was disappointed to get evasive answers in Paris, where the government was coolly concerned only with its own survival, and certainly had no time for Polish interests.

A Polish uprising in 1794 began before Kosciuszko and his friends were ready for it, but he quickly took command and led the rebel army in brilliant military successes. The most dramatic was the Battle of Raclawice, in April 1794, when he defeated a Russian force of five thousand with a Polish force of four thousand troops and two thousand peasants armed only with scythes and pikes. The rebels captured Warsaw on April 17. Kosciuszko took control of the new government and put through many reforms. In October 1794, however, he was defeated, seriously wounded, and captured by the Russians. "Freedom shrieked as Kosciuszko fell," wrote Thomas Campbell a few years later. Kosciuszko was imprisoned in Russia for two years.

Released when a new czar ascended the throne, Kosciuszko went to America, where he was warmly received and was given his accumulated Continental pension. Congress also voted him five hundred acres of land in Ohio. This he asked Thomas Jefferson to sell for him, and with the proceeds he bought slaves so as to set them free.

After a year's stay in the United States, Kosciuszko returned to France in 1798. Unlike many of the Polish nationalists, however, he was suspicious of Napoleon, did not believe that help for Poland could come through him, and refused to support him. His healthy cynicism may well have stemmed from his disappointing experience with the leaders of Revolutionary France. He died in Switzerland at seventy-one, a hero of Poland and America. Is it because his name is so much harder to pronounce that he is less honored in the United States, for which he did so much, than Pulaski? Or is it the mundane nature of the T-square and spade in contrast to the romance of the cavalry saber?

Drillmaster of the Army

Friedrich Wilhelm von Steuben, a genuine baron though not the lieutenant general he said he was, arrived at Washington's headquarters in January of 1778. Washington was dubious about accepting another foreigner—only Lafayette had won his full acceptance, and even he was pesky in his constant pleas for a division to command—but the lively, balding Prussian brought a sprightly charm that warmed the Valley Forge chill. He also brought first-hand knowledge of the military organization and tactics of Frederick the Great's Prussian army, the most respected in the Western world. Because von Steuben's skills were highly regarded in Europe, Benjamin Franklin and Silas Deane—and the remarkable Frenchman Pierre-Augustin Caron de Beaumarchais—had decided to finance his voyage to America from the treasury of the mysterious Hortalez and Company, which Beaumarchais had set up to help the American cause. They knew Congress wanted no more foreign officers, but they thought von Steuben would be useful, and that he could make a place for himself if he arrived bearing the rank of lieutenant general. They therefore rapidly promoted him from captain, the rank he had held at the end of the Seven Years' War, and von Steuben did not refuse.

Von Steuben came from an upward-mobile Prussian family, not from the old aristocracy. His grandfather had inserted the *von*, and he himself was the first baron von Steuben, having received the title not in Prussia but from the Prince of Hohenzollern-Hechingen, the tiny German state where he had gone to work when the Seven Years' War and his military career ended simultaneously. The prince, like von Steuben himself, was a generous spender, and it was his employer's constantly imminent bankruptcy that forced von Steuben to look for new employment just at the time when the American Revolution was attracting so many European soldiers.

Despite the contrast between the high rank and aristocratic background in which von Steuben cloaked himself and the considerably plainer reality, he was not a soldier to be condescended to. He had fought with distinction in the Seven Years' War and had been chosen to serve as aide-de-camp to Frederick himself, a post which for two years gave him personal contact with one of the great military men of history.

At Valley Forge von Steuben found an army that was poorly trained and poorly disciplined, under leaders who were, most of them, ignorant of what was needed to improve matters. It is a common fallacy that the American Revolution was won by frontier sharpshooters who used hit-and-run tactics to destroy regiments of red-coated automatons. Sniping farmers were indeed effective in harassing the British column pulling back from

Concord, but in several pitched battles after that the American cause failed because American troops were hard to move into position quickly enough and once there had a tendency to break under fire. Good military discipline was desperately needed, and the Continentals did not fight well with any consistency until they got it—from von Steuben.

When Washington asked von Steuben's help in training the army, the baron took three steps to change things. First, he developed a system of drill, so that there would be standard ways of handling weapons, marching, and giving commands. Then he wrote up the system in clear regulations—no small task even without a language barrier, and quite an accomplishment for von Steuben and his assistants, for he formulated the rules in German, translated them into French, which he knew, and then had them translated into English by two French-fluent American aides. Finally, and crucially important, von Steuben trained the instructors who would drill the men. At the same time, he himself was drilling a model company of a hundred men, whose enthusiasm and increasingly military appearance stimulated the rest.

Most striking in von Steuben's methods was his obvious respect and affection for the men he was training. He won their cooperation through his willingness to work as hard as they did, and his sense of humor. Paradoxically, it was this drillmaster from the country of Frederick William and Frederick the Great who taught the American army to instill discipline while respecting the dignity of the individual soldier, rather than using harsh physical punishment.

The Continentals' spirits rose as the cold and hunger of Valley Forge began to count for something and they could feel themselves becoming part of an effective army.

Von Steuben had come to Valley Forge on February 23; by April 30 he had made such progress that Washington asked Congress to make him inspector general of the Continental Army with the rank of major general, a request Congress granted.

The new Continental Army proved itself in the campaigns of 1778, and during the winter of 1778-1779 von Steuben converted his hastily produced drill procedures into the *Regulations for the Order and Discipline of the Troops of the United States*. The book went through a process of translation and editing even more complex than had been necessary for the drills of the previous winter. Completed, it became the military bible of the Continental Army.

Most of the baron's contribution was as inspector general and as a kind of one-man general staff for Washington. He had little chance to command in the field. He had the frustrating job of trying to gather, conserve, and transport supplies for Nathanael Greene in Virginia in 1780, and he lost many of them to Benedict Arnold, Banastre Tarleton, and William Phillips. Once Lafayette arrived in Virginia, von Steuben served under him. He did command a division at the siege of Yorktown, where he had a chance to offer his experience in European siegecraft.

Always popular with Americans, von Steuben stayed in the United States after the war, spending his winters in New York City and his summers at his country estate. Generous to a fault, he had borrowed money after the Yorktown victory so that he could appropriately entertain the defeated British; in his later years he continued his extravagant generosity, and his many friends, including Alexander Hamilton, often had to rally to stave off his bankruptcy.

And Many Others

Despite the valor and skill of de Kalb, Lafayette, von Steuben and Kosciuszko, Washington frequently complained about the foreigners who were foisted upon him. He had reason.

Irish-French Thomas Conway may have been the worst troublemaker, as leader of the so-called Conway Cabal that sought to remove Washington as commander in chief and replace him by Horatio Gates. Arrogant Tronson du Coudray, whose demand for special privilege caused trouble even as he boarded ship to sail for America, antagonized the many American officers he wished to precede on the seniority list. It was a considerable relief to all concerned when he managed, through sheer recklessness, to drown himself in September 1777. Matthias Alexis de Roche Fermoy, a hard-drinking Frenchman from Martinique, was given command of a brigade for Washington's crossing of the Delaware, and endangered the victory at Princeton by leaving his troops before the battle; he later managed to bungle his mission at Ticonderoga by setting his own quarters on fire.

But there were many others who made substantial, even essential, contributions. When Washington groaned about the foreign officers, he always excepted not only Lafayette but "the engineers." Military engineers—men who were trained to assess terrain, plan fortifications, and supervise their construction—were exactly the experts the new army needed. Congress asked France for as many as four such officers as part of its first request for aid, two years before the alliance was signed. Louis le Beque de Presle du Portail and two others arrived in July 1777, and du Portail, especially, became immediately and increasingly respected for his skill, hard work, and devotion. Not surprisingly, he clashed early with the arrogant du Coudray. Du Portail rose from colonel to major general entirely on his merits. He was responsible for much of the siege engineering at Yorktown.

At least two more Frenchmen were worthy of the best Americans they fought beside. François Louis Teissedre de Fleury was in fact a hero of two armies in the Revolution. Coming first as a volunteer, he distinguished himself at Piscataway and also at Brandywine, where his horse was shot from under him; Congress voted him a new one in appreciation. At Stony Point he won the $500 prize Anthony Wayne had promised to the first man who made it through the two abatis and over the parapet. When France entered the war, de Fleury went home on leave, came back with Rochambeau in the Saintonge Regiment, and was decorated for his part in the Yorktown campaign.

Much less known than the dashing Pulaski—but a more effective soldier—was the French volunteer who took over the battered remnants of Pulaski's Legion after the Savannah debacle. Of a noble rank that equaled Lafayette's, Charles-Armand Tuffin, marquis de la Rouerie, was known in America simply as Charles Armand. He fought well early in the war, and did a good job with what became known as Armand's Legion in the late Virginia and South Carolina operations. Armand's Legion fought at Camden, and it is little shame to him that his men were not able to withstand the force of the panicked Virginia militia that poured back through them on that disastrous day.

And so the Continental Army had an international officer corps; Frenchmen, Poles, and Germans brought to it diversity of skills, experience, personality, and character. The best and the worst came to America, drawn by a war that gave each man the chance to get ahead in his career, escape or resolve some inner pain, or advance his own country's cause. For some of them the adventure ended in death, through chance, recklessness, or the tragic errors of other men.

4

The International British Army

Much more international in its number of foreign troops than the Continental Army was the army fighting for Britain in North America. Of the thirty-two thousand men Britain sent out in 1776, twelve thousand were German. By the time the war was over the total number of Germans who fought under the British flag at one time or another had reached close to thirty thousand. The British contingent itself was not homogeneous, including many Scots and Irishmen who had not yet been fully assimilated into the British realm. The uniforms, customs, and accents of soldiers from Scotland and Ireland added an exotic element to the British ranks.

Hessians and Other Germans

When it became clear to British leaders that their American troubles had become a major armed insurrection, they soon realized that foreign military forces would be needed to suppress it quickly. The British army simply wasn't large enough.

Since the Middle Ages there had always been European countries that made a business of providing hired soldiers. In the eighteenth century, the small German states, with well-trained officer corps, disciplined troops, and financially needy princes, were the principal source. Moreover, the British royal family had ties of kinship and association with Germany; so it was naturally to them that the government turned for help.

The agreements that provided the troops to fight in America were couched as treaties of alliance between Britain and several small German states, but they were in fact cold-blooded bills of sale. The faction in Parliament that had favored conciliation with the colonies had great fun in the debates on these treaties. As Lord Camden put it,

To give this bargain the appearance of what it really is not, the whole is stuffed up with pompous expressions of alliance, founded in reciprocal support and common interest; as if these petty States were really concerned in the event of the present contest between this country and America. . . . Is there one of your Lordships who does not perceive most clearly that the whole is a mere mercenary bargain for the hire of troops on one side, and the sale of human blood on the other; and that the devoted wretches thus purchased for slaughter, are mere mercenaries, in the worst sense of the word?*

Lord North, however, could answer all complaints with the assurance that the troops had been obtained on the very best terms available, and that since the use of ample numbers of them would ensure the war's being over quickly—probably within a year—it was a good bargain all around. In any case, it did not matter very much how foolish the government members looked in this debate, since they had more than enough votes to dampen the most satirical eloquence of the opposition.

Although the German soldiers were popularly known as Hessians—in 1776 and ever since—they actually came from six German states. Hesse-Cassel did send close to 17,000 and Hesse-Hanau another 1,400; but 5,700 came from Brunswick, over 2,000 from Anspach-Bayreuth, and over a thousand each from Waldeck and Anhalt-Zerbst.

In each case, the prince of the state was paid a fixed amount of money, and the king of England also agreed to feed and supply the Germans at the same standards as British troops. In some of the treaties there was also a curious "blood-money" clause, whose meaning has been debated; it seems to have provided that for each man killed and each three men wounded, the English king would pay the appropriate German prince a set fee. This was apparently in addition to money paid for recruiting a new soldier to fill the roster. Symbolizing, as it seemed to, the sovereign's absolute right to the life of his subject, and the idea that the soldier's death diminished the sovereign rather than the man or his family, the blood-money clause evoked much hostile comment in the European liberal press.

The German officers were generally of about the same caliber

*Peter Force, *American Archives: Fourth Series* (Washington, 1837-1846), Vol. 6, p. 310.

as their British counterparts, and some were considerably better.
Lieutenant General Baron Friedrich Adolphus von Riedesel,
who led the Brunswick contingent, was a fine commander, as
were the Hessians Lieutenant General Leopold von Heister and
Lieutenant General Baron Wilhelm von Knyphausen. The British generals often failed to make full use of their German col-
leagues, however, probably largely for reasons of prejudice and
professional jealousy.

The common soldiers were a mixed crew. The princes had to
raise new levies to meet their contracts with King George, and
they did it by time-honored techniques. Quotas were assigned to
each district, and since forced recruiting of law-abiding natives
of the state was officially forbidden, recruiters combed the
streets to pounce on any reasonably healthy man under sixty
who was not readily identifiable as a productive citizen. The
press gangs often picked up travelers, perhaps from a neighboring German state, who had no powerful local connections to
protect them. Petty criminals, political dissidents, and those who
had local reputations as troublemakers or drunkards were also
fair game. A young theological student who had left school
because of religious doubts was seized as he traveled through
Hesse-Cassel. He later gave this description of his fellow
recruits:

> Here was an indescribable lot of human beings brought
> together, good and bad, and others that were both by turns.
> My comrades were a runaway son of the Muses from Jena, a
> bankrupt tradesman from Vienna, a fringemaker from
> Hanover, a discharged secretary of the post office from
> Gotha, a monk from Wurzburg, an upper steward from
> Meinungen, a Prussian sergeant of hussars, a cashiered
> Hessian major from the fortress itself, and others of like
> stamp.

The recruiters tore up this young man's university matriculation
papers so that he could not prove his identity, and he resigned
himself to the situation, feeling that if others could stand it he
could too—and after all, there were things to see on the other
side of the ocean.*

The German soldiers who fought in the Revolution have been

*Johann Gottfried Seume, quoted in Edward J. Lowell, *The Hessians*, pp. 39-40.

portrayed in American folklore as particularly despicable enemies, with *Hessian* implying savagery and refusal to give quarter. Much of this reputation probably came simply from misunderstandings growing out of the language barrier. It was also felt that because the Germans were mercenaries, in the sense that someone had paid their rulers for their services, they therefore were creatures who liked to make war for a living; this charge was actually far truer of such American heroes as Lafayette, de Kalb, and Pulaski than it was of the often-reluctant officers and brutally impressed men of the German regiments. They were, nevertheless, good fighters.

The Hessians played their part in the Battle of Long Island and in pushing Washington up Manhattan Island, across the Hudson, and down through New Jersey. They were especially effective at White Plains, and Fort Washington was virtually a Hessian victory.

This fortress was basically indefensible by the Americans in the strategic situation that existed—and Washington knew it. In 1776, however, he did not yet have enough confidence in his own judgment to say no at the appropriate time. His subordinates were sure they could hold it, and Washington did not overrule them. British General Sir William Howe entrusted the main assault effort to 3,000 Germans under General Knyphausen. They were to move in from the north, while a smaller British force was to cross the Hudson and drive against the face of the high-rising fortress. At the same time a mixed British-Hessian force was to move up from central Manhattan. Everything went smoothly for the British and Germans; 2,722 of Washington's best troops were captured, and the other 150 men in Fort Washington were killed or wounded. The British suffered 458 casualties—killed, wounded, and missing. Three-fourths of these were Hessians. The post was renamed Fort Knyphausen.

Six weeks later the same regiments that conquered at Fort Washington were to suffer one of the most humiliating and disastrous defeats of the war. As the Hessians slept off their Christmas food and drink at Trenton, and sleet-chilled sentries turned their backs to the north wind and to approaching danger, Washington led his diminished, ragged army across the Delaware River. Complete surprise was achieved, and the Hessians, good soldiers though they were, could not rally in time to make any initial resistance. Colonel Jacob Rall, commander of the Trenton outpost, quickly gathered two of his three regiments for a counterattack and ordered his band to play a march. Surrounded on three sides, however, the Hessians were doomed. Rall himself fell, and the regimental colors followed him.

When General Howe heard the news, he expressed shock that "three old established regiments of a people who make war a profession should lay down their arms to a ragged and undisciplined militia." He made old General Heister the scapegoat of the affair and had him recalled. Heister died a few months later, deeply hurt by this ending to his career. The real culprit seems to have been the brave but overconfident and careless Rall, who lay dead, and the generally complacent spirit that infected the Hessians. And who could have guessed that the defeated Washington with his tiny army would strike back so fiercely on the day after Christmas?

Meanwhile, the contingent from Brunswick had arrived in Canada in June 1776 and soon joined the British in pursuing the retreating American invasion force under Benedict Arnold. Von Riedesel, the Brunswick commander, favored taking Fort Ticonderoga before winter, but the British commander, Sir Guy Carleton, decided to wait. Von Riedesel was probably right.

The northern campaign of 1777 was Burgoyne's Offensive, an invasion of New York from Canada, led by Lieutenant General John Burgoyne; von Riedesel and his men were to serve under Gentleman Johnny. There were close to four thousand Germans, and they made up almost half the non-Indian part of the invasion force. The Americans evacuated Ticonderoga, once the British had occupied the nearby height that commanded it, and the British and Germans set out in hot pursuit. At Hubbardton, Vermont, the advance guard of Brigadier General Simon Fraser fell on an American force at breakfast. The Americans, who included the Vermont Green Mountain Boys, put up a surprisingly stiff fight, and Fraser's men were in trouble until von Riedesel himself, leading his advance detachment, rode up and saved the day.

Very different for the Brunswickers was the Battle of Bennington. As Burgoyne continued southward, he needed supplies, and especially horses. The Brunswick dragoons had none, and they were almost useless without them, weighed down as they were by heavy boots, uniforms, and swords. On the recommendation of a Tory advisor, Burgoyne ordered a foraging expedition of dragoons east of the Hudson, and the unfortunate Lieutenant Colonel Friedrich Baum led it. He found no horses and pressed on toward Bennington, just across the Vermont border, where supplies were stored. Before he got there he was taken in a murderous double envelopment by Colonel John Stark; Baum was killed, and his surviving men surrendered. Reinforcements under Brunswicker Lieutenant Colonel Heinrich von Breymann arrived too late, and soon after them came Stark's reinforcements—Colonel Seth Warner and his Green Mountain Boys. The Germans were utterly routed. Their losses were heavy—207 men killed and 700 captured. Yet they had fought bravely. They had been ordered into hostile territory badly outnumbered; horse dragoons had been sent out, weighed down by equipment never meant for slogging through summer heat on foot in rough country, to capture their own horses. It was small wonder that von Riedesel was bitter at the treatment his men received. Relations between von Riedesel and Burgoyne were not good, and Bennington was one reason.

By mid-September, Burgoyne had reached what were to be the Saratoga battlefields. The first battle, at Freeman's Farm, was technically a British victory, and the Germans played an important role. Von Riedesel commanded the left, and his attack, near nightfall, carried the day. Colonel Breymann, who had escaped, wounded, at Bennington, distinguished himself earlier in the afternoon by coming to the relief of an English regiment that was falling back, and a Captain Pausch, with two six-pounders of the Hesse-Hanau artillery, played a key role in turning the tide.

At the second Saratoga battle, Bemis Heights, von Riedesel commanded the center, with Simon Fraser on his right and a force of English grenadiers on the left. Early in the battle the grenadiers were routed, exposing the German flank, and finally the Hessian cannon were captured, and the Germans fell back. Fraser's wing held longest, but when he himself fell mortally wounded the British right also fell back. As the British and Germans retreated, Colonel Breymann, with a few men, was left holding a small redoubt at the extreme right of the line. Surrounded, Breymann was killed and his men captured.

The Convention Army

Breymann's contingent was soon joined in captivity by the rest of the Germans and British of Burgoyne's army, and it proved to be a long and peripatetic captivity. Burgoyne obtained rather remarkable surrender terms from General Gates. The instrument of surrender was called a "convention," and the British and Germans were permitted to return to their homes, as long as they promised not to fight again in the war against the United States. It was a peculiar agreement for Gates to make, since if the troops returned to Europe they could serve anywhere except America and thus make available the same number of British troops to fight the Americans. Once made, however, it should have been kept, under all the rules of honor, but it was not. Congress refused to accept the Convention of Saratoga, and the army that surrendered there began a series of wanderings about the country as prisoners of war that ended only with the war itself. They were known as the Army of the Convention.

There was a woman with this army who has left one of the most enjoyable and valuable pieces of American Revolution literature. When Baron von Riedesel received orders to go to America, his wife decided that she would go with him. Waiting only for the birth of her third daughter, the baroness set out across the ocean, accompanied by the three little girls and a family servant, to join her husband. Her journal describes all the events of Burgoyne's Offensive, the life of the Convention troops in captivity, and many details of American life, all as seen through her eyes—which were very perceptive, though naturally prejudiced in favor of her husband, Germans and Germany, and England. She generally did not like Americans who supported the Revolution. She and her husband became good friends of Thomas Jefferson, however, during the time the Convention Army spent in Virginia.

The baroness was only one of two or three thousand women who followed the Patriot, British, and German armies. (The French, somewhat surprisingly, had very few women with them.) She was one of the real heroines among them. At Bemis Heights she quieted her children so that they would not disturb the gravely wounded General Fraser, who died in her quarters. During the heavy bombardment before the surrender at Saratoga, she took refuge with the children in a cellar and soon had it cleaned and organized into a hospital for the wounded, with drinking water brought in by the courageous wife of a sergeant.

Although the war was over for the Convention troops after Saratoga, other Germans continued fighting until 1781. A few days after the Saratoga surrender, another group of Hessians fought a brave and thoroughly ill-advised battle at Redbank, New Jersey. There, sent by Major General William Howe, Colonel Karl von Donop led his 4,000-man brigade against Fort Mercer, held by about 400 Americans. Catching the charging Hessians in the ditch between the abatis and the walls of the fort, the Americans killed or wounded 370. Von Donop was wounded and captured; he died three days later.

Germans also fought and died at Charleston and Guilford Court House, against the Spaniards at Baton Rouge and Pensacola, and finally at Yorktown. German losses in killed and wounded at Yorktown were 184, close to 40 percent of all those lost on the British side. It was Hessians who were killed and captured when Redoubt 9 at Yorktown was taken by the French.

Scots for King George

Scotland was very much a nation in 1776, and only a short time before had been brought firmly within the kingdom of Great Britain. It was just thirty years earlier that the Highland clans had risen to fight for Bonnie Prince Charlie in the Jacobite rebellion (the Forty-five). Scots had invaded England then, before the rising was crushed at the bloody Battle of Culloden and in its even bloodier aftermath. One thousand prisoners taken in that battle, or most of them, were murdered or summarily executed, and every prominent Scottish supporter of the Stuarts who could be caught was treated likewise. The Bonnie Prince, Charles Edward Stuart, lingered in Scotland for months, hidden by brave supporters. Among them was a girl in her early twenties, Flora MacDonald, who disguised the prince as a woman and guided him on a long flight to the Isle of Skye, whence he eventually sailed to exile in France. Flora herself was captured, and was imprisoned in the Tower of London until public sympathy for her heroism brought about her release.

George II had been king of Great Britain then, and the Scottish Jacobites had vehemently hated the House of Hanover. The

Seven Years' War (1756-1763) was something of a unifying force, however, as many Scottish regiments fought "the French for King George upon the throne." Then George III acceded to the throne in 1760. He announced, "I glory in the name of Briton," and although this is often taken as an affirmation of his identity with England rather than with the Germany of his immediate ancestors, George may have intended rather to stress all Great Britain in contrast to England alone. He did in fact appoint a number of Scots to high posts and did make many efforts to heal the wounds of the Forty-five.

There were four or five Scottish regiments serving with the British army in the Revolutionary War. One of them was raised by Simon Fraser (not the general killed at Bemis Heights), a Jacobite leader who had lost his title of Master of Lovat after the Forty-five, but who had since raised and ably led a regiment in the French and Indian War. It still comes as something of a shock, however, to find the Jacobite heroine Flora MacDonald, as a woman of fifty-two who had recently immigrated to America, rallying Scots in North Carolina in support of the Hanoverian king.

Studies have shown, in fact, that most of the Scottish immigrants in North Carolina—many of whom had fled home to avoid living under the Hanoverian kings — were Loyalists, and that most of the Loyalists in North Carolina were Scottish immigrants. Much can change in thirty years. The Scots had been given generous land grants and had taken oaths of loyalty in return, and perhaps their fervent past loyalty to a king (albeit a Stuart) made them especially suspicious of republican ideas. Certainly an oath given meant much to them, as did loyalty to their leaders. When Flora MacDonald and her husband, Allan, rallied behind the two Scots officers—Donald MacDonald and Donald McLeod—sent by the British in early 1776, the clans of North Carolina rose with a skirl of bagpipes and flash of dirks and broadswords. Flora, mounted on a white horse at Cross Creek, exhorted the gathered Scots in Gaelic and reviewed the columns of troops. Despite her inspiration and the battle cry, "King George and Broad Swords!" these Scots, fifteen hundred of them, were shattered at Moore's Creek Bridge on February 27. The Loyalist cause did not reappear in North Carolina as a force to be reckoned with until much later in the war.

III

THE ROLE OF
FRANCE

5

The Search for Supplies

When the Revolutionary War began, the rebelling colonists had almost no ammunition with which to fight it. The small stores seized at Portsmouth and Newport, and those hoarded at Concord, soon ran out. Little gunpowder was produced in the colonies. Much of the saltpeter (potassium or sodium nitrate) that is an essential ingredient of gunpowder was imported by the European countries that did make it—much coming from Bengal, in British India. By Christmas 1775 General Washington did not have so much as one pound of gunpowder in his magazines.

The story of how the colonists, and then the newly independent states, got the arms and ammunition to hold off the British until 1778, when the French alliance simplified supply problems, involves hundreds of merchants, ships' captains, diplomats, Patriot Americans serving in Congress, and European rulers and their ministers. The complicated network of supply touched London, Paris, Amsterdam, Texel, Nantes, Le Havre, and dozens of Caribbean islands. It can perhaps best be told by focusing on the activities of four men, none of them adequately recognized for this work—Pierre-Augustin Caron de Beaumarchais, Silas Deane, the comte de Vergennes, and Benjamin Franklin. And it cannot be told without some mention of a rocky little island in the Caribbean, now called St. Eustatius but then appearing on maps as St. Eustatia and popularly known as Statia in all the maritime households, shipping offices, and dockside taverns of the late eighteenth century.

Statia

Martinique, Guadeloupe, St. Lucia, and many other West Indies islands were important in supplying the Americans with war goods, but none played as crucial a role as Statia. The reasons for this are not immediately obvious.

St. Eustatius is a tiny volcanic eruption, displacing about eight square miles of blue Caribbean. The cone of its long-dead volcano rises sharply two thousand feet above the sea. The volcano's crater encloses a tiny tropical rain forest, but there is little fertile land on the island for cultivation. Nor is it gifted with a magnificent natural harbor. It had only one port in the eighteenth century, and that one quite ordinary. And it had no significant fortifications or armaments.

Yet in 1780 Admiral Sir George Rodney wrote, "This rock of only six miles in length and three in breadth has done England more harm than all the arms of her most potent enemies, and alone supported the infamous American rebellion."* He had some personal interest in making Statia sound formidable and dangerous, but his assessment was not far wrong.

St. Eustatius today yields no clues to the source of its eighteenth-century glory. Still called Statia, and sometimes "the Golden Rock of the Caribbean," it boasts no luxury resorts and attracts few tourists. The brochure for its one small hotel invites visitors to "come and see . . . why the Dutch, French and English wanted this magical island," but going and looking at the island will not solve the intriguing puzzle.

For the secret of Statia's importance was its location, and it was a location that had meaning only in its eighteenth-century context.

St. Eustatia (Sint Eustachius) was and is Dutch territory, and, since the Netherlands had given up strict adherence to mercantilism, it was a free port. Its facilities were open equally to ships and traders of all nations, and no duties were levied on goods shipped to Statia and stored there for reshipment elsewhere. More significantly, it was a free port located in the Leeward Islands, just nine miles northwest of the important British island of St. Kitts (St. Christopher), with the French island of St. Barthelemy lying about forty-five miles to the north, the Danish island of St. Croix about a hundred miles to the west, and Spanish Puerto Rico lying beyond St. Croix. Statia was thus able to serve the commercial needs of many nations and to become a rich trading center. Before the American Revolution, it was ideally situated for American vessels evading the British Navigation

*Quoted in Helen Augur, *The Secret War of Independence*, p. 51.

Acts and smuggling forbidden goods into North America. In peacetime it thrived. When Britain and France were at war, and the Netherlands was neutral, as in the Seven Years' War, Statia's roadstead was constantly white with the sails of a hundred ships or more.

Edmund Burke described Statia's unique position in the House of Commons in 1781, after the British had finally seized it. After stressing its lack of fertility, fortifications, and anything else that could mean strength, except trade, he said: "Its utility was its defence. The universality of its use, the constant neutrality of its nature . . . was its security and its safeguard. It had risen, like another Tyre, upon the waves. . . . Its wealth was prodigious."*

Well before Lexington and Concord, it became clear from activity at Statia that someone was expecting to need more supplies in North America and was planning ahead. By the end of 1774, the British ambassador to the Netherlands reported from his intelligence sources that there had recently been a sharp increase in trade through the island. Some of this increase was undoubtedly due to the "Association" of the Continental Congress, a pledge not to import any British goods. Americans were naturally buying more merchandise of all sorts from the countries of continental Europe, since they had promised not to buy from England. But there were unmistakable signs of preparations for war as well. Two Boston agents were in Amsterdam all that winter, specifically to buy gunpowder, and the gunpowder was to be shipped by way of Statia. The British ambassador had also reported in August that the Dutch were shipping "a pretty large quantity" of gunpowder to Statia.†

As contraband trade through Statia increased, and war came nearer, the British ambassador made urgent protests to the Dutch government. In March 1775, with Massachusetts declared by Parliament to be in a state of rebellion, the Netherlands officially forbade exporting ammunition and other war goods to the British colonies in America. Protocol was satisfied, but the Dutch merchants paid little attention. The prohibition was not enforced. Some American merchants who took it seriously and tried to order gunpowder elsewhere found they had merely delayed matters by not going straight to the Dutch. It

*Quoted by J. Franklin Jameson, "St. Eustatius in the American Revolution," p. 684.
† *Ibid.*, p. 687.

became quite customary for ships to load at Amsterdam for African ports, set sail in that direction, and then pick up the prevailing trade winds and continue straight to Statia. When Statia became closely watched by British men-of-war, in early 1776, American ships began to land first at a nearby French port, take out French—that is, neutral — papers, and then sail merrily on to Statia. Later, when France entered the war, and French ports and ships were no longer neutral, the traffic at Statia multiplied. The British navy, involved in fighting the French, could not control what happened at the little island. Even British merchants on nearby British islands stored goods in its warehouses for safekeeping. A Dutch admiral reported that 3,182 vessels sailed from Statia during the thirteen months he spent there in 1778-1779.

St. Eustatia was to play several other roles later in the war. It was to shelter American privateers, and to act as a depot for foreign volunteers heading for America. It would be a way station for Benjamin Franklin's diplomatic correspondence, and for war supplies. Its glory was to have a disastrous end. But in the war's early years it lay secure and prosperous in the tropic sun, its acres of warehouses crammed with supplies, its stored ammunition increasing in price—twofold, threefold, fourfold, and more—and its roadstead full of sails.

Beaumarchais

Pierre-Augustin Caron de Beaumarchais was a man of tremendous vitality, interested in everything, at home everywhere, skilled in many crafts. He was a man of letters and of action in the great eighteenth-century tradition, although more uninhibitedly adventurous and less profoundly intellectual than Voltaire, Jefferson, Priestley, or Franklin.

Beaumarchais was the son of a watchmaker named Caron. He signed his name *Caron, fils* in his youth, and he later made it clear that the name of his hero, Figaro, who spoke for Beaumarchais himself, was based on an anagram of this youthful signature.

Watchmaking was still a relatively new technology in the mid-eighteenth century, with much room for innovation, and it held great fascination for ladies and gentlemen of rank and wealth. Caron, apprenticed in his youth to his father, invented a new watch part before he was twenty, had the credit for it stolen from him by another watchmaker, fought the issue out in the press, and was invited to the court at Versailles as a result of the publicity. He then made a tiny watch fitted into a ring for Madame de Pompadour, charmed the king's four lonely daughters, and became the court watchmaker.

Caron was a musician as well. He played the harp and flute, and invented an improved pedaling arrangement for the harp. He gave the princesses harp lessons and became their friend. Soon he became a minor court official. Along with his rise in the world came marriage to a rich widow from a village called Beaumarchais, and Caron added the village name to his own as a symbol of his enhanced social status. Madame de Beaumarchais died less than a year after their marriage, probably of typhoid fever, but the name of her hometown went into French literary history.

Two or three years later, Beaumarchais made friends with a wealthy businessman named Joseph Paris-Duverney, a financier who had helped Voltaire make his fortune. With Paris-Duverney's help, Beaumarchais himself began to make money. He purchased a better government office, one that carried with it a good income and noble status. In 1768 he married for a second time, well and happily.

Then things began to go wrong for Beaumarchais. His wealthy patron, Paris-Duverney, and his second wife both died in 1770. He became involved in onerous litigation with Paris-Duverney's heir. Then a jealous duke murderously attacked him for real or imagined attentions to the duke's mistress, and— largely because he defended himself, and because of the duke's influence—Beaumarchais was imprisoned. Court proceedings in both cases dragged on. After a corrupt judge, Louis Goezmann, ruled unfairly on the charges brought by Paris-Duverney's heir, Beaumarchais took up his pen and moved to the court of public opinion, as he had earlier in seeking credit for his watch invention. The pamphlets he wrote in his defense won much attention for his case and caught the eye of the great Voltaire. Especially striking for later readers is one passage from his fourth pamphlet:

I am a citizen! I am a citizen! That is to say, I am neither a courtier, nor a churchman, nor a gentleman, nor a businessman, nor a favorite, nor anything that is regarded as power-

ful nowadays. I am a citizen! That is to say, what you should
have been for the past two hundred years, what you will be
perhaps in twenty years.*

Beaumarchais became a popular cause. He was acclaimed "the
French Wilkes" in the same year (1774) in which John Wilkes of
England was triumphantly elected Lord Mayor of London amid
cries of "Wilkes and liberty!" In England the tempestuous
Wilkes had fought for and come to represent freedom of the
press, freedom of the voters to choose their own representatives,
and freedom in general; Beaumarchais was becoming a symbol
of the same kind.

After an official investigation Beaumarchais was sentenced to
be *condamné au blame*, an official reprimand that deprived him of
most privileges, including the judgeship that gave him much of
his income. But Goezmann was also *condamné au blame* and lost
his job. The verdict was greeted as a great moral victory for
Beaumarchais. However, he was financially ruined and in royal
disfavor.

The lively watchmaker-musician-businessman-writer was not
a man to nurse his wounds for long. He decided to start restoring
his fortune and favor by volunteering for the delicate mission of
arranging to quash the publication in England of a revealing
four-volume biography of Madame du Barry, who had become
the mistress of Louis XV after the death of Madame de Pompadour. Since the purpose of the book's shady publisher was to
obtain blackmail in return for halting publication, Beaumarchais's mission was basically one of striking the best bargain
possible without embarrassing the king and his mistress. This he
accomplished, but when he went home to claim his reward he
found Louis fatally ill with smallpox, and du Barry about to be
banished from court so that the king could receive the Church's
sacraments. There was nothing to do but start all over with the
new king.

Blackmailing royalty with scandalous books was apparently a
fairly common occupation of the period, for it soon developed
that young Louis XVI and his wife were to be slandered in a
publication based on the inoffensive fact that they had been
married for four years and did not yet have any children. This
time Beaumarchais's travels took him not only to London, where

*Quoted in introduction to *The Barber of Seville*, trans. and ed. by Brobury Pearce Ellis.

some copies of the book were destroyed, and to Amsterdam, where others were, but also to Nuremberg and Vienna. This last part of the mission seems to have been overdramatized by Beaumarchais, to the extent of his scratching himself with his razor to give the impression of gunshot wounds. In any case, he came back from Vienna with a large diamond which he said had been given to him by the empress Maria Theresa in gratitude for his service to her daughter, Marie Antoinette.

In the midst of all this, he was preparing his play *The Barber of Seville* for production in 1775. He had written into it bitter references to his own troubles, and the first performance was hissed for its excessive length and distasteful jibes. Ever resourceful, Beaumarchais revised the play in forty-eight hours, and it played thereafter to enthusiastic crowds. Its success pales, however, beside Beaumarchais's later work *The Marriage of Figaro*, which was the hit of the century. The plays, which are obscured for many non-Frenchmen today by the operas based on them, are witty, charming, and full of subtle but telling social comment.

Beaumarchais's experience of injustice had made him an advocate of the underdog, and his energetic temperament made him always eager for an adventure. With his reputation as a secret foreign agent for the Crown now well established, Beaumarchais set out for London again in the spring of 1775. This time he was entrusted with a more serious mission—reporting to the comte de Vergennes, the French foreign minister, on British politics and economic matters, as part of that shrewd minister's plans for revenge on England. Beaumarchais was well qualified. He apparently already knew John Wilkes, who was idolized by the American activists and was in touch with many of them. And he also knew Lord Rochford, Secretary of State for the Southern Department, the branch of government dealing with the North American colonies. Beaumarchais had met Rochford in Madrid ten years earlier on one of his numerous foreign adventures, when business and a problem involving his sister's marriage had taken him to the Spanish capital.

In London, Beaumarchais was soon reporting on British sentiment and finances, while at the same time successfully negotiating with an emotionally unstable transvestite French agent for some letters that compromised earlier French spying activities in Britain—all in a day's work for Beaumarchais.

He was also becoming emotionally committed to the American

cause and began to develop a strategy for aiding it. At dinners given by Wilkes, Beaumarchais met Arthur Lee, one of the numerous Lee brothers of Virginia and an agent for the colonies in London. He also met many Englishmen who sympathized with the colonies, some of them willing to risk treason to help the Americans. Some of these men were friends of Benjamin Franklin, a more famous colonial agent who had already returned to America, and Franklin had almost certainly worked with some of them to start getting supplies to the colonies. Soon Beaumarchais was traveling to Flanders, probably in connection with shipping supplies to America.

Once news of Lexington and Concord arrived, and it was clear that Great Britain had serious trouble across the ocean, Beaumarchais began bombarding Vergennes and the king with long letters urging aid to the colonies. This was the burden of his pleas: Britain was France's great enemy. The colonies were too weak to hold out long against Britain. It was in France's compelling interest to help the colonies just enough, with arms and supplies, to keep the war going a long time. Naturally enough, Beaumarchais said nothing about the justice of the American cause, which would not have been an effective argument. He urged speed and secrecy; nothing must happen that would bring France into a war with England.

On this last point Vergennes was in full agreement. Ever ready to strike a blow at England, he understood the need to do it without involving France in any official way. He and Beaumarchais together worked out a plan for a cover organization, an instantly created great commercial trading house, headed by Beaumarchais and christened by him Roderigue Hortalez and Company. An imposing building in the Faubourg du Temple, once the Netherlands Embassy, was chosen as headquarters.

Beaumarchais, who was a businessman and had been the protégé of a famous financier, was not ill qualified for the job of the company's director. He wanted 3 million livres from the French government to spend on what the Americans needed. Vergennes gave him 1 million livres from the French treasury, for which Beaumarchais signed a receipt and made himself accountable. The other 2 million livres were scraped together from the Spanish—Bourbon cousins of Louis XVI and fellow enemies of Britain—and from several wealthy individuals. The Americans were to pay what they could in the form of commodities—especially tobacco.

The next month, July 1776, Silas Deane of Connecticut arrived in Paris with Congress's request for 200 cannon, 30 brass mortars, 200,000 pounds of powder, and tents, clothing, and small arms for 25,000 men. Thanks to a recent change in weapons by the French army, there was a good deal of surplus available, and the supplies were assembled at Le Havre and Nantes. Deane had agreed to supply ships to transport them, but none appeared.

Beaumarchais went to Le Havre under an assumed name to supervise things, and promptly blew his cover by directing rehearsals for a local production of *The Barber of Seville*. At the same time, he himself arranged and paid for the ships to take the precious cargo to America.

Meanwhile, the British ambassador to France, who knew almost immediately everything Beaumarchais and Deane did, vigorously protested the sailing. Vergennes properly acquiesced and halted the ships. The largest, *Amphitrite*, had already sailed, but she put back into port when Philippe Tronson du Coudray, who was sailing to America as a volunteer, complained about his sleeping quarters.

Then, as Beaumarchais and Deane waited anxiously, Vergennes let the ships slip out, one by one, deferring to each British protest, but releasing a ship each time the ambassador's attention was diverted.

The ships sailed into the harbor at Portsmouth, New Hampshire, on April 30 of the next year, fateful 1777, and were welcomed by a happy crowd of townspeople. These were the French guns, small arms, clothing, and powder that made possible the great victory of Saratoga that year. And it was Saratoga that persuaded the French government to do more than send arms—to sign a treaty of alliance and enter the war against England.

The alliance did not mark the end of Beaumarchais's work for the United States. After its signing, he fitted out a warship, which he named the *Fier Roderigue*, and sent it off to escort a convoy of ten merchant ships loaded with supplies, also sent by Beaumarchais. Unfortunately, the *Fier Roderigue* was commandeered by Admiral d'Estaing for a naval battle off Grenada in the West Indies. She fought well, but she was badly damaged, her captain was killed, and all the well-laden merchant vessels were captured or sunk.

Out of all this work and money expended, Beaumarchais

probably received less than nothing for himself. It is impossible to be sure because of the Arthur Lee/Silas Deane controversy that erupted in 1776 and is still not entirely resolved. Arthur Lee wrote Congress that the French government wanted no payment for the war supplies, and described Beaumarchais's pleas for return cargos of tobacco as "the perseverance usual to adventurers of his type."* Yet correspondence survives that shows Lee understood from the beginning that tobacco was to be sent in return for war goods.† Congress never paid the French or Beaumarchais in money or in kind for the supplies.

And of course the French government would never admit that Beaumarchais had been acting for Vergennes. Even in the nineteenth century, during the Bourbon restoration, Beaumarchais's heirs were unable to get from their government any acknowledgment that Louis XVI and his ministers could have done anything so improper as to aid a group of rebels whose existence as a nation France had not recognized. Finally, after traveling all the way to Washington, Beaumarchais's daughter and grandson were able to get from Congress the equivalent of 800,000 francs—probably a small fraction of what Beaumarchais had contributed.

Although by December 1777 Beaumarchais was writing Congress truly that both his money and his credit were exhausted, his enthusiasm for the American cause was undimmed. He was visiting Benjamin Franklin in his French home and headquarters—at Passy, outside Paris—when news came to Franklin that Burgoyne had surrendered his army at Saratoga. Beaumarchais set off immediately to take the news to Paris, and traveled with such eager speed that his carriage overturned on the way. He wrote Vergennes, "My right arm is cut, the bones of my neck were nearly crushed . . . but the charming news from America is a balm to my wounds."‡

Silas Deane

Silas Deane's mission to neutral France had to be secret. He was the first representative sent abroad by the rebelling colonists. They had not yet declared independence when he left

*Quoted in Cynthia Cox, *The Real Figaro*, p. 117.
†Augur, *The Secret War of Independence*, pp. 269-270.
‡Cox, *The Real Figaro*, p. 117.

America early in 1776, and he represented no nation. It had been agreed that he would pose as a rich Bermuda merchant and discreetly make contact with the French government, sounding French officials on the possibility of aid to the colonists. Then, in whatever way was possible, he was to arrange to get arms, ammunition, cloth, and blankets shipped to America.

When Deane arrived in Paris it was July 1776, and independence was being voted in Philadelphia, but neither Deane nor the French knew this until October. Deane's only lever on the French government—and he was too idealistic and unsophisticated to grasp it at first—was the colonies' power to hurt England.

A Connecticut blacksmith's son, Deane was nonetheless well educated, with a degree from Yale, and was a successful merchant-shipper and political leader. His second wife was Elizabeth Saltonstall, whose family was as prominent then as now in New England. She had brought him the connections that launched his political career, and she was a devoted stepmother to his only child, a young son.

Active in colonial protest movements since the days of the Townshend Acts, Deane was a member of the Continental Congress from the beginning. Along with Franklin, Robert Morris, and other members of the Secret Committee, he was one of the practical, energetic men who did what needed doing in the earliest days of the war. It was Deane, for example, who organized and financed Ethan Allen's successful attack on Fort Ticonderoga.

Deane was to be much condemned in his lifetime and after it for his activities in Paris. Although he lost his money and health in the American cause, he has been termed a war profiteer. A complex man, he certainly made errors, and he may well have hoped to make some money for himself. In the eighteenth century there was little squeamishness about public officials' acquiring wealth while helping supply their country. Nor was there any concern about conflicts of interest. Most of the members of the Continental Congress's Secret Committee were merchants or had family connections with merchants, and it was these firms that received contracts to supply the Continental soldiers and sailors. In any case, Deane himself ended up no richer after his exhausting service in Paris.

Deane's chief sin in the eyes of military men, then and now, was his indiscriminate overrecruitment of volunteer European officers for Continental service, but there were some extenuating circumstances in that matter. Deane was, after all, two or three months away in message time from Philadelphia, and it was hard for him to visualize the impact of his recruitments there. He also felt that he had to stay on good terms with the French court, where many of the eager volunteers had powerful friends and relatives. And it was through Deane, after all, that some great volunteers, notably Lafayette and von Steuben, came to aid the Revolutionary cause. His really grievous error was writing to the Secret Committee in December 1776 that it would be well to replace Washington as commander in chief with a distinguished European officer like the comte de Broglie. His contributions are further clouded by the fact that toward the end of the war he began to have misgivings about the American cause, to feel it was hopeless, and to resent the criticism and charges that shadowed his diplomatic accomplishments of 1776-1778. He wrote letters urging reconciliation with England without American independence, and the letters were published. He had dealings with a British agent in Paris that were probably treasonous. Unwelcome in America, he lived the last of his life in poverty as an exile in England.

But all this was far in the future in the summer of 1776, when thirty-nine-year-old Silas Deane drove out to Versailles escorted by his French connection, a scholarly old friend of Benjamin Franklin's, Dr. Jacques Barbeu-Dubourg. At Versailles Deane met a man whose keen grasp of power diplomacy and cold hatred of Great Britain would give him the arms he wanted.

Vergennes

When the comte de Vergennes became foreign minister to young Louis XVI in 1774, he inherited the voluminous intelligence files of the duc de Choiseul, and he brought with him the same hatred for England that had animated his great predecessor. Fortunately for historians, Vergennes had the habit of putting his views on paper.* At the beginning of his ministry, he summed up his ideas on what French foreign policy should be: The Family Compact with Spain must be maintained for the necessary support it provided against England; the Austrian

*As Samuel Flagg Bemis has remarked. (*Diplomacy of the American Revolution*, pp. 17-18.)

alliance of 1756 should be maintained too, but strictly as a defensive alliance, needed because of England's alliance with Prussia; there was to be no war with England unless success was sure.

Vergennes was pleased with news of the Boston Tea Party and the Intolerable Acts, but he was cautious. When word came from the French Embassy in London that friends of the rebels had made approaches about an alliance, Vergennes did nothing except, probably, allow some subsidies to merchants supplying the Americans. He could still visualize the situation abruptly reversing itself, with an American insurrection bringing the fall of the British government, and a new government coming to power that would be headed by the earl of Chatham (William Pitt's title since 1766), France's implacable foe. Britons and Americans might then unite to seize France's West Indies islands. (This seemingly unlikely possibility was frequently mentioned by the French.)

Then, with 1775, Massachusetts was declared in rebellion, and shots were fired at Lexington. The British had blundered into a war.

That summer of 1775, Vergennes sent an experienced agent, Julien Achard de Bonvouloir, to America. He was to arrange to meet members of the Continental Congress and assure them, strictly unofficially, that France wished them well, welcomed trade with them, and had no desire to take advantage of the British-American troubles by retaking Canada. Achard de Bonvouloir arrived in Philadelphia in December, traveling incognito as a merchant from Antwerp, and rendezvoused with members of Congress's Committee of Secret Correspondence, including Franklin. They met after dark, and each member of the committee took a different path to the appointed house. The French agent delivered his messages and granted an urgent request made by the Americans: France—unofficially, of course—would send them two skilled military engineers.

While Achard de Bonvouloir was in America, Vergennes was receiving a barrage of letters from Beaumarchais in London. Vergennes would probably have been persuaded by a less insistent advocate; the idea of setting up a make-believe firm of merchant shippers to send arms to America fitted in very well with his own ideas. Roderigue Hortalez and Company was born.

Then Silas Deane arrived at Versailles. The aristocratic master of European diplomatic intrigue greeted Deane with a warmth

that the American took to signify genuine concern for the cause
of the colonies and for Deane himself. Vergennes assured him
that French ports were open to Americans, suavely indicated
that although France could not openly encourage the shipment
of war goods, nothing would be done to prevent powder-laden
ships from sailing. He also warned the American against all
Englishmen in France—they might well be spies. Deane thought
he was being careful, and he knew he was being followed
everywhere, but neither he nor any American, nor Vergennes,
suspected that Edward Bancroft, Deane's private secretary and a
friend of Franklin's, was a British spy. Bancroft, an American
who had been living in England, was a double agent throughout
the war, and no other American seems to have known this until
sixty years after his death. It is little wonder that the British knew
of all Deane's purchases and sailing dates; the remarkable thing
is how well the American armies were supplied from France
despite the superb British intelligence network.

Vergennes never put a word in writing to Deane; France was
neutral. All messages to Deane came from Conrad Alexandre
Gérard, First Secretary of the Foreign Ministry, who had interpreted for Vergennes and Deane at their meeting. Gérard's
messages were guardedly phrased. When Deane received a
puzzling letter from Beaumarchais suggesting that he could be
very helpful to an American trying to buy arms, Deane asked
Vergennes what it meant, and the assurance came back that
Beaumarchais "could be relied on." Finally Deane understood:
Beaumarchais was acting for the French Foreign Ministry and
with money it was advancing and guaranteeing. But Vergennes
would never admit that the government of France was giving
military aid to American rebels.

Franklin

When Benjamin Franklin arrived in Paris in December 1776
—as massive reinforcement for Silas Deane's diplomacy—he was
seventy years old. He had behind him a fully lived, many-sided
eighteenth-century life, rich with business and literary success,
scientific discoveries, public service, love affairs, and friend-
ships. In humble background, breadth of interests and abil-
ities, and frequency of romantic involvement, the older man
had a good deal in common with Beaumarchais. But while

Beaumarchais was well known only in Europe, Franklin's reputation shone throughout the western world.

He had been born one of the youngest of a huge family of
children, son of a Boston soap and candle maker, had become a
printer, had run away to Philadelphia, and had become its leading citizen. Everyone knew him as the author of the practical
maxims of *Poor Richard's Almanac*, for his important discoveries
about electricity, and for his demonstration that the lightning in
a stormy sky is itself electricity. He was also known for his public
service to the colonies, and especially for his long representation
of them in London.

He had served in London as colonial agent—that is, representative, lobbyist, and business agent—for Pennsylvania and other
colonies during most of the seventeen years before 1775. A
notably convivial person, he had made many friends. British
opposition politicians sympathized with him on American
rights, American sea captains passing through London checked
in with him, and scientists and men of letters in Britain and
France conferred with him and invited him to join their
societies.

When Franklin came to France in 1776, he was greeted not
only as a man of accomplishment but as a symbol, as the epitome
of everything that was wise, good, simple—and American.
Whenever he appeared in public he was mobbed by an idolizing
crowd. His portrait was cherished on medallions, porcelain coffee cups, and countless adulatory engravings. Vergennes and his
aides may have helped America for entirely cynical reasons, but
many Frenchmen of all classes loved America through Franklin,
the quintessential American.

It was fitting that Franklin should return to Europe to conduct
the delicate negotiations that led to the French alliance and all
the aid it would bring, for while in London he had been the first
American to start war supplies moving toward the colonies.

Just when Franklin had become convinced that independence
was the road for America to take, and that war was thus inevitable, is still not clear. There is now more controversy than ever
about this shrewd and complicated man. It seems likely,
however, that by January 1774 Franklin had come to believe that
independence and war were inevitable. It was during that month
that he was submitted to the humiliation of being officially
denounced in London before the Privy Council by the Solicitor
General of the realm for allegedly having created a plot for "a

great American republic." The Solicitor General did not have
evidence for his rantings at Franklin, and there is general agreement that Franklin did not decide for independence because of
this insult to himself. He was, however, shocked by the aggressive anti-Americanism of powerful Englishmen, as dramatized
before the Privy Council that day, and the experience did so-
lidify his decision.

This was the time of reaction to the Boston Tea Party. Soon
Parliament was debating an act to close the port of Boston, and
the other Intolerable Acts. In March a member of the House of
Commons declared that "the town of Boston ought to be
knocked about their ears, destroyed. *Delenda est Carthago*."*

The Intolerable Acts all passed easily, despite the brilliant
rhetoric and telling arguments against them of Edmund Burke,
Isaac Barre, and the earl of Chatham. Franklin, in London, got
the full, immediate force of the government's determination to
coerce the colonies; colonial leaders in America got it months
later. Experienced as Franklin was in British public life, he could
have no doubt as to what would happen. And he had the means
to do something about it.

Franklin saw American sea captains regularly. He understood
European power politics and knew how happy France and Spain
would be to cause England some trouble at little danger to
themselves. He also had friends in France, and while these were
mostly bookish men not used to state affairs, they were gentlemen, they could gain access to the royal ministers, and they
tended to sympathize with the American cause, which spoke for
the human freedom and justice they themselves espoused.

Although it cannot be proved from Franklin's papers, there is
reason to believe that he was in touch with Vergennes in 1774
through Dr. Barbeu-Dubourg, the same man who later drove
with Silas Deane to Versailles. Franklin may also have been in
contact with the sieur Montaudoin, a merchant of the great port
city of Nantes, who was Franklin's friend and fellow Freemason.
Nantes was full of Freemason merchants, many of them sympathetic to the Americans, and all of them eager to do business
with them. More and more ships left Nantes for the North
American colonies, usually by way of the West Indies. Two new
vessels were named *L'Americain* by their Nantes owners in 1774,
and two more were named *Boston* and *Iroquois*. Eventually, in

*Peter Force, ed., *American Archives: Fourth Series* (Washington, 1837), vol. 1, p. 46.

North America, their cargoes joined those of the fleets that sailed from Amsterdam for Statia.

If Franklin in 1774 was arranging subsidies by Vergennes for merchants supplying the colonists with war supplies, and if he was making arrangements for the shipment of arms, he was probably technically guilty of treason and was risking his life. Henri Doniol, who studied the French records of the period in the late nineteenth century, decided that he was.*

In any case, when Franklin returned to Europe in 1776, things were very different. The United States had declared its independence, and Franklin had signed the Declaration. In November, a foreign fort—appropriately, at St. Eustatia—had fired a salute to the new nation's flag, heralding the beginning of international recognition. Franklin was the senior member of a team of three commissioners—Franklin, Deane, and Arthur Lee—charged with negotiating a commercial treaty with France. This was all they were to work for, originally. If France signed a commercial treaty, the act would automatically mean official French recognition of American independence. It would mean increased supplies from France. And it would avoid what were considered by Congress to be political entanglements.

At the same time, French recognition and a commercial treaty would put Great Britain in a difficult position. Other European countries might be expected to follow France's lead. Then Britain either would have to go to war to enforce its naval regulations—that is, no war goods shipped to its colonies by any nation—or would have to allow neutrals to trade with the United States and thus recognize the erstwhile colonies as a belligerent nation.

*Cited in Augur, *Secret War of Independence*, p. 17.

6

The Franco-American
Coalition

Of the four nations that joined in the war against Britain, only one made a really significant contribution, and that contribution was crucial. The great joint enterprise of France and America approached its climax in the early fall of 1781, as de Grasse's ships stood off the Virginia coast and four thousand Frenchmen marched the long, dusty roads from the Hudson to the York. Behind the ships, the march, and the victory ahead lay years of patient diplomatic work and many disappointments.

The Treaties of Alliance

From the day the decision for independence was made, American policy had sought to bring France into the war against England. The new country was weak, Great Britain was powerful, and the members of Congress were not fools. Although Benjamin Franklin arrived in France with instructions to seek a commercial treaty only, the congressmen who sent him fully understood that if France recognized the United States as a sovereign nation by signing any treaty at all, Great Britain and France would probably soon be at war.

The model treaty Franklin brought with him is usually called the Plan of 1776; it had been hammered out by Congress, with John Adams taking the lead, through that hot summer, and it later served as the model for most U.S. treaties of the eighteenth century. It stated that citizens of France should have the same commercial rights in the United States as American citizens, and vice versa. It provided for freedom of the seas and defined neutral rights. It also provided that, if the treaty should lead to

war between France and Great Britain, the United States would
not aid Great Britain.

The model treaty was not especially tempting to the French
government, which of course then aimed only at keeping the war
well stoked up and preventing any reconciliation between Britain and America. Franklin, Deane, and Arthur Lee, who had
been named U.S. commissioners for negotiating a treaty with
France, spent much time in polite but unavailing talk with
French diplomats, and in equally unavailing attempts to keep
British spies from reading—and even writing—their correspondence.

Then came the news of Saratoga, and Vergennes immediately
opened serious negotiations. It was not so much that the French
now felt the Americans had a chance to win. It was rather that
they feared that a stunned British government would make the
Americans an irresistible peace offer, the war would be over,
independent America would vanish, and a reunited British
Empire would confront a vulnerable France.

The treaty Vergennes approved was actually two treaties, and
they were signed on February 6, 1778. The Treaty of Amity and
Commerce was much like the model treaty on which it was based.
However, instead of the provision that citizens of the allied
nation would have the same commercial privileges as citizens of
the nation itself, a most-favored-nation clause was inserted; that
is, neither France nor the United States would grant to any other
nation more favorable commercial terms than they granted each
other. Instead of the model-treaty clause about the United States
not helping Britain against France in case of a war, there was the
separate Treaty of Conditional and Defensive Alliance.

This second treaty was termed conditional because it was to go
into effect only if and when war broke out between France and
Britain. If that happened—as was expected—the two countries
were to work and fight together against the common enemy.
France also promised not to try to retake any North American
land it had held before the Seven Years' War, such as Canada.
Both sides promised not to stop fighting until U.S. independence had been secured, and both promised not to make peace
with Britain until both had agreed on it.

The treaty was surprisingly favorable to the United States,
considering the relative strength and prestige of the two parties.
This graciousness was probably a public-relations decision by
France. The French king and government did not want to

appear on the world stage as greedy opportunists; rather they
wanted the sympathy and cooperation of the neutral powers of
Europe, whose ships would be needed to carry supplies, and
whose continued benevolent neutrality on the continent of
Europe was necessary. Whatever the motivation, the generous
French terms formed a smooth and solid basis for Franco-
American cooperation throughout the rest of the war.

Franklin, Deane, and Lee, now representatives of a fellow
sovereign nation, were ceremoniously received at the French
court by Louis XVI in March 1778.

France's Envoys and the American Public

The alliance with France demanded the first of several about-
faces in feelings toward other countries that Americans have
made. France had not been loved in America before the war.
The French king and government were widely termed "popish,"
a word that connoted not only Roman Catholic religion but
suppression of the religious liberty of others. A sizable number
of Americans were descended from Huguenots who had fled
France for England and America to escape religious persecu-
tion, and they feared popery. New England Congregationalist
preachers also railed against it. A measure of the feeling against
France and Catholicism is the fact that Parliament's Quebec Act
of 1774, an enlightened document that gave Catholic French
Canadians freedom to practice their religion, was considered by
many Americans to be an Intolerable Act—along with the closing of the port of Boston the same year.

France also was feared for its suspected territorial ambitions in
America, was hated as the enemy fought by Americans in the
French and Indian War, and was despised as the user of Indian
"savages" against English settlers. There was an American
stereotype of the Frenchman—a mincing, affected dandy, not
much good for man's work. If this hypothetical Frenchman took
to diplomacy, he was wily and not to be trusted.

And, also, there was still a strong American feeling of kinship
with Britain that lingered well after the Revolution had brought
a declaration of independence. Many American leaders, especially the moderates who had been reluctant to support independence in 1776, felt regret at the blow to England, mingled
with satisfaction in America's strengthened position, when the

alliance was sealed. Despite the celebrations, there was doubt and suspicion. How smoothly the alliance moved forward would depend to a large extent on the men France sent to America.

France's first minister to the United States was Conrad Alexandre Gérard, who had conducted the treaty negotiations. He seemed eminently qualified for the post. Son of a well-off middle-class family, he was no haughty aristocrat but a sensible, competent civil servant. He had been first secretary of the foreign office since 1766, first under Choiseul and later under Vergennes. Having worked with Silas Deane from the beginning of Deane's mission, he was comprehensively informed on every aspect of French-American relations. He knew that the Americans would probably press for U.S. rights to the Newfoundland fisheries as war aims, that they might also press for U.S. sovereignty over Nova Scotia, or even all Canada, and that France was not to fight for such U.S. territorial gains. Gérard was instructed to discourage any American attempts to conquer Mississippi territory that Spain had designs on, and generally to persuade the Americans not to anger Spain. Yet he could not speak officially for Spain, which was not yet in the war, and whose participation France was carefully working to procure. All this Gérard understood, and he was generally successful in carrying out his tasks.

What he did not understand was American society or politics. He knew and trusted Silas Deane, who had worked hard to achieve the alliance and who was a merchant, a member of the merchant-moderate group among the American leaders, and an opponent of the Lee-Adams group, generally called the radicals, for convenience, by modern-day historians. On the issue that caused Deane's recall from Paris, Deane was probably in the right and Arthur Lee probably in the wrong. And Deane really was not fairly treated by Congress. But the tangles of American politics were too complicated for Gérard. Prejudiced in favor of his own merchant class, Gérard distrusted farmers and artisans, many of whom were politically active in New England. Seeing that the Adams cousins and the Lee brothers were suspicious and hostile toward Deane, Gérard concluded, in a wild flight of logic based on badly mistaken premises, that the Lees, Adamses, New Englanders in general, and the whole "radical" faction were enemies of the French alliance. He bizarrely termed them "the English faction"—a strange term indeed for the men who had maneuvered and propagandized ceaselessly for independence, moved the independence resolution, and forcefully argued it through. Later, at Vergennes's insistence, he dropped this term, modifying it to "anti-Gallican"—a description only slightly less inaccurate, since the radical group had pushed for the alliance from the beginning, and had worked for immediate independence partly in order to achieve a French alliance.

If few American leaders, despite their old prejudices, were against the alliance, many soon became anti-Gérard. His crowning blunder was his involvement in Deane's troubles.

As the Congressional investigation of Deane's alleged profiteering and corruption dragged on, and as it became clear to Deane and Gérard that Deane would not receive an open-minded hearing from Congress, Gérard's side-taking showed clearly. His championship of Deane led him to meddle in U.S. affairs to the extent of urging that John Jay be appointed American commissioner in Madrid in place of Arthur Lee, Deane's accuser.

Gérard's considerable problems in Congressional relations were exacerbated still further by illness, probably malaria. He reported that he was sick five of his first seven months in the United States. Since he had to confer with Congressional leaders in his own house, and since he was not inclined to invite men whom he considered hostile, his knowledge of American politics and society became more and more restricted.

Gérard sailed back to France in October 1779, pleading health problems, which were certainly real enough. By and large, his mission had not been successful, crippled as it was from the beginning by his ignorance of American life and his inability to adapt his diplomatic skills to the give-and-take style of representative government. He had done little to dispel American preconceptions about wily, insincere French diplomats—despite the fact that he was, if anything, too sincere in his advocacy of Silas Deane and in his generally forthright pushing toward French goals.

The man who replaced Gérard, the chevalier de la Luzerne, was a different person altogether. He had been a military man, not a diplomat, for most of his life, and had entered the diplomatic service only two years before he was sent to America. Short, plump, and friendly, he had a more tolerant disposition than Gérard. Luzerne was able, for example, to accept the idea that certain Americans could demand fishery rights and Canadian territory for the United States, war aims that were not

France's, and could still favor the French alliance. He saw the alliance as an enterprise beneficial to both sides, rather than as the magnanimous French favor it had seemed to Gérard.

Where Gérard had assumed that all the Lee-Adams-radical group were disloyal to the alliance, and even to the revolution, Luzerne carefully distinguished between a man's personal views—which might be anti-Catholic and opposed to French policy—and his dedication to the United States and loyalty to the alliance. In his letters to Vergennes, Luzerne stressed the loyalty and usefulness to the alliance of Samuel and John Adams, despite their disagreements with some aspects of French policy. While Vergennes, from Paris, had had to correct some of Gérard's more distorted views, he received from Luzerne an education in American life and politics. Apparently Vergennes was unable to profit fully from the lessons, however, for he persisted in the Gérard-engendered view that opponents of the merchant-moderate faction were anti-France.

Luzerne was especially fascinated by American ideas of freedom of the press and religion. He respected the place they held for Americans, and quickly recognized that although he could tone down anti-French propaganda in the press by quiet persuasion or bribery, there was no point in trying to get Congress or a state government to censor a newspaper. He could accept, with regret, the Protestant requirement for officeholding in Massachusetts and also appreciate the freedom that was granted to Quakers and other sects in Pennsylvania. By the time he returned to France, he had become a convert to equality and republicanism, at least for the United States.

Luzerne's personal charm helped erase the bad impression Gérard had made and also won affection for himself. He was a popular guest at every party, and even men prejudiced against France seem to have had nothing bad to say about him. He was able to work directly and effectively with congressmen, building a coalition of Southern and Middle States delegates that generally supported what France supported. In this he was greatly helped by his first secretary, François Barbé-Marbois, a trusted assistant who had worked with him before his American assignment. Together the two men reinforced and buttressed the alliance, and also did their effective best to mold American policy to fit French needs.

France Sends Ships and Men

The signature of the treaties of alliance meant not only the sending of diplomatic envoys to Philadelphia but, more significantly for the American cause, the overt provision of money and goods.

On April 13, 1778, about a month after France's ambassador informed the British government that his government recognized the independence of the United States, the first French fleet set sail from Toulon for America. There were twelve ships of the line,* escorted by three frigates, under the command of Vice Admiral Jean-Baptiste Charles Henri Hector Theodat, comte d'Estaing. D'Estaing was new at such a large command, having served in the army until the age of thirty-four, when he transferred to the navy. He then served as governor of the Antilles from 1763 to 1766. While his service there made him acquainted with the West Indies and its importance to France, his views of naval strategy were those of a man trained to the strategy of land forces. His promotion to vice admiral over the heads of many other officers provoked the jealousy of his subordinates, some of whom went so far as to fail to carry out orders on occasion.

D'Estaing sailed slowly west, with orders that once he was 120 miles or so west of Gibraltar he could engage any British vessels he found. His destination was the mouth of Delaware Bay, where Admiral Lord Richard Howe was supporting the British army in Philadelphia, but the French government leaked the false word as d'Estaing sailed that he was bound for Brest. This ruse succeeded in confusing the British, who didn't find out that d'Estaing was headed for America until he was already eight weeks out of Toulon. Promptly thereafter, thirteen British ships of the line, which had just been prepared for sea, were dispatched to New York, commanded by Vice Admiral John Byron, known as "Foulweather Jack" from his propensity for running into stormy seas.

D'Estaing at Newport

D'Estaing reached the mouth of the Delaware River on July 8,

The United States: The Theater of War in North America

83

1778, to find that Howe had returned to New York from Philadelphia on June 28. So he followed him north. Word of d'Estaing's approach reached Howe in time for him to prepare his defense. At the northern end of Sandy Hook, which commands the western edge of the entrance to New York Harbor, Howe placed five guns. Inside the Hook he stationed an east-west line of seven ships, echeloned to the north and facing east, but so moored that they could swing to face north and deliver a broadside head on to ships coming up the channel. Other ships were placed at the far side of the entrance, and three were stationed outside, where they could rake the French ships as they tried to cross the bar a couple of miles outside Sandy Hook.

It was the bar that settled the outcome of this potential engagement, for although the tide was full when d'Estaing approached it, he was not convinced that his large, deep-draft ships could safely cross. After feinting in that direction he abandoned the project and headed south until he lost the British scouts sent to keep track of him. Then he turned northeast for Narragansett Bay, where plans had been made for a combined operation to capture the British garrison at Newport.

Major General John Sullivan had been put in charge of a force assembled by Washington for this purpose. It included a division of two brigades under Lafayette, a second division under able Major General Nathanael Greene, and six thousand militia commanded by Major General John Hancock. These troops were to cross to the north end of Rhode Island and proceed south to Newport, while d'Estaing landed four thousand soldiers and seamen from his ships on the west side of the island. Together they would attack the four- to six-thousand-man British garrison and wrest the valuable harbor of Newport from British control.

In preparation for the action, starting on July 30 the French ships moved into Narragansett Bay in position to threaten Newport Harbor. The British, who had five frigates and some smaller vessels in the bay, tried to move them to the security of Newport Harbor. But the water was too shoal to cross, and they finally destroyed the frigates and two sloops, taking off their guns and other usable items to improve their defenses on land.

The French-American "coordinated attack" was a fiasco. General Sullivan crossed to Rhode Island on August 8 while d'Estaing's ships were still moving into position, so enraging d'Estaing that he considered not carrying out his part of the operation at all. But he did finally land four thousand men on Conan-

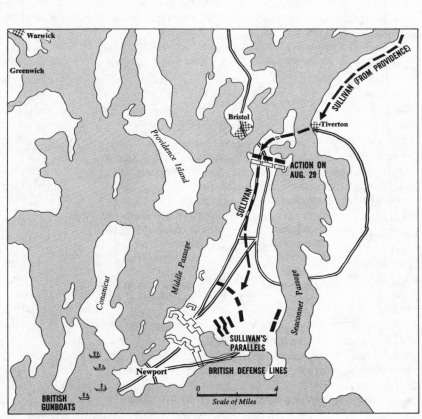

The Siege of Newport

icut Island, where they were to be organized preparatory to crossing to Newport. Before they were ready to proceed, however, Lord Howe and his fleet appeared off Point Judith, twelve miles from d'Estaing and only seven from the entrance to Narragansett Bay. Whether d'Estaing felt insecure in his position or whether he was anxious to fight the British is not clear. In any case he took his men back aboard and headed out at seven in the morning on August 10.

Howe at this time had one ship of the line with 74 guns (the first of Byron's ships to arrive), seven with 64, and five ships with 50; 50s were not usually considered ships of the line although they frequently fought as such. D'Estaing had fewer vessels but more guns, having one ship with 90, one with 80, six with 74, three with 64, and one with 50. Heading out on the port tack with the wind out of the northeast, he also had the weather gauge, that is, he was to windward of the British fleet.

Not waiting for the French to come within range, Lord Howe put to sea, also heading south on the port tack. At that time of year, the wind normally blows from the southwest in that area, and Howe was hoping that a wind shift to the southwest would give him the windward advantage. But the wind moved only a couple of points to the east, and after sailing all day and all night the two fleets were still in the same relative position. During the day d'Estaing maneuvered into position two or three miles astern of the British line, which had shifted to a northerly course, but before he could get into position to attack the wind freshened and rain began. By sunset the wind had reached gale force. All the next day the storm continued, scattering the ships of both fleets widely over the ocean. Many were badly battered, and although there were some minor encounters between isolated vessels, there was no possibility of assembling either fleet for a full engagement. Most badly damaged was the *Languedoc*, 90,* d'Estaing's flagship. The storm had completely dismasted her and broken her tiller, and she could fire only her two stern guns when the *Renown*, 50, opened fire and damaged her even more. She was saved by darkness and by six French ships of the line which arrived the next morning and drove off the *Renown*.

The British rendezvoused off Sandy Hook on August 17, where they repaired their damage, which was mostly minor. D'Estaing anchored temporarily at sea off Cape May on the

---

*A figure following a ship's name indiates the number of guns she carried.

fifteenth to make repairs and then headed back to Newport.
Some of his other ships, as well as the *Languedoc*, had been
seriously damaged, and in spite of Sullivan's pleas that he return
to Newport, d'Estaing insisted that he could not repair his ships
adequately there. He sailed on to Boston, where he arrived on
August 28, followed three days later by Howe. But Howe did not
attempt to pass the fortified islands of Boston Harbor and soon
returned to New York.

Sullivan meanwhile had advanced to within fifteen hundred
yards of the British fortifications at Newport. But without the
support of the French fleet and its four thousand men he could
not hope to take the town. He withdrew.

It is hard to fault d'Estaing, who considered his first responsibility the preservation and restoration of his ships; but one
cannot but sympathize with the Americans who saw him apparently deserting the cause he had come to serve. The historian
William Gordon, writing ten years later, described the reaction
at Newport:

> Upon the fleet's sailing for Boston, it was said —"There
> never was a prospect so favorable blasted by such a shameful
> desertion." A universal clamor prevailed against the French
> nation; and letters were sent to Boston containing the most
> bitter invectives, tending to prejudice the inhabitants
> against D'Estaing and all his officers.*

Lafayette, who felt and acted like the American officer he was
until France was insulted, came close to fighting a duel with a
sneering American at this point. He wrote to Alexander Hamilton, "Would you believe that I, one who has the honor of belonging to the leading nation of the world, to a nation which . . . is
respected and admired by all Europe . . . have personally been
put in the position of hearing the name of France spoken without respect, and perhaps with disdain, by a herd of Yankees
from New England."†

Washington counseled Sullivan to be prudent and maintain a
united front with the French despite his disappointment, but to
no avail. In his general orders of August 24, the outraged
American accused the French of abandoning the United States.

*Quoted in William Stinchcombe, *The American Revolution and the French Alliance*, p.51.
†*Ibid.*, p. 52.

Although he tried to retract the statement two days later, this really could not be done, and certainly not with the clumsy self-justifications Sullivan employed. D'Estaing was through with the Newport operations and Sullivan was stranded.

American leadership now rallied to shore up the alliance. Washington gave the cue. The failure was to be officially ascribed not to d'Estaing or Sullivan but to the storm at sea. D'Estaing responded with moderate statements, and Congress, at Minister Gérard's request, passed a resolution thanking d'Estaing for his aid. But the French admiral and the American general had undoubtedly strained the alliance by their tactical errors and undiplomatic behavior.

Once in Boston, the French officers and sailors of d'Estaing's fleet generally behaved in an exemplary way. Abigail Adams wrote her husband in praise of the "chastity, temperance, industry, frugality, sobriety, and purity of morals" of the French and was distressed that any Americans could have the "low vulgar prejudices" she had heard some express.* There was apparently prejudice indeed, because there were four riots between French and American sailors in Boston during September and October 1778. The first riot started over a bread shortage; at least one Frenchman was killed. During this same period, three people were killed in Charleston, South Carolina, in similar riots. The upper ranks of French and American society got along together very well, but the seamen could not converse with each other, did not have bilingual liaison officers to interpret for them, had not been influenced by Enlightenment views on intercultural toleration, and were also subject to such irritating factors as hunger induced by lack of bread.

Savannah

Once d'Estaing's ships were refitted, he sailed for the West Indies, a key area in the world power struggle of the Revolutionary War and the customary winter base for both the French and English fleets during the war. At St. Lucia he was no more successful than at Newport in his attempt to seize British-held territory by naval and amphibious operations. However, he did somewhat redeem himself by capturing St. Vincent (June 16,

*Ibid., p. 58.

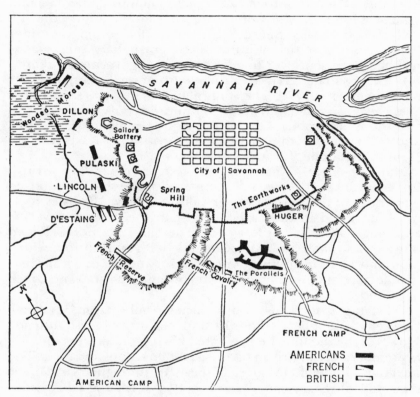

The Siege of Savannah, September-October 1779

1779) and Grenada (July 4). After a naval battle off Grenada, from which d'Estaing pulled away too soon to gain decisive results, he sailed for Savannah, which had been captured by the British in December 1778 in the most stunning early success of their new southern strategy.

D'Estaing had been invited to Savannah by Governor John Rutledge of South Carolina and Continental Brigadier General William Moultrie, who were laying plans to recapture the city and needed naval support. By this time all Georgia was under British control; so firm was the British grasp that a royal governor had been sent over to administer civil government there.

D'Estaing's fleet arrived at the mouth of the Savannah River on September 8, 1779. The admiral had twenty-two ships of the line, eleven frigates, and almost a hundred transports, carrying five thousand troops. One of the eight regiments was a black one, from Santo Domingo, which had on its rolls twelve-year-old Henri Christophe, future king of Haiti.

Major General Augustine Prevost, commanding British forces in the south, was in Savannah with twenty-five hundred men, most of them American Loyalists. Thirteen British vessels were anchored in the harbor. D'Estaing seemed to have the advantage, as he had at Newport, especially since he was joined outside Savannah by Major General Benjamin Lincoln with a thousand men, including Count Pulaski and his five-hundred-man legion, and by militiamen who brought the attackers to ten thousand.

D'Estaing landed his troops thirteen miles from Savannah between September 9 and 16 and began to invest the city. However, by the time he presented his surrender demands, on September 16, the British had also landed troops and guns. The next day, after eight hundred of these British regulars had made their way into Savannah, Prevost rejected d'Estaing's demands.

The heavy French siege guns still had to be gotten off the ships, across the marshes, and into positions. This was slow work and they were not in place until October 3. D'Estaing, who had been so cautiously methodical about opening the siege, belatedly became nervous about prolonging it. He feared the fall hurricane season, and he had heard, truly, that a British fleet, summoned by a last-minute message from Prevost just before the French had bottled up sea access to Savannah, was on its way. Although not only the Americans but most of his own officers protested that more preparation bombardment was needed, d'Estaing insisted that the city must be assaulted on October 9. The assault was made by thirty-five hundred Frenchmen and about a thousand Americans, including Continentals, militiamen, and two thousand of Pulaski's cavalry. The British, warned by an American deserter, were ready. Everywhere the allies were thrown back. One French column did not even reach the entrenchments. The Frenchmen and Americans of the main force fought their way into the main redoubt, but were forced to withdraw after hard fighting. Pulaski's cavalry charged the abatis. They, too, fell back, and Pulaski—gallant and unwise to the end—was mortally wounded.

Nine days later d'Estaing raised the siege. He put his men and guns on board his vessels, and on October 20 he sailed away. Nothing had been accomplished for the allies at Savannah. However, the attack proved of considerable importance, for it caused Sir Henry Clinton to reassess his strengths and his problems and conclude that he could not continue to maintain operations in the South and hold both New York and Newport. He decided to abandon Newport, thereby making that strategic port available as a base for future French fleet operations.

D'Estaing had had much to contend with from Sullivan at Newport, but by the end of the Savannah siege it was clear that his basic trouble was more than simple bad luck. He had been consistently late, slow, and overcautious. His accomplishments in the West Indies—limited ones, in view of his opportunities—were significant for France. In cementing the new French-American alliance, however, and in helping it win the war, d'Estaing's sluggishness had been as ineffective as the wrongheadedness of Gérard, his contemporary in America.

New Commanders at Sea

On December 29, 1779, Admiral Sir George Brydges Rodney sailed from Plymouth to take command of the British Leeward Islands Station. With him were twenty-two ships of the line, fourteen frigates and smaller vessels, and a great many merchant ships bound for the West Indies, Portugal, and, first of all, Gibraltar. Four of the ships proceeded with him to St. Lucia, where on March 27, 1780, he took over command of sixteen more ships, which had been temporarily commanded by Rear Admiral Sir Hyde Parker. At almost the same time, France sent a

new commander to the West Indies to replace d'Estaing, Rear
Admiral Louis Urbain de Bouenic, comte de Guichen. These
men were primarily concerned with the war in the West Indies,
but they would be involved also with naval actions in North
American waters.

Rochambeau Arrives

Lafayette was in France in the winter of 1779-1780, trying,
among other things, to get the government to send troops to
help the American cause. When the project for a joint French-
Spanish invasion of England was abandoned and troops became
available, the French government decided to send six thousand
of them to America. Named to command this force, instead of
the disappointed Lafayette, was General Jean-Baptiste Donatien
de Vimeur, comte de Rochambeau. It was probably a wise
choice.

Although Rochambeau had never been to North America and
spoke no English, he was a capable commander, a veteran of
European wars, and a man of tact and intelligence. Commanding forces in combined operations with a foreign ally turned out
to be a job for which he was especially suited.

Lack of available shipping cut Rochambeau's force to five
thousand men before they sailed in the late spring of 1780,
escorted by Commodore Charles Louis d'Arsec, chevalier de
Ternay, with seven ships, headed for the abandoned British base
at Newport.

When the fleet had been at sea for ten days, Rochambeau
opened his sealed orders. They provided that he was to be
subordinate to General Washington, and that he and his troops
were to serve under Washington, and Washington only. The
French government leaders were determined to protect their
men from incompetent American commanders.

The Frenchmen's immediate welcome at Newport, on July 12,
was chilly. The ships arrived in a heavy fog, and no one on shore
could see that the one or two shadowy hulks dimly visible in the
harbor represented seven ships of the line, five frigates, and
transports packed with five thousand French troops. After their
experience with d'Estaing, the Newporters were a bit dubious
about Frenchmen anyway, and rumors had it that the French
were only stopping briefly for supplies, not staying to fight.

Within a day or two, however, Rochambeau—through an

interpreter—had reassured the town's leaders that his force was a large one, that it would stay, and that more troops and ships were on the way. Soon flags were hung out, bugles pealed, fireworks crackled, and Newport's main streets were ordered illuminated in honor of the French visitors.

Perhaps the most important reassurance Rochambeau and his companions gave the local citizens came from their appearance and bearing. "Neither officers nor men are the effeminate beings we were heretofore taught to believe them," wrote Ezra Stiles in his diary, quoting his friend William Channing.* It turned out, too, that General Rochambeau, despite his lack of English, had a language in common with some of the inhabitants. He had been intended for a church career until he was almost fifteen, at which point his older brother had died and left him heir to the family title. He remembered much of his Latin and could converse in it with clergymen like Stiles and other classically educated Americans.

The officers represented the best France had to send. All four regiments were distinguished, and their commanders able as well as noble. Rochambeau's three top commanders—called *marechaux de camp*—were the baron de Vioménil; his brother, the vicomte de Vioménil; and the chevalier de Chastellux. Newport viewed the Vioménil brothers largely in physical terms: "Both of a commanding height," said one American, and another described them as the best-looking men in the world.

The chevalier de Chastellux, who spoke English and soon became friendly with Washington, acted as the commander in chief's informal liaison with Rochambeau. A lively-minded man, he was eager to see everything in America. The months spent by the French marking time at Newport gave Chastellux an opportunity to travel about the country, recording his impressions of eighteenth-century America in his diary.

Rodney Comes North

Eager to make use of the French troops as soon as possible, and well aware of the importance of naval support, Washington was hopeful that de Guichen would sail north from the Caribbean to join de Ternay's fleet at Newport and participate in an

*Quoted in Bonsal, *When the French Were Here*, p. 24.

operation against General Clinton in New York. His hopes found support in Lafayette. When de Guichen, having escorted a Spanish fleet to Cuba, anchored at Haiti, he found messages from Lafayette and from the French minister in the United States urging him to sail north to cooperate with Washington. But de Guichen refused. He preferred to honor his orders to escort ninety-six ships laden with valuable sugar and coffee to France. He sailed on August 16, taking nineteen ships of the line with him to protect the merchantmen.

Meanwhile, British Admiral Rodney, in the West Indies, had heard of the arrival of de Ternay at Newport. Receiving word of de Guichen's departure, and recognizing the strategic importance of combining the two French fleets, he assumed that de Guichen planned to leave the convoy at sea with a few ships to protect it and head with the rest for Narragansett Bay. Without announcing his own plans, Rodney, having decided to challenge the French fleets in the north, sailed at the end of July 1780, pleading the desirability of getting away from the islands during the hurricane season. To the surprise of all the British commanders at New York, he turned up at Sandy Hook with ten ships of the line on September 14.

Word of Rodney's arrival was a final blow to Washington's hope for naval support, for de Guichen's refusal to come north had already arrived. For the British, on the other hand, it created the possibility of action against de Ternay's fleet and the French troops at Newport.

On July 13, Vice Admiral Marriot Arbuthnot, commander of the British fleet at New York, had happily greeted Rear Admiral Thomas Graves, who had arrived from England with six ships of the line and a frigate. Upon receipt immediately thereafter of the news of de Ternay's arrival, Arbuthnot took his whole force, nine ships of the line and a 50-gun ship, up to the waters off Rhode Island. He anchored in position to observe the entrance to Narragansett Bay, and there he stayed until September 13, when he sought the protection of Gardiner's Bay at the end of Long Island. From that vantage point he hoped to observe, and if possible intercept, de Ternay's ships if they left, following the usual pattern, to spend the winter in the West Indies.

Despite the welcome reinforcements, Rodney's sudden appearance was far from pleasing to Arbuthnot. Rodney, who was senior, promptly assumed command of the combined British fleets, ordered Arbuthnot to watch for de Ternay, and told

Graves to proceed at once to cut off the French ships before they could reach Martinique, in case they eluded Arbuthnot. He also stationed frigates along the coast of South Carolina "to support the Commerce of the Important Colony, and destroy the Rebellious Pyratical Vessels which infested it."*

Rodney found General Clinton less than eager to attack the French at Newport. The position was so strong, he said, that it could not be taken without a regular siege. There were not enough British troops available to undertake a siege, and Washington would undoubtedly take advantage of any transfer of men from New York to attack there. Convinced by his arguments, and unable to convince Clinton to send some troops to the West Indies to take Martinique, Rodney left New York on November 16 to return to the warmer waters of the Caribbean. De Ternay wintered at Newport and Graves returned to New York.

The fall of 1780 was a season of heavy storms. On the first day out of New York, Rodney's ships encountered heavy gales that scattered them and damaged many of them. He found on arrival at Barbados that a series of unusually strong hurricanes had swept through the islands in October, wreaking great havoc on Barbados, damaging many ships, and destroying two ships of the line and nine smaller vessels. With wood for repairs in short supply, Rodney was glad at the end of the year to greet Rear Admiral Sir Samuel Hood, who came to serve as second in command, and who brought with him wood and other supplies, as well as eight ships of the line.

Winter at Newport

In Newport, meanwhile, Rochambeau had set about strengthening the fortifications while he waited for the promised second division of his army. He had accepted the command on condition that the army comprise a full six regiments and the Lauzun Legion. Consequently he was not as disappointed as Washington and Lafayette when de Guichen refused to come north, for he was not willing to leave Newport in any case until the rest of his men arrived.

*Despatch, Rodney to Philip Stephens, Secretary of the Admiralty, October 10, 1780, in *Letter-books and Order-Book of George, Lord Rodney*, Vol. 1, p. 30.

The tedium of the winter of 1780-1781 at Newport was lightened for the French officers by a great deal of dancing and flirtation. Among the girls of Newport, a pretty Quaker named Polly Lawton was especially intriguing. As Franklin's wise head was enhanced for Parisians by his fur hat, so Miss Lawton's beautiful figure was glorified for Rochambeau's officers by her plain white dress. Her Quaker thees and thous gave Frenchmen the feeling that they were being addressed in the equivalent of the intimate French *tu* by this otherwise demure young lady, and her firm stand against all wars and fighting charmed the king's officers, if it did nothing to change their martial careers.

With the coming of spring, Washington and Rochambeau talked strategy and looked southward. The months of waiting would soon be over.

7

The French and the Yorktown Campaign

In May of 1781, Rochambeau was still waiting at Newport, the second division of his army still had not come, and he had received word that it would never come. The fact was that the American war was bankrupting France, and expenses had to be cut. It was bitter news, but since there was nothing to be done about it, Rochambeau accepted it and made do gracefully with the six hundred replacements that were sent.

There was good news to soften the blow. Admiral François Joseph Paul de Grasse had sailed with a powerful fleet—twenty ships of the line and other vessels in proportion—from Brest for the West Indies. So in the third week of May, Rochambeau and Chastellux set out on horseback to meet Washington at Wethersfield, Connecticut, where they would plot strategy. Washington and his aides made a hard two-day ride from their positions on the Hudson to reach the rendezvous point, a charming village that was coincidentally the home of Silas Deane, then in France and tragically engaged in compromising, perhaps treasonous, contacts with a British agent.

Rochambeau and Washington had in common a strong sense of grand strategy and a solid grasp of the importance of seapower. Before leaving Paris to take command, Rochambeau had prepared a document for the Minister of Marine listing the equipment he required. It began with the statement, "Rien sans la marine preponderante." The important new factor in the discussions of the French and American commanders was de Grasse's fleet. It could give them that preponderant seapower.

The British land forces were divided between two major power centers—New York and the Chesapeake Bay area. If a sea

force could isolate one of these centers, Washington and
Rochambeau reasoned, there was a good chance that it could be
destroyed by joint land-sea operations. The advantages of New
York over Virginia were weighed and found convincing. Virginia meant a very long march, all sorts of transport problems, a
climate thought by many to be unhealthy in the summer, and
opportunities that would tempt the desertion-prone American
troops. New York was the agreed first choice.

Washington promptly (May 23) wrote French Minister
Luzerne at Philadelphia, asking him to call de Grasse in from the
Indies. Luzerne sent the word to de Grasse by a French frigate
picked for speed. Washington himself wrote to an anxious
Lafayette, commanding Continental forces in Virginia, that
New York would be attacked. Fortunately, he did not mention
Virginia as a second-choice objective.

This letter was intercepted by the British, and since Washington had no cipher for use with Lafayette, it gave the plan away.
The British also read a letter from Chastellux to Luzerne.
Washington, however, was able to learn through his agents that
the British knew of his intention to move against New York.

Circumstances were thus converging toward a move to Virginia. But preparations for New York proceeded.

The first step, no matter which final objective was chosen, was
for Rochambeau to join forces with Washington on the Hudson.
The French set out from Newport on June 10, most of them in
splendid white uniforms, and each regiment identified by
brightly colored coat facings and collars. They were an impressive sight as they marched through the New England coun-
tryside. The first division, the Bourbonnais and Royal Deux-
Ponts, was commanded by baron de Vioménil. The Bourbonnais, whose coats had crimson facings and pink collars, were a
proud unit that had fought side by side with Rochambeau's old
regiment, the Auvergne, at the Battle of Kloster-Kamp in 1760.
Rochambeau's son was the Bourbonnais's second in command.
The Royal Deux-Ponts, in blue uniforms with lemon-colored
facings, were a German-speaking regiment from a little Duchy
in the Saar Basin; the dukes of this state were traditionally allied
with France, and the regiment was commanded by a member of
the ruling family, the comte de Deux-Ponts.*

The Soissonnais and Saintonge regiments marched out the

*Uniform colors are taken from Arnold Whitridge, *Rochambeau*, pp. 146-147.

next day. The Soissonnais, with whom Rochambeau had fought on Minorca, wore rose-colored facings, sky-blue collars, and yellow buttons—a rainbow that was to devastate the ladies of Philadelphia as the French moved south. The Saintonge wore green facings and cuffs, and yellow buttons; they were commanded by the comte de Custine, later a general of revolutionary France. Serving in the regiment was Major Francois Teissedre de Fleury—already a hero of the American Continental Army. He had been the first man over the parapet in Anthony Wayne's masterful capture of Stony Point, New York. Home on leave, he had rejoined the French army in time to sail with Rochambeau.

Finally, there was the Lauzun Legion, or as much of it as had been squeezed onto the transports at Brest. It was a proprietary unit, and commanded by the duc de Lauzun, a notorious rake but a highly respected officer. The legion was a colorful assemblage of volunteer soldiers of various nationalities—Poles, Germans, Irishmen, and Hungarian Hussars. With Lauzun was the second battalion of the Dillon Regiment, commanded by Robert Dillon, descendant of a Stuart loyalist who had fled to France with James II; the regiment's rolls were full of Moores, O'Farrells, O'Neils, Kellys, and Lynches who would soon be fighting against Hanoverian England in the New World.

In twenty-five days the French marched the 220 miles from Providence, their first night's camp, to Philipsburg in Westchester County, where they met the Americans. They arrived on July 5 and awaited orders.

At about this time, Washington learned that Cornwallis, who had been marching about at will through Virginia, raiding Patriot supplies and almost capturing Governor Thomas Jefferson, had headed down the peninsula that is known in Virginia as *the* Peninsula, and was camped at Williamsburg. This behavior, ordered by General Sir Henry Clinton, put him in position to be trapped by the allies unless he managed to escape by sea.

On August 1 Cornwallis moved to Yorktown, at the tip of the Peninsula. "Should a French fleet now come to Hampton Roads," Lafayette wrote to Washington, "the British army would, I think, be ours."* This missing piece of the design to trap the British was found on August 14, when a message from de Grasse informed Washington that he was sailing for Chesapeake

*Quoted in Larrabee, *Decision at the Chesapeake*, p. 118.

Bay with thirty-three hundred French troops and twenty-eight ships of the line. His fleet would be at Washington's disposal until mid-October.

De Grasse had taken these troops from Santo Domingo, where they had been stationed by the French government to be used by the Spanish for an expedition they were contemplating in Florida. With some difficulty, because the Spanish were very demanding allies, de Grasse had persuaded the French governor to lend them on his promise to return them by November. He embarked them and went to Havana, where he obtained 4 million livres, which was more than enough to pay for his fleet's expenses, with the remainder going to Rochambeau.

Accomplishing a masterpiece of planning and preparation, Washington and Rochambeau were ready to start their troops toward Virginia just five days after de Grasse's message was received. During this period, they persuaded Commodore Count Louis de Barras, who, after de Ternay's death of a fever, had taken command of the French squadron that had escorted Rochambeau's troops to Newport and was still stationed there, to give up a plan for an expedition to Newfoundland and to sail to join de Grasse at Chesapeake Bay, bringing with him French siege guns and ammunition.

It was a time of high excitement for the allied commanders, but not one element necessary for springing the trap was yet sure. No one could know whether de Grasse's ships would survive storms and British ships and get to the Chesapeake before British Rear Admiral Thomas Graves moved his fleet down from New York; or whether the ground troops could make the long march in time; or whether Cornwallis would stay put; or whether the destruction or capture of his army could be accomplished before de Grasse had to leave in order to get his borrowed troops back to Santo Domingo. Lafayette was ordered to keep Cornwallis from escaping, but he did not have the strength to stop a determined effort.

The March

The entire French force and twenty-five hundred Americans set out for Virginia on August 19. There were cavalry and engineers as well as infantrymen, horse-drawn artillery, and numerous military bands, all making the long trek south. Commanding the Americans was Major General Benjamin Lincoln.

Washington and Rochambeau, with Chastellux and their staffs, rode ahead. Back at West Point, thirty-five hundred Americans were left to keep an eye on the Hudson River.

The French line of march has been preserved in maps exquisitely drawn by Captain Alexandre Berthier, one of Rochambeau's aides and the man who was to become Napoleon's chief of staff.* The first leg of the journey was made as a feint toward New York. By halting opposite Staten Island and Sandy Hook until the rear elements of his column came up, Washington gave the impression of a wheeling movement directed toward the port city itself. By building an oven for the baking of French bread, assiduously spreading rumors, and gathering boats from every dock in the area, the allies made the ruse succeed and were well on their way south before the British realized what was happening.

The march from New York to Williamsburg took from late August to late September. In 1781 this generally steamy month included an unusually intense heat wave. Although the officers tried to use the coolest part of the day for marching, four hundred men in the woolen uniforms of the day fell from the ranks in exhaustion on one especially hot day's march. Rochambeau's chaplain, the Abbé Robin, described his daily routine of being wrenched from sleep by drum rolls at two o'clock in the morning and riding off behind "the poor infantryman trudging along under the weight of his knapsack." When the men reached their new campsite, the abbé said, they often had to wait without food or water through the hottest part of the day until the baggage wagons pulled in. "Stretched on the dusty ground, panting with thirst, I have often wished—like the Rich Man in the parable—that another Lazarus would dip the tip of his finger in water to quench my thirst." He was impressed with the unexpected fortitude of the aristocratic young officers, despite the pampered lives they had led at home. The vicomte de Noailles, Lafayette's brother-in-law, who was second in command of the Soissonnais Regiment, marched at the head of his men all the way to Yorktown. So did the comte de Custine, commander of the Saintonge.

Despite the suffering, there was a great deal of fun and sociability along the road to Virginia. Everywhere the French

*Originals of the maps are in the private collection of Mr. Paul Mellon. They have been meticulously reproduced in *The American Campaigns of Rochambeau's Army*, translated and edited by Howard C. Rice, Jr., and Anne S. K. Brown, Vol. 2.

camped, Americans were curious to meet them, and the Frenchmen seem always to have been ready to play band music for their
guests and to join in dancing with them. The Abbé Robin
delighted in the democratic atmosphere in which officers
and soldiers, Frenchmen and Americans—including American women—danced together. "It is the feast of equality," he
wrote.*

The disturbing news that the combined fleets of Graves and
Hood had sailed from New York reached General Washington
at Philadelphia early on September 1. Might they get to
Chesapeake Bay before de Grasse? Or intercept de Grasse and
defeat or badly damage his fleet? Or intercept de Barras, with his
precious cargo of artillery and supplies? Any of these developments would threaten the allied plan.

Washington shared his worries with Rochambeau until September 5, when they left Philadelphia by different routes,
Washington riding south, and Rochambeau choosing to go by
ship down the Delaware as far as Chester, to examine some forts
and obstructions of the 1777 campaign. About three miles south
of Chester, a courier met Washington on the road and gave him
the good news that de Grasse had arrived in the Chesapeake
ahead of the British. Washington sent off dispatches to Congress
and French Minister Luzerne, and then rode back to Chester to
be on the dock when Rochambeau's vessel arrived and pass the
word on to him. It was a joyful meeting. Although the two
commanders could not know it, de Grasse's ships had already
sailed out of Lynnhaven roadstead again and were beginning
the Battle of the Chesapeake against Graves and the British fleet.

The American and French armies meanwhile had marched
into Philadelphia, the Americans on September 2 and the
French on the fourth. The French halted a mile short of the city,
brushed the dust from their coats and trousers, and marched in
in splendor. Crowds cheered the sparkling white uniforms with
their bright-colored facings. Members of Congress, after some
discussion as to the appropriate way of returning the French
salutes, doffed their hats in unison in response to each one. The
next day the Soissonnais Regiment gave an impressive precision-
drill exhibition, and that night the French officers dined as
guests of the chevalier de la Luzerne. During the banquet,
Washington's message to Luzerne was handed to him, and he

*Abbé Robin's journal is quoted in Whitridge, *Rochambeau*, pp. 152-153.

read it to the assembled officers. De Grasse had reached
Chesapeake Bay. The Frenchmen cheered. Word spread quickly through the city, and everyone knew very well what it meant.
People ran shouting through the streets, houses were illuminated, handbills announcing the news were printed, and wits
preached mock funeral orations for Lord Cornwallis. A cheer-
ing crowd gathered outside Luzerne's residence.

Rochambeau and Washington had planned for all the troops
to be taken by water down Chesapeake Bay, but when they
reached Head of Elk, the embarkation point, they found very
few usable craft. The men and materials most urgently needed
to start siegeworks were sent ahead on the vessels available, and
the rest of the force marched to Baltimore. There were only a
few craft there, too, and what there were the French yielded to
the Americans. Rochambeau's men prepared for another long
march, but on the first night of the journey a messenger arrived
with word that de Grasse was sending transports to Annapolis;
the safe arrival of de Barras from Newport had made this possible. So most of the French troops did go by water from Annapolis to Williamsburg. Finally Berthier could write on
his list of campsites: "Camp a William's Burg, le 26
septembre . . . Fin."

De Grasse off Virginia

De Grasse reached the entrance to Chesapeake Bay on August
26, anchored at Lynnhaven Bay roadstead, and landed his
troops on August 30. He stationed some ships in the James River
and across the mouth of the York River, to prevent Cornwallis
from escaping to the south, and posted a frigate outside Cape
Henry as a lookout.

The British meanwhile had been vigorously, although not
entirely effectively, shifting their fleets to meet the challenge.
When Admiral Rodney, in the West Indies, learned from
Graves, in New York, that a French fleet was expected to sail to
North America from the Caribbean, and learned from his own
intelligence sources that de Grasse was preparing to sail from
Cap François, Haiti, he alerted Admiral Hood to prepare to sail
north. There were a number of delays, and Hood actually left
Antigua for the Chesapeake Capes on August 10, five days after
de Grasse had left Cap François. Nevertheless, Hood and his

fourteen ships of the line reached the Capes three days ahead of
de Grasse. Finding Chesapeake Bay empty of naval vessels, he
sailed north.

Hood arrived off Sandy Hook on August 28, only a short time
after advance word of his imminent arrival had reached Graves,
and shortly before the report came that de Barras had left
Newport three days earlier with all his ships, carrying artillery
and French troops. Graves joined Hood on the thirty-first, bringing with him five ships of the line and a 50-gun ship, and took
command of the entire fleet. It sailed at once for the
Chesapeake.

At 8:00 A.M. on September 5 de Grasse's lookout frigate outside Cape Henry spotted Graves's fleet steering southwest before a northeast wind for the mouth of the Chesapeake. De
Grasse at once ordered his ships to sea. His fighting fleet was
down to twenty-four ships of the line because he was using some
ships to block the York and James rivers, and he was also short-
handed, since he had put two thousand of his seamen ashore
with the troops. He headed out of the bay on the ebb tide to avoid
being caught at a disadvantage within it. Some of the ships had to
tack several times to clear Cape Henry, and they emerged from
the bay still not in an orderly line of battle.

Graves was at a disadvantage in numbers, nineteen to twenty-
four ships of the line, but he had the advantage of the windward
position as the French ships sailed out, forming a line as they
headed east, close hauled to the northeast wind. Graves continued on his southwesterly course until his flagship, the *London*,
in the center of the line, was abreast the French van, which was
proceeding about three miles to leeward. Then his ships wore
together, hove to while the French line moved abreast, then
moved east on a converging course.

Graves altered his course twice, toward the southeast, in order
to close the range between his line and the French. Each time, his
ships followed in line behind their leader, so that when those in
the British van were close enough for action seven toward the
rear of the line were much too far away. They never got into the
fight. Just after 3:45 P.M., Graves gave the signal to bear down
and engage the enemy. Since the signal for line ahead continued
to fly, the ships in the rear did not bear down until that flag was
finally taken down almost two hours later, too late for them to
close with the French. The *London*, meanwhile, bore down to
close range, and then luffed up to fire a broadside. Since the

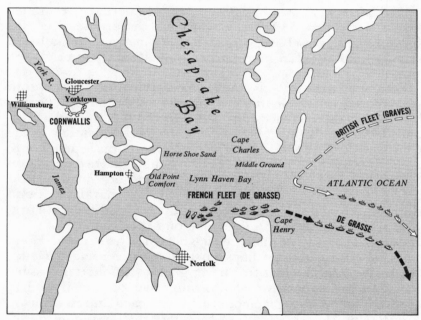

Battle of Chesapeake Bay

ships ahead had been slower to turn, the *London* partly blanketed the one ahead of her and had to heave to in order to permit the ships in front to pull ahead. In spite of all this confusion, during which the French were trying to order their line and were returning the British fire, the ships within range were engaged in furious combat until just after sunset, when de Grasse ordered his van to drop off. This broke off the action. Ninety British seamen had been killed, and 246 wounded. Several British vessels were badly shot up, and the *Terrible*, 74, was so badly damaged that Graves finally ordered her burned; she was set afire on September 10. French losses are not accurately known. However, the *Diademe*, which had come under fire from several British vessels, reportedly lost 120 men and her sails and rigging, and had 125 holes in her hull, 12 of them below the waterline.

For the next several days the two fleets remained at sea, within sight of each other. Neither commander tried to engage, Graves because he thought his ships had suffered too much damage, and de Grasse because he was anxious to return safely to the Chesapeake. The wind turned fair after dark on September 8, and de Grasse took advantage of it. When he reached the bay on September 11 he found that de Barras and his squadron had arrived the day before. Graves approached two days later, found thirty-six French ships at anchor, and proceeded to New York, where he anchored at Sandy Hook on September 19.

Graves's conduct of this battle has been much discussed. Hood was very critical of it, perhaps partly in self-defense, since it was his squadron in the rear that never got into action. It is possible that Graves might have won an important victory if he had ordered a general engagement early, with each ship tackling the French ship closest, instead of keeping his ships in line ahead. And he could probably have headed off the French and returned before them to Chesapeake Bay, which Hood advised him to do. As it was, the result of the battle was a decisive and very important victory for the United States and France.

Pageant at Yorktown

With the French fleet blocking escape by sea and the American and French armies cutting off escape by land, Cornwallis was now isolated in the Peninsula, and allied victory at Yorktown was almost inevitable. The strategic vision of Washington, the masterful concentration of forces gathered from land and sea, from distances of a thousand miles, capped by de Grasse's narrow victory—these had the drama of suspense, fear, and hope. The drama of the siege of Yorktown was of a different kind.

The investment of the town, the stylized laying of the siege according to a pattern set in the seventeenth century, the storming of the outlying redoubts, the bold but hopeless sortie of the defenders, the drum beating a parley, and the final ritual of surrender all seem part of a great pageant, a ceremony of victory and defeat. It was, at times, a bloody ceremony, and suspense was all too real for many individual participants, but the end was never seriously in doubt, and the losses were light considering the number of men involved.

A touching, and sometimes humorous, motif of this long ceremony was the chivalrous rivalry between Frenchmen and Americans, and within each army, for the honor of firing the first shot, leading one of the few — and therefore especially precious — attacks, or planting a regimental standard on surrendered earthworks. Washington had called for a "spirit of emulation" to set the tone of the campaign, and the French and American officers took up the challenge, each trying to outdo the other.

The last of Rochambeau's artillery arrived from Head of Elk on September 30, and the concentration was completed. Washington had under his command an allied force of slightly more than 18,000 men. Cornwallis had about 8,800. Most of them were in Yorktown, but there was also a contingent across the York River at Gloucester Point, under the famous cavalry commander Banastre Tarleton. Of Washington's 18,000, 9,500 were Americans under General Lincoln, and 7,800 were Frenchmen under Rochambeau. Rochambeau's force included the roughly 4,000 troops who had made the march from Newport, about 800 marines landed by de Grasse, and the 3,300 regular army troops brought in de Grasse's ships from the West Indies; this last contingent was under the command of the marquis de Saint-Simon, a general described by the duc de Lauzun as "a good and brave man," but easily angered and "given to making scenes with everybody."*

Saint-Simon's force, a new ingredient in the French camp,

*Freeman, *George Washington*, Vol. 5, p. 348n.

comprised three regiments fully as distinguished as those from Newport. The Gâtinais had been formed from Rochambeau's old regiment, the Auvergne, which he commanded in the Seven Years' War; many of Rochambeau's old soldiers were thus with the Gâtinais and still felt loyalty to the regimental motto: "*Auvergne sans tache!*"—"stainless Auvergne." The Touraine was the famous old unit at whose head Lafayette's father had fallen in the Seven Years' War. The Agenois, the ranking regiment of the division, had fought, along with the Gâtinais, at the ill-fated siege of Savannah under d'Estaing. Also with Saint-Simon was the first battalion of the Dillon Regiment, the French regiment filled with Irish names, whose second battalion had come from Newport with the Lauzun Legion.

Since late August, Cornwallis's troops had been fortifying Yorktown. Once Washington and Rochambeau arrived, the British general realized that his situation was hopeless unless he received reinforcements by sea, reinforcements whose naval escort would have to fight its way past de Grasse. Cornwallis decided to contract his forces within his inner defenses and wait. That was why, on the night of September 29-30, Cornwallis abandoned three outer redoubts on the allied left, a happy surprise for the French and Americans, and probably the most serious tactical error of Cornwallis's career.

Some of the French had a chance to fight on October 3, when Lauzun's cavalrymen encountered Banastre Tarleton on Gloucester Point. Backed by firm-standing Virginia militia, the French drove the British from the field and then advanced to lay siege to the British post at Gloucester. Although unhorsed during a French charge, Tarleton escaped capture.

Across the river at Yorktown, the allies had already set about the work of preparing for a siege, a procedure in which the Americans were quite inexperienced—Washington's blockade of Boston early in the war had been only a distant and crude version of a conventional seige. Both Rochambeau and von Steuben, the invaluable Prussian volunteer who was one of Lincoln's three division commanders, had ample European siege experience, having fought on opposite sides in the siege-filled Seven Years' War. Following their counsel, the allies prepared their siege according to the book.

A series of trenches running parallel to the enemy's fortification lines, each closer than the last, had to be dug. These were called *parallels*, and usually two were enough. On the night of October 6, protected from British guns and muskets by a dark, overcast sky, French and American soldiers began digging the

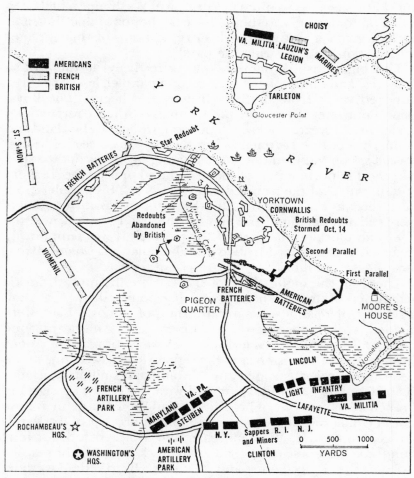

The Siege of Yorktown, September 30-October 19, 1781

first parallel six hundred to eight hundred yards from the British lines. Three days later the parallel was completed, the siege guns were emplaced, and at three o'clock in the afternoon a French gun fired into the British positions, signaling the opening of the siege. As so often at Yorktown, Washington had been called on to decide who should have the honor of that shot, and he had given it to the French in recognition of their greater contributions in preparing the parallel.

The big guns hammered away effectively at the British defenses, and on October 11 the second parallel, less than three hundred yards from the British lines, was begun. The Royal Deux-Ponts Regiment and the Gâtinais worked courageously under fire to create the French portion, while the Maryland and Pennsylvania line regiments dug the American section. Siege specialist von Steuben called the digging of the second parallel "the most important part of the siege," and praised the "bravery and dispatch" of the troops doing the work. This parallel could not stretch as far as the first, however, for two British redoubts were still manned on the far right of the allied position, near the river and blocking the path of the parallel. It was temporarily ended, therefore, in a fortified position called an *epaulement* that faced these redoubts.

Then, on the night of October 14, came the most dramatic action of Yorktown. The redoubts had to be taken. Again the assigning of missions was an awarding of honors. They were divided equally between Frenchmen and Americans, one redoubt for each. The American attack was to be made by troops from Lafayette's division, and the right to lead it was won, after a determined verbal struggle, by Alexander Hamilton. Rochambeau honored Baron de Vioménil with the right to assign the French mission to one of his officers, and Vioménil in turn chose Count Guillaume de Deux-Ponts, younger brother of the Deux-Ponts commander. Vioménil gave him a picked force of four hundred chasseurs and grenadiers—shock troops of the period—from the Deux-Ponts and Gâtinais. Baron de Lestrade, lieutenant colonel of the Gâtinais, would be Deux-Pont's second in command for the operation. Vioménil, Deux-Ponts, and Lestrade, with two carefully selected sergeants, planned the attack in detail. Lafayette's Americans under Hamilton were going to attack the other redoubt at the same time, while other French units would make demonstrations against a British redoubt on the allied left and against British defenses on Gloucester Point.

The redoubt assigned to the French has gone down in history as Redoubt 9 because it was so marked on some British maps. It was the redoubt closest to the allied epaulement, and it turned out to be more strongly held than Redoubt 10, the American objective.

As the men of the Gâtinais and Deux-Ponts moved into the trenches to await the signal, their envious comrades wished them luck, and Colonel Deux-Ponts embraced his younger brother warmly. Rochambeau himself appeared and excited the Gâtinais with the cry *"Auvergne, Auvergne sans tache!"* Some of the Gâtinais said they would fight like lions and begged Rochambeau to get them back the Auvergne name for their regiment in return—he promised he would.

The signal was six rounds fired in quick succession by one of the French batteries. When it came, the men moved out silently, led by the two sergeants—"men as intelligent as they are brave," wrote Deux-Ponts in his journal. A Hessian sentry called out "Wer da?" well before the French reached the abatis that surrounded the redoubt. Fire from the redoubt's palisade hit them as they struggled across the abatis and then across the ditch inside it and up the side of the palisade which bristled with sharpened stakes (*fraises*). Engineer troops with axes also hacked at the stakes, and finally a few attackers reached the parapet and began firing at the enemy. Once they got into the redoubt the fight was easy. The 120 defenders crowded together behind a row of casks and made a fine target. The redoubt surrendered, and Deux-Ponts, on Vioménil's orders, immediately prepared to meet a counterattack. As Deux-Ponts put it, "Our general was judging the English commander after his own pattern. That is what he would have done immediately, but the English did not advance."*

The Americans had also performed superbly in their attack on Redoubt 10. But they had faced only sixty-five men, and the defenses of their target redoubt had been carelessly constructed. The British guns blasted away as the allies furiously worked to complete the second parallel, into which they integrated their two new redoubts. The French suffered many casualties in this bombardment and throughout the actions of that night. French

*Quoted from Deux-Ponts's journal by Bonsal, *When the French Were Here*, p. 160.

losses were almost a hundred killed and wounded, American about forty.

Yorktown was doomed. The allied guns were devastating it. Cornwallis responded with what amounted to the ceremonial gesture required of a besieged general. In the dark early morning of October 16, he sent out three hundred and fifty men for a raid popularly known as Abercromby's Sortie after the officer who commanded it. Its aim was to spike the allied guns in the new batteries. The British caused seventeen casualties and temporarily spiked six guns by driving their bayonet points into the guns' touchholes and breaking them off.* Abercromby's men had made their gesture, but within a few hours the guns were firing, and the British had gained little but broken bayonet blades and a number of casualties.

Cornwallis then tried to take his men across to Gloucester by boat, desperately hoping to break through the thinner siege lines there and escape by land. A storm frustrated the effort; the French and Americans learned of it only when they saw the few boats that had gotten across come back from Gloucester the next day.

Later that same morning, October 17, the anniversary of Burgoyne's surrender at Saratoga, a British drummer mounted the parapet of the British defenses and beat the roll that called for a parley. Cornwallis was ready to give up.

During the surrender negotiations, the careful honoring of French and American privileges was scrupulously continued. Rochambeau named the vicomte de Noailles to serve as commissioner, and Washington appointed the American John Laurens. While they met with the two British commissioners at Moore House, behind the allied parallels, Washington sent two hundred Frenchmen and two hundred Americans to guard the approaches to Yorktown and prevent overeager allied troops from rushing into the town prematurely and without discipline.

The signing of the surrender document came on the morning of the nineteenth. After Washington had signed, Rochambeau inscribed his title, and since de Grasse was ill, de Barras signed, "En mon nom & celui du Comte de Grasse."

The crowning ceremony, the surrender itself, came that after-

---

*Spiking a gun effectively, as when a unit was forced to abandon its guns to an advancing enemy, required jamming or pouring metal into the touchhole, the hole through which the powder was lit, in such a way that it could not be removed without destroying the barrel.

noon. French troops lined one side of the road down which the defeated British would march, Americans the other. As always the French were by far the more striking, and by now the Americans who had fought with them knew there were strong leaders and brave soldiers inside the white uniforms with the colorful trimmings.

The British marched out of Yorktown with their flags cased, not unfurled, and with their bands playing British tunes, not American or French ones. These seemingly small points meant the difference between honor and disgrace. They had been written into the surrender terms to match the conditions imposed on Benjamin Lincoln and the Americans who had surrendered at Charleston the year before.

At the far end of the lines of allied soldiers the British troops saw Washington, waiting astride his horse on the American side, and Rochambeau mounted on the French side. The surrendering officer, Brigadier General Charles O'Hara, Cornwallis's second in command, approached Rochambeau rather than Washington, perhaps in error, but more likely in deliberate preference to surrendering to an insurrectionist. Rochambeau motioned him toward the commander in chief. Washington, in turn, upon learning that Cornwallis was ill, or pleading illness, courteously but firmly directed O'Hara to Washington's own second in command, General Lincoln. And so it was that the humiliated captive of Charleston received the British surrender at Yorktown.

The aftermath was all gentlemanly cordiality. Washington entertained O'Hara at dinner, and his guest rose to the occasion, appearing to enjoy himself as thoroughly as if he had not just participated in a devastating British defeat. All this was also according to custom, and won admiration for O'Hara and the other British officers, who behaved similarly during the next few days. The French, however, carried graciousness to the defeated foe to lengths that the Americans found hard to accept. The vicomte de Noailles lent Cornwallis a popular book on tactics, and Rochambeau lent him £10,000. Other French officers pressed generous loans on their recent enemies. Although this seemed excessive to the Americans, in eighteenth-century Europe there was still a chivalric internationalism among military men. All officers were gentlemen and brothers, regardless of nationality and ideology, and—except in actual combat— were to be treated as such.

Rochambeau carefully distributed rewards to his men. Even before the surrender, he gave two days' extra pay to the men of the Gâtinais and Deux-Ponts who had captured the redoubt, with larger bonuses for the engineer troops who had opened the way through the deadly abatis and palisade. He gave official recognition to the special contributions of Colonel Comte François d'Aboville, who commanded the French artillery at the siege, and to Colonel Querenet de la Combe, who commanded the French engineers who built the siegeworks.

The honor of taking the news to Paris and Versailles went to Lauzun and Guillaume de Deux-Ponts as "the two officers of rank who have most distinguished themselves." They sailed on two separate ships and safely reached France in late November. A mass of thanksgiving for the victory was held in the Cathedral of Notre Dame, and on the night of November 27 all the inhabitants of Paris were ordered to illuminate the fronts of their houses in celebration of what Frenchmen and Americans had done in Virginia.

The next year, after the French troops had wintered in Williamsburg and marched back to Philadelphia, the chevalier de la Luzerne gave a ball in honor of the birth of the long-awaited dauphin, a ball that served also as a victory celebration for Yorktown. There were at least seven hundred guests and ten thousand spectators outside, appropriate quantities of refreshments, a band providing "splendid entertainment," and a climax of fireworks. Dr. Benjamin Rush gave a summary of the party's mood that also summed up the paradoxical character of the great alliance:

> How great the revolution in the mind of an American! to rejoice in the birth of an heir to the Crown of France against which we had imbibed prejudices as ancient as the wars between France and England—above all how new the phenomenon for republicans to rejoice in the birth of a prince who must one day be the support of monarchy and slavery. The picture is agreeable, as it shows us in the clearest point of view that there are no prejudices so strong, no contradictions so palpable, but will yield to the love of Liberty.*

*Quoted in Bonsal, *When the French Were Here*, p. 220.

Decisive as the allied victory was in the struggle between Britain and the United States, and joyfully as it was celebrated, Yorktown did not bring an immediate end to fighting, and certainly not to fighting between the warring powers of Europe. Many battles lay ahead, for by this time the war had really become global, involving more nations of Europe, affecting nations not directly involved, and spreading conflicts far from the shores of the new United States.

IV

SPAIN JOINS THE FIGHT

8

Spain and the Great Siege of Gibraltar

The great Rock of Gibraltar, towering over the water at the western end of the Mediterranean Sea, was the primary reason Spain negotiated, finagled, threatened, and bribed—and finally fought—during the American Revolutionary War. Lying near the southern tip of Spain and separated by just fourteen miles of water from Morocco, the Rock had been captured by British Admiral Sir George Rooke in the War of the Spanish Succession early in the eighteenth century and formally ceded to Britain in 1713. Regaining it soon became an important objective of Spanish governments. To Prime Minister José Moñino y Redondo, conde de Floridablanca, England's preoccupation with a revolt in America seemed to present a promising opportunity.

First Floridablanca tried diplomacy. After the Franco-American alliance was signed in 1778, but before any shots had been fired between France and England, Spain offered England a bribe: Despite the Bourbon Family Compact, Spain would remain neutral if England would yield Gibraltar; and Spain might well be able to persuade France not to fight England at all, still assuming that England would hand over Gibraltar.

This offer was not accepted. The next year, with France applying pressure to get Spain into the war, the Spanish made another offer to Britain. Spain would try to get France out of the war on terms of (1) Gibraltar being given to Spain; (2) the United States being treated as independent, *de facto*, during negotiations; and (3) each country, including the United States, keeping only the territory it effectively controlled at the time. This last point would recur over and over during wartime negotiations, and posed a serious threat to the territorial integrity of the United States. For Spain, however, the key point

119

was Gibraltar. The proposal, presented as an offer to mediate, cloaked a threat. If it was not accepted, Spain would enter the war against Britain. It was not, and Spain did.

France and Spain signed a secret treaty, the Convention of Aranjuez, on April 12, 1779. They agreed that France would assist Spain to recover Minorca, Mobile, Pensacola, the Gulf of Honduras, and the coast of Campeche (on the Yucatan peninsula), and above all that no peace would be signed until Gibraltar was restored to Spanish sovereignty.

During the next two years, as the dashing Bernando de Gálvez conquered important posts in the Mississippi Valley and West Florida for Spain, another prime Spanish aim was to emerge. With a colonial system still based on mercantilism, Spain's rulers looked on the Mississippi River and even the Gulf of Mexico as valuable economic possessions to which they wanted exclusive rights. Never allied with the United States, despising and fearing revolutionaries and revolution, the Spanish rulers became almost as determined to wrest exclusive rights to the Mississippi from their co-belligerent, the United States, as they were to wrest Gibraltar from Britain.

Serious designs on the Mississippi were well in the future, however, in the summer of 1779. The Spanish focus was sharply on the Rock as the Spanish ambassador packed up and left London on June 16. Five days later the British garrison on Gibraltar learned that Spain was at war with England.

The Rock

The British garrison at Gibraltar in 1779 was under the command of General George Augustus Eliott, a dour Scot, who had arrived two years before. He had found fortifications and garrison in sorry condition, but in two years, with hard work and stern discipline, built up the defenses and spruced up the men. His ramrod control would serve them well in the years ahead.

Gibraltar, with a single narrow approach from the Spanish mainland across a strip of sand, seemed highly vulnerable to a siege combined with a blockade from the sea, when the Spanish governor of adjacent San Roque, Lieutenant General Don Joaquin Mendoza, announced to Eliott that he had been ordered to cut off communications by land. Eliott's garrison numbered about seven thousand men, including three regiments from

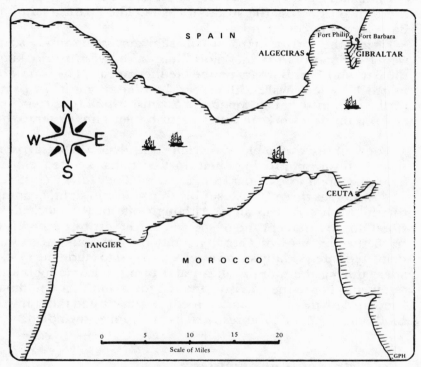

Gibraltar and Nearby North Africa

Hanover. He had well over four hundred pieces of artillery, a figure that would be increased to 663 in the years of the siege, including 18-, 24-, and 26-pounder guns, mortars, and howitzers. A single sloop, three frigates, and one ship of the line, under Admiral Duff, were the only naval force at hand. It could hardly keep a sea lane open in the face of a determined blockade. To enforce the blockade the Spanish had fifteen cruisers based at Cadiz, an assorted collection of vessels at Algeciras, and the use of a port across the strait, at Ceuta. The Spanish admiral Barcelo was in command.

Facing the fortifications of Gibraltar across the sandy strip were two Spanish fortresses, Fort Philip at the west, overlooking the bay, and Fort Barbara on the Mediterranean. The two were joined by a long wall, with several bastions along it. In front of the wall in the siege years the Spanish would dig trenches and put up siegeworks in order to push their guns closer to the Rock.

The first test of the blockade came on July 5, 1779. Garrison troops, busily improving their fortifications, spotted eleven Spanish ships approaching from the west. They hove to just out of gunshot, as three British supply ships came in sight, heading for the harbor of Gibraltar. Although one of the blockaders stood out to intercept them, she was driven off by cannon fire from the defenses of Gibraltar, and the precious cargo was delivered safely. Many such vessels managed to elude the blockaders during the months ahead and bring welcome food and other supplies to the garrison and the town, but they could not keep up with demand. Eliott immediately instituted rationing of food, and tightened the restrictions as supplies dwindled.

Rodney off Cape Finisterre

The plight of Gibraltar's garrison and of the defenders of the British base on the island of Minorca, also under siege, was not unheeded in England. The departure of Admiral Sir George Brydges Rodney, distinguished veteran of the Seven Years' War, to take up command of the Leeward Islands Station offered a great opportunity in the fall of 1779 to send provisions and reinforcements to the beleaguered men on Gibraltar. On December 29 a huge fleet set sail from Plymouth—twenty-two ships of the line, fourteen smaller naval vessels, and an assortment of ships carrying men, equipment, and food, as well as a number of merchantmen bound for trade in the West Indies.

Southwest of Cape Finisterre on January 8 British sailors sighted twenty-two Spanish ships, including a ship of the line, the *Guipuscoana*, 64, six smaller naval vessels, and other ships carrying naval stores and provisions to Cadiz. Rodney's ships gave chase and captured the lot. Putting a crew aboard the *Guipuscoana*, he gave her charge of escorting the captured provision ships to Gibraltar.

And Cape St. Vincent

Moving on down the coast, the British fleet had just passed Cape St. Vincent in the early afternoon of January 16 when it encountered a Spanish squadron, commanded by Admiral Don Juan de Langara, comprising eleven ships of the line and two 26-gun frigates. As Rodney's vessels bore down upon them, the Spaniards, with a strong westerly wind, formed a line of battle on the starboard tack, heading southeast toward Cadiz, which was about a hundred miles away. Rodney's faster, copper-bottomed ships came up from the leeward, passing between the Spaniards and the shore and engaging each in turn as they came within range. Battle was joined at about four in the afternoon. Within an hour the *Santo Domingo*, 70, had blown up with all hands, and an hour later another Spanish vessel struck her colors. Darkness fell, and the seas were high; although the battle off Cape St. Vincent is often called the "Moonlight Battle," the moonlight was fitful. The fighting continued until two in the morning, when the leading Spanish ship struck and the firing ceased. Four of the Spanish ships had escaped, two had been driven ashore, and the *Santo Domingo* had been lost. Rodney added the other four to the British fleet and with them headed for Gibraltar, carrying aboard the captured Spanish admiral.

Word of the approach of the convoy had been carried to Gibraltar by two British brigs. The first had preceded the slower-sailing convoy by several days; the second brought news of the battle off Cape Finisterre. Admiral Barcelo, apparently aware of the imminent arrival of a formidable British force, remained close in port at Algeciras as the defenders of Gibraltar strained their eyes into the mist that lay to the west on January 17. Heavy seas, head winds, and the current running through the strait held up the British vessels and carried many beyond the Rock. The first ships anchored at Gibraltar that afternoon, with news of the battle off Cape St. Vincent. The rest struggled in, and it was January 26 before Admiral Rodney, in his flagship, the *Sandwich*, 90, arrived. As the British defenders of Gibraltar exulted, the Spanish across the bay could gaze in dismay at the harbor full of British vessels. On many masts Spanish flags flew beneath the British colors of their captors, and goods intended for Spanish use were being unloaded for the British defenders.

While provisions and reinforcements were put ashore at Gibraltar, other ships continued to Minorca with supplies for the British there. Upon their return, on February 13, Rodney departed for the Leeward Islands. Admiral Duff, who had shown no great ability as commander of the naval force at Gibraltar, left thereafter with a detachment from the Channel fleet that had accompanied Rodney. En route to England this force encountered and attacked a French convoy bound for the Indian Ocean, escorted by two 64-gun ships. With his small force Duff took one of the warships and three supply ships.

The Spanish Attack

With the British ships out of the way, Admiral Barcelo emerged from behind the protective boom he had had installed across the harbor at Algeciras and took up blockade duty. Life on Gibraltar settled back to the routine of siege. Gunfire exchanges between besiegers and besieged became a regular pattern. In March, rationing, relaxed when supplies were plentiful, was reinstituted. With few vessels making it through the blockade, scurvy began to plague the defenders and the people of the town.

Rumors reached Gibraltar during the spring that the Spaniards at Algeciras were preparing fireships to use against the small naval force that remained at Gibraltar — one ship, the *Panther*, 60, commanded by Captain Harvey; a frigate, the *Enterprise*, under Captain Lesley; two other smaller ships; and some armed transports. They, and a few small merchant vessels, were at anchor in the harbor on the night of June 6, 1780, when the watch on the *Enterprise* sighted a vessel approaching. It proved to be a Spanish fireship, one of nine that the Spaniards were bringing up to set loose to drift down upon the anchored British vessels. Fire from the *Enterprise* was answered with a rain of burning missiles. As the fireship and its companions burst into flames, Lesley cut his anchor line and stood in toward shore to avoid the drifting fire brands. While the Spanish crews, having abandoned the fireships, rowed off homeward in the longboats they had towed astern, British seamen took to boats, got lines aboard the burning vessels, and towed them away from the harbor. Seven were brought to the beach, where they provided the garrison with a stock of wood, and two disappeared harmlessly at sea.

Later in June, the *Panther* was attacked by four Spanish ships. Although she gave a good account of herself and managed to escape to the protection of the guns of Gibraltar, she was damaged in the action. Rodney had left her behind contrary to his instructions and now she was ordered home. Evading the blockade, she sailed for England.

The Siege Continues

There were two diplomatic developments in the summer of 1780 that affected Gibraltar. Secret negotiations for peace between England and Spain came to naught as the British military position worsened and France promised help in the siege of Gibraltar. And the emperor of Morocco joined the alliance against England. The effect of his move on the Gibraltar garrison was immediate, for the British consul in Tangier had been invaluable as a source of intelligence and an organizer of supply shipments.

The summer dragged on, hot and uncomfortable, with little to relieve the monotony. Smallpox in the town added to the misery of the civilians, and military and civilians alike suffered from scurvy, until in October a Danish ship loaded with citrus fruit was blown in close enough to be brought into harbor. Her cargo, carefully husbanded by Eliott, soon arrested the scurvy. The blockade was made more effective when the Spaniards produced a gunboat with a single 26-pounder in the bow that not only harassed shipping but had speed enough to come in close, fire at the fortifications under cover of darkness, and escape.

During the dreary winter the fire of the opposing batteries continued. Deserters crossed from both sides to join the group that seemed from their vantage point to have a pleasanter life.

But both were uncomfortable, the garrison on the Rock and the Spaniards living in trenches on the low land. In early spring Vice Admiral George Darby brought a convoy of a hundred vessels from England and sailed into the harbor without opposition, bringing delight to the inhabitants of the town and the garrison and fury to the Spaniards who watched, unable to interfere. In their frustration the allies directed heavy fire not only at the fortifications but at the town of Gibraltar itself, a rare instance in the eighteenth century of striking at civilians and their homes. The townspeople fled south beyond the range of the guns, which fired fifty-six thousand rounds of shot and twenty thousand shells in the next six weeks. The battered town was left to troops and sailors, who roamed the streets, drinking, looting, and raising hell, until Governor Eliott found it necessary to tighten discipline, to the point of hanging on the spot men found looting in the town.

On April 20, 1781, the British vessels, having suffered only slight damage from Spanish gunboats in night raids, sailed for England, taking with them many women and children.

The heavy bombardment went on for months, reducing the town to ruins, causing many casualties, and damaging the fortifications. But the British defenders continued to return the fire, and although their flagpole was shattered by a shell, they nailed the flag to the stump and held their ground. Their stubborn defense was a bright spot for England in 1781, as in America allied forces converged on Yorktown.

During that summer the Spanish besiegers took advantage of the good weather, following an exceedingly rainy spring, to build more siegeworks and advance their guns closer to the Rock. Their strength had been built up to twenty-one thousand men, opposing six thousand British and Hanoverians, and their fleet increased to the point that very few ships were able to sneak into the bay with provisions for the defenders. But before the Spanish could mount a major assault on the fortifications of Gibraltar, Eliott decided to attack.

The British Sortie

On November 27, 1781, at two in the morning, Eliott, with almost half of his force, moved out from the shelter of his defenses and headed for the Spanish lines. The sortie had been carefully planned and was as carefully executed. Not until the rapidly advancing British soldiers were almost upon them did the Spanish sentries detect the attack and sound the alarm to the sleeping troops. With little attempt to defend their positions, the Spanish abandoned their fortifications and withdrew to safety. Quickly moving in behind the infantry, British engineers spiked guns, destroyed walls, and set dumps and stores afire. The only Spanish resistance was sounded by the big guns of the forts, which opened fire on the Rock, answered by the batteries of Gibraltar. As the volleys flew back and forth overhead, the work of destruction proceeded. Finally, the attackers withdrew, touching off a line of powder that detonated the main Spanish powder magazine in a great explosion. Debris and bits of burning wood flew far and wide, spreading the fire to areas that had been left untouched. While the British returned to their exulting comrades, the Spaniards surveyed their losses, hanged some men judged guilty of negligence, and set about building new positions, pushing them even closer to the British fortifications.

The glow of success soon faded as the British garrison settled back to the routine of life in besieged Gibraltar. The daily exchange of gunfire continued, taking a toll in both death and damage. Between April 1781 and January 1782, 122 British troops were killed, and 400 wounded, 45 of these so badly that they were sent back to England. Scurvy broke out again, rationing went on, and only a few supply ships managed to slip through the blockade.

The Last Great Assault

In February 1782 the last British position on Minorca fell to the French, and Gibraltar stood alone. French soldiers who had been stationed at Minorca were transferred to the siege lines at Gibraltar, where they and other reinforcements added nine thousand men to the force. The duc de Crillon took command in May, determined to put an end to the years of siege. He started preparing at once for a great attack, from sea and from land, and the word was spread abroad that the garrison would be battered into submission. The French king's brother, the comte d'Artois, arrived to watch, and the duc de Bourbon headed the list of lesser nobles who gathered for the show.

The summer months were spent preparing ten unique vessels that were to pound the fortifications from the sea. They were old men-of-war, cut down on one side, and having the other side reinforced with three layers of heavy timber and one of wet sand, to a thickness of three feet, with a lining of cork. Behind this barricade stood the gunners, their guns poking out through the wall. Above their heads was a slanting sort of roof of cordage and wet hides, so designed that cannonballs landing on it would roll off into the sea. Commanded by Admiral Bonaventura Moreno, the battery ships carried 142 guns at the ready and 70 in reserve.

It was evident to the British that a large-scale attack from the sea was about to take place, and Governor Eliott prepared his men to resist it. He had a new weapon, iron shot heated red hot so that when it hit it would burn as well as damage its target. Grates and furnaces for heating shot were installed in all the batteries, and test firings on the Spanish fortifications met with great success, striking one battery and spreading fire. The Spanish responded with fifty-five hundred round shot and twenty-three hundred shells from their land guns, and more from gunships, in a period of two days.

On September 12 the combined fleets of Spain and France assembled at Algeciras for the attack that was to follow the anticipated devastating success of the battery ships. There were over forty ships of the line, uncounted frigates, zebecs, bomb-ketches, and landing craft, and three hundred troop transports.

A light northwest breeze the following morning propelled the battery ships toward the harbor of Gibraltar. Before they had dropped anchor and prepared to go into action, the Spanish land batteries opened a heavy fire, and the garrison's guns responded to that before the British guns pointing seaward began to exchange fire with the battery ships in the harbor. It was two in the afternoon, and the seaward wall and bastions of Gibraltar bore new marks from the naval attack, before one of the British red-hot cannonballs scored on the 21-gun *Talla Piedra*, one of the largest of the battery ships, commanded by the prince of Nassau. Fire raged out of control aboard her in the strong wind, by then blowing from the southwest, and the crew was ordered to abandon ship. One by one the other battery ships were set afire, and their crews ceased firing and went over the side. The land batteries continued to fire across the low land of the peninsula during the night, but on the water there was no further fighting. Boats from Gibraltar moved among the wreckage picking up Spanish survivors, many of them badly injured. From time to time an explosion aboard a burning vessel broke into the background noise of gunfire, flames, and general chaos. When the sun rose three ships had been sunk or blown completely apart, and the rest of the battery ships were burning. All would sink before day was done. The harbor was full of corpses and wreckage. About two thousand seamen had died; three-hundred and fifty were prisoners in Gibraltar, many of them gravely injured. The gunners of Gibraltar had fired eighty-five hundred rounds, using up seven hundred and fifty barrels of gunpowder. The total for both sides has been estimated as high as forty thousand rounds.

The great attack from the sea had been a dismal failure, but the Spanish land batteries continued to fire, maintaining a daily schedule of over one thousand rounds.

The Rock Holds Out

The defenders of the Rock were soon to be rewarded. On September 11, 1782, Admiral Lord Richard Howe sailed from England with thirty-four ships of the line, an assortment of other naval vessels, and more than a hundred merchant ships. Some of them headed for the West Indies, but Howe brought most of the fleet with him, through heavy storms off Cape Finisterre and Cape St. Vincent, and sailed serenely and unopposed into the harbor of Gibraltar. The grateful Eliott at once put his new supplies of powder and shot to work against the Spaniards.

The Franco-Spanish fleet, which had watched from its moorings as Howe's ships sailed in, followed the British fleet out when Howe headed back to the Atlantic on October 19. Off Cape Spartel the British awaited the allies, and a minor action developed. But the allies broke it off, and Howe sailed on to England, unmolested thereafter.

The end was at hand. In October French and Spanish units withdrew from the advance fortifications, and firing dwindled to sporadic bursts from a land battery or a gunboat as peace negotiations proceeded in Paris. On January 20, 1782, preliminary peace terms gave Minorca and Florida to Spain. But Gibraltar remained in British hands. After three years, seven months, and twelve days, on February 2 the longest continuous siege on record came to an end, a proud memory in British annals. It was an embarrassing defeat for the allies that sharply limited their bargaining power during the peace talks.

9

Bernardo de Gálvez Clears the Mississippi Valley for Spain

Bernardo de Gálvez is a Revolutionary name seldom heard, at least in the eastern United States, and yet this Spaniard's skill at military leadership, his success as a statesman, his personal magnetism, and his dashing, romantic style should make him a natural popular hero. His exploits could provide material for films and novels by the score. This "last of the Conquistadores" formed competent and devoted armies by combining Spanish regulars with the French civilians, Anglo-American settlers, German and Swiss immigrants, free blacks, Indians, hunters, and vagabond eccentrics who lived on the southwestern frontier. With them he took Manchac, Baton Rouge, Natchez, Mobile, and Pensacola—wresting the lower Mississippi Valley and all West Florida from Britain. He was the hero of Louisiana and all Spanish America in his own time. His proud motto was "*Yo Solo*"—"I alone"—granted by Charles III in gratitude for Gálvez's bold forcing of the entrance to Pensacola Bay.

Gálvez was a golden boy from birth. Child of an extremely influential family of the Spanish aristocracy, he was brought up for a military career. After serving as a lieutenant in operations against Portugal late in the Seven Years' War, he was sent in 1769 as captain and second in command on a Mexican expedition against a group of Apache Indians. This assignment was an honor that jumped him over senior officers, but, as in his later career, Gálvez was equal to the position in which his birth placed him. With determination and inspiring leadership he pressed on with limited supplies and rallied his men at a critical moment in the campaign; he was successful in devastating Apache villages and winning security for the Spanish frontier for a time; and he

131

gained a reputation for treating his Apache captives humanely. Returning to Spain, Gálvez took a leave of absence from the Spanish army and went to France to study military science. Then, back in Spain in 1775, he took part in an unsuccessful landing in Algiers, an effort in which he managed to distinguish himself. After a few months as a lieutenant colonel, still propelled onward and upward by the Gálvez name, he was sent in 1776 to Louisiana to be colonel of the regiment there — the *Tercio de Louisiana*. At that time his father was viceroy of New Spain, and his uncle José de Gálvez, still more powerful, was minister for the Indies and one of the strongest figures in the Spanish ministry. Bernardo was his favorite protégé. When he was about thirty years old, a few months after he landed in Louisiana, Bernardo de Gálvez was made its governor.

The American Revolutionary War had begun, and the effects were felt in Gálvez's territory. The Spanish government was neutral, but it was eager to use any opportunities that might arise to make difficulties for England. Spain was also concerned by the vulnerability of Louisiana and wanted its defenses strengthened against possible British attack. Gálvez worked to accomplish these aims. He seems also to have had the additional motivation of a pro-American bias, a bias the Spanish government definitely did not share.

Gálvez came as governor to a Spanish territory that had earlier been French for two generations, and where five men had been hanged just seven years before for leading resistance to Spanish rule. His charm and ability soon made him popular, however, and his marriage to a French Louisianan, the charming widow Félicie de Maxent d'Estréhan, increased his popularity to the point of adulation. Although without experience in government administration, he immediately showed a statesmanlike grasp of Louisiana's needs—both its immediate, military needs and its long-range economic ones. He took measures to encourage agriculture and commerce. By seizing British ships on charges of trading in contraband, and encouraging trade with France, he shifted Louisiana's chief trading activities from England toward France. Seeing a need for population increase if Louisiana was to have the kind of economic development it needed, Gálvez encouraged the immigration of white settlers and also the importation of black slaves. English and American refugees from the Revolution, especially Loyalists from Patriot-controlled areas, streamed into neutral Louisiana in sizable numbers, and Gálvez welcomed them. Galveztown (not to be confused with Galveston, Texas) was founded by these refugees sixty miles northwest of New Orleans and was named for the governor.

Having participated in Spanish Indian fighting, Gálvez could compare the French approach to the Indians that he found in Louisiana with the Spanish approach of constant warfare that he had seen in Mexico. He found the friendly French approach more effective and adopted it.

For the first two years of his governorship, Gálvez was on the sidelines of the war being fought primarily on the eastern coast of the continent and on the seas. But he could not avoid occasional involvement with those whose activities took them to the Mississippi River.

Oliver Pollock and the Ammunition for Fort Pitt

A close associate of Gálvez's was the Irish-American Oliver Pollock, another unsung hero of the Revolution. Pollock had emigrated from Ireland to Pennsylvania in his early twenties and had become a merchant and trader. Trade with the West Indies had taken him to Havana, where he worked for a prominent commercial house, became fluent in Spanish, and made the acquaintance of another Spanish-speaking Irishman, Alejandro O'Reilly. O'Reilly, one of the many eighteenth-century Catholic Irish who chose to live somewhere other than Ireland in the aftermath of the exile of James II, was considered by many to be Spain's best general in the late 1760s, when he and Pollock met. He had fought all over Europe, and for France and Austria as well as Spain. It was this veteran soldier whom the king of Spain sent in 1769 to put down an insurrection in New Orleans, and it was O'Reilly who ordered the five rebel leaders there hanged.

Pollock went with O'Reilly from Havana to New Orleans and soon became intimate with other Spanish leaders there. When the Revolution came, his strong American patriotism led him to use his considerable influence, and also his money and credit, for the Patriot cause. He became the local commercial agent for the Continental Congress.

In the summer of 1776, before Gálvez took over as governor

from Luis de Unzaga, two American officers, Captain George Gibson and a Lieutenant Linn, appeared in New Orleans. They were disguised as traders, and they were seeking gunpowder desperately needed by the Americans defending Fort Pitt (later Pittsburgh) and Fort Henry (later Wheeling). They found Pollock; he persuaded Governor Unzaga to let him have a sizable quantity of powder; he then passed it on to Gibson and Linn. Pollock paid for the powder with a draft on the "Grand Council of Virginia" for 1,850 Spanish dollars. Until some official American body covered the draft, Pollock stood responsible for it. Meanwhile, Linn took most of the powder up the Mississippi and then up the Ohio to Forts Pitt and Henry. Gibson was ceremonially arrested to protect the good name of Spanish neutrality, briefly imprisoned, and then released with the rest of the powder.

Help from Gálvez during Spanish Neutrality

When Gálvez became governor, this quietly beneficent policy toward the United States continued. The new governor encouraged trade with America as well as with France. He also seems to have given refuge to at least one American privateer.

The government in Madrid was also giving surreptitious help by this time, as part of its policy of sapping British strength. In February 1777, Madrid sent cloth, muskets, powder, bayonets, and quinine, through a merchant and ostensibly as an ordinary commercial operation, to the rebelling North American colonies. When the shipment arrived in New Orleans, its size and obviously military nature made it conspicuous, and word soon leaked out that the "merchant" was no merchant and the shipment belonged to the king. Gálvez handled the matter with great finesse. Openly declaring that these were government supplies for the king's military forces, he still managed to get them all to the Patriot forces by various ruses. The cloth was pronounced motheaten and was rejected so that it could be sold to an American agent who was disguised as a merchant. The supplies in barrels, including the gunpowder, were sold as nonmilitary commodities of the same weight. For the future, however, Gálvez suggested to the government in Madrid that supplies for the Americans be carefully smuggled in rather than shipped under such transparently false commercial procedures.

Although supplies flowed freely, Gálvez made a careful judgment in the summer of 1777 not to allow New Orleans to be used as a staging base by George Morgan, commander at Fort Pitt, who was planning attacks on Pensacola and Mobile, the two key British posts in West Florida. Gálvez told Morgan he could help him with supplies, but that no aid could be given that would appear to come from Spain and thus compromise Spanish neutrality. He sent the boats that had brought a request from Morgan back to him loaded with weapons, ammunition, and supplies.

Morgan never attacked Mobile and Pensacola, but George Rogers Clark did attack and seize the frontier post of Kaskaskia in 1778, and he captured Vincennes twice, once in the fall of that year and again in a surprise winter attack after the British had retaken it. Most of Clark's powder came from Pollock and Gálvez. His original supplies were from the lot brought to Fort Pitt from New Orleans by Lieutenant Linn in 1776. In the summer of 1778 Clark also received a large shipment of supplies from New Orleans, and Pollock sent him, at his request, about $7,200 worth of goods in September. Just before the winter march to Vincennes, five hundred more pounds of essential powder arrived.

Clark paid for these supplies, and also paid the other bills of his commissary department, by drawing drafts on the state of Virginia. Virginia's credit was not very good, however, and the drafts were negotiable only to the extent that Pollock was able to get them covered. His usual practice was to ask Gálvez to cover the drafts, and Gálvez usually did; when he did not, Pollock used his own money, and when that ran out, his credit. On one occasion he borrowed enough money at 12.5 percent discount to cover a $12,000 draft, and he later mortgaged some property to cover another draft. One way or another, Pollock was able to pay Clark's drafts at par in New Orleans when Continental currency was worth only 12 cents on the dollar in the east. Pollock was eventually reimbursed for most of his money, but he had to wait until ten years after the Revolution for some of it.

The Willing Episode

Among all the colorful and controversial men who appeared on the Mississippi during Gálvez's governorship, James Willing had perhaps the most spectacular career. The proverbial black sheep of the proverbial distinguished East Coast family, Willing was the brother of Robert Morris's partner, Thomas. He had moved to Natchez in 1774 and become a merchant there, but he was not energetic, productive, or successful. He appeared to enjoy easy living more than business. Still he was a staunch patriot, and when the Revolution broke out he was strongly pro-independence.

Willing went to Philadelphia in 1777 and persuaded the Commerce Committee of Congress to commission him a captain in the navy and to authorize him to pick up supplies from the Spanish at New Orleans and bring them up the Mississippi and Ohio. There is controversy as to what else he was authorized to do, but he probably was instructed to seize British property and expel British forces and Loyalists from settlements along the Mississippi.

At Fort Pitt, Willing took command of an armed boat called the *Rattletrap*. With thirty volunteers he left Fort Pitt in January 1778, picking up more crew as he moved down the Mississippi.

Accounts of what Willing did on his way to New Orleans vary, but there is no doubt that many of the new crew members joined up for the fun of breaking wine bottles, drinking confiscated brandy, and dividing up the spoils of the British settlements at the end of the voyage. At Natchez, the first major post he reached, Willing gave a promise to respect civilian property, and he seems to have kept it fairly well. As the *Rattletrap* moved downriver, however, and the expedition gathered momentum, livestock was slaughtered, slaves seized and carried away, buildings burned, furnishings looted, liquor enjoyed, and white civilian populations terrorized.

As the *Rattletrap* and her crew neared New Orleans in late February, volunteers swelled the force to over a hundred. The crew's destructive reputation preceded it, and frightened Loyalists from West Florida, which extended to the Mississippi, sought refuge in Louisiana. Eager to make his force seem larger than it was, Willing spread rumors that the *Rattletrap* carried only the advance guard of an army of thousands. As she sailed down the river, with several British craft captured along the way, a group of Spanish riverboats happened to be following close behind. The effect was of a great flotilla moving majestically downstream. Reports reaching West Florida exaggerated Willing's force to five thousand men or more.

Willing had official dispatches from Congress to give his arrival in New Orleans legitimacy, and Pollock greeted him and found space in army barracks for his men. He also made arrangements for Willing to auction off some of the property he had taken, the most valuable of which was a hundred slaves.

Gálvez, who placed the Willing group under Spanish protection, had to deal with the inevitable British protests. The governor was firm and somewhat cocky with the British; he was not afraid to be a little provocative. One British naval officer, a Captain John Ferguson, was asked not to refer to anyone under Spanish protection as a rebel, and it was further pointed out that Ferguson's ship had neglected to salute the Spanish flag. Gálvez was well ahead of the government in Madrid in tacit recognition of American independence and in pro-American action. Yet he managed to shelter Willing's Americans and stand up to the British while still offering refuge to fleeing Loyalists. He also returned property Willing's men had seized along the way, whenever he judged it was not taken as fair prize of war.

Willing and his men lingered in New Orleans, living the good life and becoming an awkward burden. They had succeeded in disrupting British supply operations on the Mississippi and in crippling British naval forces on the river, but they were clearly not going to hold any British Mississippi posts permanently. They had made anti-Americans out of many neutral Anglo-American settlers, and in West Florida defenses were being strengthened in response to their threat. So much friction developed between Willing and the helpful Pollock that by the end of May Pollock did not trust himself to speak to Willing. Gálvez eventually got Willing's crew out of the city and northward through Spanish territory, carefully avoiding the British settlements they had terrorized on their way south. Willing himself was sent by sloop to Philadelphia, which he did not reach; a British vessel captured the ship, and Willing was interned in New York.

How to Defend New Orleans

From the time he became governor, Gálvez had worked to build up the defenses of New Orleans and Spanish Louisiana.

To defend the mouth of the Mississippi he had three launches built, each with an 18- or 24-pounder gun. Of shallow draft, and having oars as well as sails, these vessels were well equipped to deal with any naval vessel with a draft shallow enough to enter the mouth of the Mississippi.

Gálvez also strengthened his ground forces—although the increased figures still seem pathetically small. Regular Spanish forces were about two hundred when Gálvez took command of the *Tercio de Louisiana* in 1776. By June 1778 they were 437, and a year later they were 769. Militia at New Orleans increased from 136 in 1777 to 302 in 1778. Gálvez was adept at making soldiers of whatever human resources were at hand.

Word that Spain was at war with England reached Gálvez in July 1779, together with instructions to direct military efforts in Louisiana toward driving the British from their posts on the Mississippi and from Pensacola and Mobile in West Florida. But his primary mission was to hold New Orleans. At the British post of Manchac, just 115 miles upriver, four hundred men had recently arrived, bringing the total of British regulars at the various river posts to eight hundred.

After letters were intercepted indicating that the British were planning to send fifteen hundred men down from Canada and another fifteen hundred by sea from Pensacola for a two-pronged attack on New Orleans, Gálvez called a council of war of his military advisors on July 13. He shared with the other members his information on British intentions and capabilities and pointed out New Orleans's vulnerability. Possibly to keep the news from leaking to the British at Pensacola and Mobile, he did not tell the council about the declaration of war. Almost unanimously the members recommended strengthening New Orleans's defenses.

Well-trained soldier that he was, and mindful of the king's instructions, Gálvez was determined to defend New Orleans by taking the battle to the enemy, but he told no one of his plans except his commissary of war, Juan Antonio Gayarré.

Gayarré gathered supplies, and a little fleet was assembled, composed of Gálvez's three gunboats and a number of other vessels for transport. Departure for Manchac was set for August 23. Gálvez still made no announcement of the declaration of war, and he continued his customary correspondence with the British governor of West Florida as though nothing had changed. Then, on August 18, one of the hurricanes that plague the Gulf Coast struck New Orleans. In three hours all the vessels that had been collected were sunk, most of the supplies were destroyed, and crops in the fields were devastated.

This was the kind of calamity on which Gálvez thrived throughout his career. He pushed ahead harder than ever, finding more boats and supplies, and always keeping up the story that these things were being concentrated for the defense of New Orleans. By August 27, just four days late, the force was ready to depart from New Orleans. Typical of the groups with which Gálvez fought, this one consisted of 170 veteran Spanish regulars, 330 new recruits (some of whom had recently arrived from Mexico and the Canary Islands), 20 carabineers, 60 militiamen and volunteer habitants (French farmers), 80 free blacks, and 7 American volunteers, including Oliver Pollock, who was Gálvez's aide-de-camp.* There were ten artillery pieces, but the artillery officer was reported "very sick." There was no engineer.

Gálvez himself pressed ahead of the main body. Collecting militia and recruiting as he passed Acadian and German river settlements, he gathered 160 Indians and 600 other men of various classes, colors, and nationalities. His force thus reached over 1,400, but it was down by one-third, largely from illness, when the van sighted Fort Manchac on September 6. It was only then that Gálvez told his men that the objective of their expedition was to seize Manchac, Baton Rouge, and Natchez.

Manchac turned out to be an easy conquest. The British main force there had been transferred to the more important post at Baton Rouge, leaving only a token garrison. Not anticipating a large-scale attack, the British had never completed the fortifications at Manchac. At dawn on September 7 the fort was taken easily by direct assault by the militia, a fine morale-builder for them.

Baton Rouge, the next target, was harder. Manned by about 400 regular troops, plus 150 settlers and blacks, and equipped with thirteen guns, it was surrounded by a ditch eighteen feet wide and nine feet deep. Outside the ditch was a palisade and

---

*The carabineers were troops armed with the eighteenth-century carbine, a relatively short firearm, about thirty inches long. Since it was the standard cavalry weapon, these men may have been mounted, but the problem of transporting horses and lack of mention of them makes this unlikely. It seems more probable, since they were listed separately from the regular troops, that they were a constabulary on foot, armed with carbines.

apparently also *chevaux de frise* (frameworks set with sharpened stakes). Gálvez at this point had 384 regulars and 400 blacks, Indians, militiamen, and other settlers. His ten artillery pieces were of larger caliber than the more numerous British guns.

Gálvez seems never to have used formal siege techniques involving more than one parallel in any of his operations. At Baton Rouge, he was determined to take the fort quickly because his supplies were short and many of his men were ill. Yet a direct assault on such a strongly fortified position would have been out of the question even if he had outnumbered the British far more than he did. What he did was to improvise, making use of a deception, with great success.

The most obvious point from which to attack the Baton Rouge fort was a grove of trees that stood close to it and seemed to offer concealment for digging trenches. Gálvez set militiamen, black troops, and Indians to work hacking away at trees and spading earth there; they attracted much British fire, which was ineffective. Meanwhile, the Spanish emplaced their guns on the opposite side of the fort in a garden that was within range—both artillery and musket—of the Baton Rouge defenses. When the Spanish guns opened fire from this unexpected quarter, the British defenses were badly damaged. At midafternoon on September 21, the British surrendered. The fort's commander, Lieutenant Colonel Alexander Dickson, not only surrendered Baton Rouge with its 375 regular troops but also promised the surrender of the fort at Natchez, Fort Panmure. The white and black civilian volunteers who had helped defend Baton Rouge were released, according to a contemporary account, "because of the generous heart of our commander, and because of the impossibility of guarding them."*

Colonel Dickson sent a letter to the commander of the Natchez fort instructing him to surrender, and Pollock sent along a letter addressed to the civilians of Natchez that praised the blessings of American liberty and the generosity of Governor Gálvez, who protected those blessings. The commander of Fort Panmure surrendered to Captain Juan Delavillebeuvre in response to Dickson's letter, and Natchez thus came peacefully under Spanish control. In one month, Gálvez had taken all the east bank of the lower Mississippi from the British.

Gálvez's dynamic initiative had effectively discouraged British

*Quoted in John Walton Caughey, *Bernardo de Gálvez in Louisiana, 1776-1783,* p. 157.

plans to attack New Orleans from West Florida. There was some effort made from Canada, however. Spanish St. Louis was attacked by a British force in May 1780, but its little garrison held out and the effort was abandoned. The British had various problems, including dissension among their Indian allies, but one factor in their giving up the attack was their knowledge of Gálvez's success farther south. The other prong of the British attack on New Orleans would not move, and they knew it.

10

Gálvez Takes West Florida

Spain, in the person of Gálvez, had cleared the British from the lower Mississippi Valley. The next objective was to clear them from the coast of the Gulf of Mexico. When Britain took East and West Florida at the end of the Seven Years' War, the Gulf of Mexico ceased to be a Spanish sea. With treasure ships sailing yearly through the Gulf for Spain, the Spanish found the presence of British bases along its shores highly undesirable.

The two significant British ports in West Florida were Mobile and Pensacola. With the Mississippi campaign triumphantly completed, Gálvez set out to capture the West Florida ports.

King Charles III had specifically named Gálvez to carry out this mission. The responsibility could have been given to the command in Cuba, whence many of the men and supplies were to come. But Charles designated Gálvez, citing his experience, the fact that he had already made plans for the operations (which he had, even before the Mississippi expedition), his knowledge of the country and the enemy, his friendly relations with the Choctaw—who were the dominant tribe in the area— and with other Indians, and, finally, the fact that he had the respect of the U.S. Congress.

Soon after he learned of the declaration of war, Gálvez asked Jacinto Panis, who was to be one of his three subordinate commanders in the Mississippi campaign, to make plans for taking Mobile and Pensacola. Panis had already done some investigation of their defenses. He drew up plans, but this was before the hurricane of August 18; after that event, the West Florida plans had to be scaled down.

As soon as Gálvez returned from Baton Rouge, he began putting the plans into effect. Again he made Gayarré his commissary, and the last weeks of 1779 were spent in gathering supplies for the new campaign. A number of British vessels had been captured in late 1779 on Lake Pontchartrain and on the

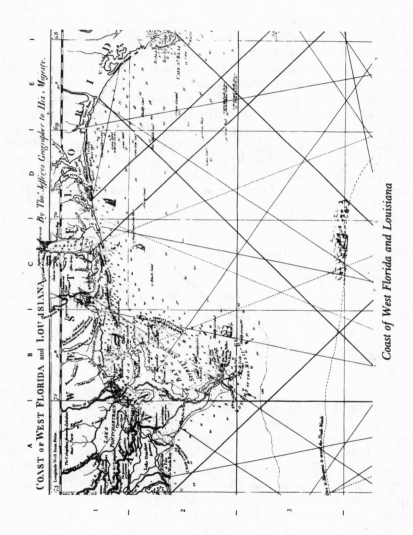

Coast of West Florida and Louisiana

143

Mississippi, and these were converted to transports for the West Florida expedition. The supplies loaded included captured British goods, some stores from Louisiana, and some shipments of powder and shot from Havana.

Gálvez needed more men and artillery from Havana. He had asked Diego José Navarro, Captain General there, for two ships of the line, six frigates, other craft, and 4,000 men in August 1779, but Navarro demurred, feeling he couldn't spare any. He told Gálvez that he could take Mobile and Pensacola by naval bombardment alone, without landing any guns, but Gálvez knew there were 36- and 42-pounders emplaced at the entrance to Pensacola Bay and in front of the fort. He insisted that he must have artillery. Navarro suggested an alternative: attack overland, approaching first Mobile and then Pensacola from inland, thus flanking the seaward-pointing guns and taking the forts "without bloodshed." To Gálvez, knowing the terrain, marshes, flora, and insect life of the region as he did, this proposal did not merit much consideration. Since Navarro would not or could not send reinforcements, Gálvez decided to go ahead with a limited operation to take Mobile only. He tried once more, however, sending Estevan Miró, another of his chief lieutenants, as his personal representative to Navarro with another request for 2,000 men for Mobile and Pensacola by mid-February at the latest. This delegation shook loose 567 men, who left Cuba in four transports on February 10.

Mobile

Meanwhile, in New Orleans, Gálvez set January 10, 1780, as mobilization day for the Mobile operation. On the eleventh, he reviewed his men as they embarked. There were 754 in all—141 regulars from the Louisiana regiment, 93 regulars from Spain and Havana, 14 artillerymen, 26 carabineers, 323 white militiamen, 107 free blacks, 24 slaves, and 26 Anglo-American volunteers. The fleet that carried and escorted them was made up of twelve vessels, including the frigate of war *Volante*, the galiot (sometimes identified as a sloop) *Valenzuela*, and the brigs *Gálvez* and *Kaulican*. They reached the mouth of the Mississippi on January 18, waited ten days for good weather, and sailed into the Gulf. On February 6, the fleet was struck by a tropical storm and scattered. Although one vessel was shipping water, all arrived off Mobile three days later.

Entering the bay turned out to be a major problem. The *Volante* and *Gálvez* led the way in on February 10, and both grounded on a bar. The *Gálvez* was floated free, somewhat the worse for wear, but the *Volante* stuck fast and was pummeled by a storm the next day. Other vessels also grounded and were worked free. Most of them finally anchored in the bay, but the *Volante* and one other vessel had to be abandoned.

Gálvez kept up morale despite the shipwrecks and loss of supplies. He salvaged the guns from the *Volante* and emplaced them on Mobile Point, commanding the entrance to the bay. He was preparing to move up the bay to Mobile when a small fast ship arrived from Havana with word that the men Miró had extracted from Navarro were approaching. With their arrival on February 20, the Spanish had well over a thousand combat-ready men, with allowance made for illness, and the British garrison had about three hundred.

Gálvez landed troops on the south bank of the little Dog River, and had the *Valenzuela* fire her 24-pounder at Mobile's Fort Charlotte. On February 28 he crossed the Dog and set up a new camp about two thousand yards from the fort. Then he began negotiations with Captain Elias Durnford, its commander.

All the dealings between the Spanish and English were marked with the graciousness that eighteenth-century warfare between gentlemen so often produced. Francisco Bouligny, Gálvez's envoy, asked Durnford to surrender. Durnford replied, in effect, that he would like to, but that since his position was the stronger it would be dishonorable for him to do so. Each man drank the health of his adversary's sovereign, and they then sat back to assess each other's positions. Bouligny exaggerated the size of the Spanish force and made light of the shipwreck losses. Durnford had received distorted reports that the Spanish had lost seven hundred men with the destroyed vessels and apparently preferred to accept his own figures and risk an attack. Bouligny returned to Gálvez without the surrender, and siege operations and defensive measures proceeded. However, the British commander sent the Spanish some wine, chickens, fresh bread, and mutton, and the Spanish commander reciprocated with both French and Spanish wine, citrons and oranges, tea biscuits, corn cakes, and cigars.

Gálvez and Durnford then opened a literary correspondence of exquisite courtesy. Durnford had ordered some houses in Mobile burned to prevent their being used as concealment for Spanish batteries. Gálvez wrote him a gentle rebuke for this destruction of people's homes and suggested that if Durnford would not burn any more houses, Gálvez would not establish batteries behind any. Durnford thanked him, on behalf of Mobile's residents, for his promise, which Durnford understood to mean he would attack from the other side of the fort, and he gave it as his opinion that Gálvez would find the terrain on that other side quite suitable for launching an attack. Gálvez then hastened to clarify his promise. It was conditional only, and he had given no promise not to attack from the residential side of the fort. However, if Durnford felt that Gálvez had in fact given his word, he would in all honor behave as though he had. Durnford promptly assured Gálvez that he did not consider the conditional promise binding, and would not hold him to it. Meanwhile, the Spaniards moved up their guns, presumably on the more vulnerable side of the fort—the records are not clear. The British hoped for reinforcements from Pensacola. Durnford was playing for time, as Cornwallis would at Yorktown, and Gálvez was aiming at a quick victory.

By March 9 the large bundles of sticks (fascines) that would protect the men digging trenches had been prepared, and at nightfall two hundred armed troops and three hundred men assigned to digging marched out of the camp to open the first trench. At dawn they were hit by heavy and damaging British fire. By March 12, however, the first parallel was apparently completed and a siege battery was emplaced. Fire was exchanged, and before sundown a breach was opened in the British fortifications. With the setting sun, the British ran up a white flag.

It was just in time for the Spaniards. Some of Gálvez's Indian allies reported that Brigadier General John Campbell was moving overland from Pensacola with eleven hundred men, two field guns, a howitzer, and some Creek allies to reinforce Durnford. Campbell, the Indians told Gálvez, had reached the area of the Tensaw River, not far from Mobile, on the other side of the bay. But when Campbell heard that Mobile had fallen, he began withdrawing toward Pensacola.

The terms of surrender gave the garrison the privilege of marching out of the fort with full honors of war. The three hundred men of the garrison, and the approximately one hundred habitants and blacks who had helped defend the fort, were taken prisoner. Gálvez gave his men, in the king's name, one-third of everything of value found in the fort, to be divided among them.

In writing to his Uncle José, Gálvez expressed regret, and some bitterness, that he had not had as many reinforcements from Havana as he had requested. With them, he felt, he could have cut off Campbell and his large force, "just as at Saratoga."* Pensacola, of course, would also have fallen, as Campbell had left only a tiny garrison there.

Gálvez's main accomplishments at Mobile, like Washington's at Yorktown, were in strategy, logistics, and diplomacy, not in the taking of Fort Charlotte. This last was a foregone conclusion, once the reinforcements had been wrested from Navarro, storm and sand bars had been overcome, and Gálvez's operations had outpaced Campbell's advance.

Pensacola

Pensacola was the major British base in Florida, and the best defended. It served not only as a naval base on the Gulf but as a center for treating and trading with British Indian allies. It was in fact essential to British-Indian collaboration in the area. The major objective of the Spanish Gulf Coast campaign, it was to pose Gálvez's strongest challenge.

As soon as Mobile surrendered, Gálvez wanted to move on to Pensacola. Even though the chance to cut off Campbell from his base had been lost, there was still the opportunity to strike Pensacola when the expedition had just returned and the defense was likely to be disorganized, and before the British reinforcements Gálvez knew were coming could arrive.

The current strength at Pensacola was formidable enough. There were thirteen hundred British regulars, six hundred armed habitants and hunters, three hundred armed blacks, and three hundred British sailors. Gálvez had about thirteen hundred men at Mobile, and he was well aware of his need for more than that in order to take Pensacola.

Navarro, despite his former refusals to send reinforcements

*John Walton Caughey, *Bernardo de Gálvez in Louisiana, 1776-1783*, p. 184.

to Gálvez, had actually sent out an expedition from Havana to Pensacola on March 7. But the ships never got close enough to shore to attempt to silence the guns of the defending forts, and they sailed back to Havana without accomplishing anything.

The taking of Pensacola, Gálvez believed, would have to be done from the sea, but besides being inadequately supplied with men he was also inadequately supplied with ships. In fact he had eight, the largest of which carried twenty-two 8-pounder guns. Two others carried one or more 24-pounders. There was not a frigate, much less a ship of the line, among them. Again he asked Navarro for men and for two frigates.

In April word reached Gálvez at Mobile that eleven British ships, including two naval vessels and nine armed merchantmen, had arrived at Pensacola. When no reinforcements for him had come by May 4 he abandoned the idea of attacking, left a small garrison at Mobile, sent the rest of his force back to New Orleans and Havana, and set out for Havana himself, determined to get the ships and men he needed.

Gálvez was in a strong position. He had recently been placed in charge of all Spanish military operations in America, probably because of his Uncle José's power as well as his own success at Mobile. The council of war in Havana approved his plans and gave him thirty-eight hundred men, together with provisions for six months. Another two thousand men were to be requested from Mexico, and as many as could be spared were to be sent from Puerto Rico and Santo Domingo. On August 29 Gálvez had almost four thousand men, in four divisions. The fleet and troops were to gather in Vera Cruz, Mexico, and to proceed from there to Pensacola.

On October 16, 1780, the fleet set sail. Very different from Gálvez's little squadron of the previous spring, this small armada comprised seven ships of the line, five frigates, a packet boat, a brig, an armed lugger, and forty-nine transports. But again the weather was calamitous. On October 18 a hurricane struck. It lasted three days and effectively demolished the fleet. The vessels were scattered, one was lost, and many were seriously damaged. The expedition that had started with such high hopes, as Gálvez finally had the men and ships to do his job, had to be abandoned. The assault on Pensacola was postponed until the next year.

Once Campbell learned of this reprieve he decided to strike while the Spanish were off balance. On January 7, 1781, a force from Pensacola, including a regiment of Germans, attacked an outpost east of Mobile. The garrison held, and the attackers withdrew, having lost several officers, including the German colonel, and sixteen men. They had killed fourteen Spaniards and wounded twenty-three.

Meanwhile Gálvez had gone back to Havana, where he urged the council of war to launch a new expedition. Marshaling all his eloquence, he pointed out that the British fleet en route to attack Charleston had run into weather that scattered their ships "as far as the very coasts of England." But, he reminded the council, they had "found themselves, reunited, and attacked with happy result. . . ." Spain, he said, should do likewise.*

The council acquiesced in a new expedition, but thought it should not be launched during the winter. Mid-March, they decided, would be a good time for setting a date that would be sometime still further in the future. Then the British attack on Mobile stimulated them to approve a prompter, although smaller, effort against Pensacola. They would give Gálvez 1,315 men, and he could draw on troops under his command in Louisiana to fill out his force. Since they knew that large vessels could not enter Pensacola Bay, they decided no ships of the line were necessary, but instead they assigned the frigate *Santa Clara*, 36, the sloop of war *Chambequin*, 20, and a packet boat, the *San Pio*, 18. The council then learned that three English frigates of forty guns each had sailed from Jamaica to cruise off Cuba's western tip. As protection against this threat, they added the ship of the line *San Ramon*, 74, and the frigate *Santa Cecilia*, 36.

The Raid on St. Joseph

While the fleet was gathering at Havana for Gálvez's attempt on Pensacola, a Spanish raiding party thirteen hundred miles to the north was laying claim to a large chunk of the Northwest Territory, on the Atlantic side of the Mississippi. Francisco Cruzat, the Spanish commander at St. Louis, ordered the raid, partly in response to the British attack on his post the year before and partly to lift the morale of the Spaniards' local Indian allies. Cruzat sent a force of 120 Indians and militia under Captain Eugenio Pourré to attack the trading post and lightly defended

*Caughey, *Bernardo de Gálvez in Louisiana*, p. 197.

fort of St. Joseph, on the St. Joseph River, a good two hundred miles east of the Mississippi, on the site of the present small city of Niles, Michigan. Pourré and his men surprised the garrison on February 12, captured the fort, and held it for twenty-four hours. They destroyed supplies at St. Joseph and claimed the valleys of the St. Joseph and Illinois rivers for Spain. It was this raid that the Spanish peace negotiators later cited when they claimed a wide swath of land east of the Mississippi from Canada to the Gulf.

The Approach to Pensacola

The day after St. Joseph was attacked, Gálvez boarded the *San Ramon* in Havana. He had apparently been ill, for it was reported that he had not completely recovered from a "severe hemorrhage." Nothing more seems to be known about the nature of his sickness, and it did not seem to handicap him in the coming days.*

Gálvez went aboard as commander, not only of the land forces but of the naval forces as well. The naval commander under him was Captain José Calbo de Irazabal. On February 28 the fleet sailed, a fresh southwest wind taking the ships out of sight of land within three hours—a good omen for the endeavor.

More forces were converging on Pensacola. Gálvez had ordered Pedro Piernas, one of his key subordinates, to bring some troops from New Orleans, including those that had straggled back there after the collapse of the ill-fated October expedition. And to complete the attacking force he ordered José Ezpeleta, his commander at Mobile, to march toward Pensacola with as many men as possible.

The fleet from Havana sailed straight for Pensacola, apparently unbothered by the patrolling British frigates. On March 9 the men sighted Santa Rosa Island, the long sand bank that guards Pensacola Bay. That night Gálvez landed on the island with grenadiers and light infantry. They marched along the beach to the fort on Siguenza Point, which proved to be unoccupied. Nowhere on Santa Rosa was there resistance. The Spaniards landed guns, emplaced a battery, and drove off the

Ibid., p. 199.

two British frigates—one of thirty-six guns, the other much smaller—that were the bay's chief defense.

Then began the task of moving the ships into the bay. As at Mobile, so at Pensacola, it was not easy. The *San Ramon*, leading the fleet, grounded as she tried to cross the first bar. She was worked free, came about, and remained out in the Gulf. With the rest of the ships outside with her, the next two days were spent in landing supplies on Santa Rosa Island and making the island base secure. The *San Ramon* was lightened in anticipation of another attempt to get her through, but naval commander Calbo was not satisfied that she could maneuver across the bar. In fact, Calbo declared that he was unwilling to try to force entrance to the bay at all, considering the circumstances—there were sand bars, the Spaniards had no pilot to guide them across, and the guns of Fort Barrancas Coloradas (Red Cliffs), high on a point commanding the bay entrance from the ships' port side, would be trained on any vessel attempting to get through.

At this point Gálvez made his crucial decision. He knew there was no way to take Pensacola without bringing the fleet into the bay. And although he theoretically commanded the entire fleet, there seemed little prospect of winning Calbo's cooperation. Four of the ships, however, were Louisianan, not Spanish, vessels, and therefore were under Gálvez's direct command—the galiot *Valenzuela*, the brig *Gálveztown*, and two armed launches. With these, Gálvez decided to force the entrance to the bay.

With the kind of bravura that can inspire selfless heroism, and also anger fellow commanders, Gálvez sent to the *San Ramon* an officer carrying a thirty-two-pound cannon ball and the message from Gálvez that although this ball had been fired by the British fort commanding the entrance to the bay, and although more of the same could be expected, he nevertheless invited all who had honor and valor to follow him and the *Gálveztown* as they entered the bay. Calbo was furious.

Gálvez then boarded the *Gálveztown*. He had a broad pennant — one that signaled the presence of a rear admiral—run up and ordered a salute of fifteen guns fired as he boarded, so that no one on either side could doubt that the commander of the expedition and of Spanish forces in America was on board. With Gálvez on the quarterdeck and all sails set, the *Gálveztown* approached the bay's entrance and crossed the bar. The other three ships followed. The guns of Fort Barrancas Coloradas fired away, but seemed unable to get the Spaniards' range and did no damage. The four ships anchored under the protection of the Spanish battery on Siguenza Point, and Gálvez fired a light-hearted salute to Fort Barrancas Coloradas.

Gálvez sent a careful description of the channel to Calbo, and that offended officer gave in to his subordinates' pleas that he sail into the bay. The next day, March 19, all the rest of the fleet except the *San Ramon* crossed the bar. Calbo sailed back to Havana on the *San Ramon* several days later, declaring that his part in the action had been completed.

Gálvez's style had won out over Calbo, the sand bars, and the British, and his "*Yo Solo*" legend was born.

During the next day or two the forces from Mobile, New Orleans, and Havana were consolidated on the mainland. Gálvez had a total of 3,550 men matched against a little more than 1,100 British. This was a good margin of superiority, even for attacking strong fortifications. Later the same year Washington was to outnumber Cornwallis by a margin of only two to one.

The British were greatly assisted, however, by Indian allies. Choctaws, Creeks, Seminoles, and Chickasaws all helped defend Pensacola. Most of these men were led by whites who had long lived as Indians, or by half-Indians who had ties to the British. Most Spanish casualties in March and April were inflicted by the Indians, who harassed the Spaniards as they moved their camp from Santa Rosa Island to the mainland, and as they inched forward and studied the British fortifications at Pensacola—Fort George and its surrounding defenses. On March 26, two parties of Spanish soldiers, taking different paths to the same destination, mistook each other for the enemy, and the resulting fire killed and wounded several men. There was suspicion that the Indians had in some way set up this misadventure.

On April 19 there was great excitement when some unidentified ships were sighted. Fears that they were British vanished when they proved to be a sizable Spanish naval force from Havana, commanded by Chief of Squadron José Solano, bringing Field Marshal Juan Manuel de Cagigal and 1,600 troops. With them were four French frigates with 725 more troops. The defenders of Fort Barrancas fired on the ships as they sailed into the harbor and landed their troops. But again the fort's guns did no damage, and by April 23 Gálvez had more than 7,000 men ready to take Pensacola. The question now was how long the British could hold out.

Count Casimir Pulaski. A nineteenth century engraving. *National Archives (U.S. Signal Corps).*

Jean de Kalb. Portrait by Charles Willson Peale. *Independence National Historical Park Collection.*

Tadeusz Kosciuszko. The portrait is attributed to Joseph Grassi (1758–1838) and may well have been painted from life. Kosciuszko is wearing the U.S. Order of the Cincinnati and the Polish Order Virtuti Militari. *National Archives (Minor Congressional Committee).*

Baron von Steuben. Painting by Ralph Earl. *National Archives (Minor Congressional Committee).*

General du Portail, the French volunteer in the Continental Army who was responsible for much of the siege engineering at Yorktown. From the Charles Willson Peale portrait in Independence Hall. *National Archives (U.S. Signal Corps).*

Pierre-Augustin Baron de Beaumarchais. Portrait by Paul Constant Soyer, after Jean Baptiste Greuze. *Print from the Musées Nationaux, Paris.*

Comte de Vergennes, French foreign minister and master diplomat. Portrait by Albert Rosenthal, after an unidentified artist. *Independence National Historical Park Collection.*

Chevalier de la Luzerne, French Minister to the United States. Portrait by Charles Willson Peale. *Independence National Historical Park Collection.*

Comte de Rochambeau. *National Archives (U.S. Bureau of Ships).*

Admiral de Grasse. *National Archives (Minor Congressional Committee).*

Bernardo de Galvez. *Louisiana State Museum.*

Catherine II of Russia in 1785. Engraving by F. Bartolozzi, after M. Benedetti. *National Portrait Gallery, Smithsonian Institution, Washington, D.C.*

John Paul Jones the Pirate. A contemporary engraving published in London. This is one of several British caricatures of Jones that have survived. *National Archives (U.S. Office of War Information).*

John Paul Jones. An engraving made by J. B. Fosseyeux in 1781 from a 1780 drawing by J. M. Moreau, Jr. *National Archives (U.S. Bureau of Ships).*

The fight between the *Serapis* and the *Bonhomme Richard*. The engraving is from a painting by Richard Paton, probably done in 1779 or 1780. *National Archives (Minor Congressional Committee)*.

Henry Laurens, the fourth American peace commissioner. Painted by John Singleton Copley in 1781, while Laurens was still a prisoner in the tower of London. *National Archives (Minor Congressional Committee)*.

The Capture of Pensacola

Hundreds of men began on April 28 to dig a long covered trench leading to a small hill that commanded part of the British fortifications. For three nights they dug, and on May 1 a battery of six 24-pounders was emplaced on the hilltop, looking down on the crescent, or advanced redoubt, of Fort George.

Continuing their digging, the working parties pushed the trench along to a higher spot, called Pine Hill. The Spaniards were starting to emplace a battery there on May 4, when British artillery commenced firing on them. Then the British infantry sortied from the fort. They captured Pine Hill and seriously wounded four Spanish officers who were left behind as the others fell back to their first redoubt. After spiking the four guns already in place, the British soldiers returned to their own fortifications. Like Abercromby's sortie at Yorktown, this one at Fort George did no lasting harm to the besiegers. The damage was soon repaired, and both batteries went into action, bombarding the crescent.

After an assault on the fortifications planned for May 7 was aborted because someone had leaked word of it to the defenders, Gálvez's men made a lucky hit. On May 8 a shell from a Spanish howitzer landed on the British powder magazine. There was a dramatic explosion that killed at least eighty-five men, and the fortifications of the crescent lay in ruins.

Dust and smoke were still rising as Ezpeleta and Geronimo Giron, exploiting the opportunity, led light troops into the area. Spanish guns and howitzers were brought forward, and the new battery opened heavy fire on the central British redoubt of Fort George shortly after noon. The first bombardment wounded an officer and thirty men. At three o'clock General Campbell ran up a white flag. He asked for a cessation of hostilities until the next day at noon, with terms of capitulation to be prepared during the cease-fire. At one o'clock on the morning of May 10, the terms were agreed on.

The British gave up Pensacola, Fort George, Fort Barrancas Coloradas, and all of West Florida. With the forts the Spanish captured 1,113 prisoners, 4 mortars, 143 guns, 6 howitzers, 40 swivel guns, 2,142 muskets, 8,000 flints, and 298 barrels of powder, plus sizable amounts of other supplies. The Spaniards had lost 74 men killed and 198 wounded. The day of the British sortie had been the most costly single day of the campaign for the besiegers, and the advance on May 8, following the explosion, had also cost many lives.

The British prisoners were taken to Havana and then returned to British authorities in New York, where they arrived on July 12. This expeditious return of enemy troops to their own armies was strongly protested by American leaders, whose troops could expect to face them. Gálvez apparently thought of Great Britain as primarily Spain's enemy and did not consider the effect his generosity would have on his cobelligerents.

Gálvez at once set about improving the defenses of Pensacola. Well aware of the poor record the guns of Fort Barrancas Coloradas had made against his own ships, he relocated them closer to the channel, in a better position to hit any approaching British vessels. He also ordered a fort built at Siguenza Point on Santa Rosa Island, knowing how much such a fort could have done to prevent the Spanish landings. Recognizing the effectiveness of Britain's Indian allies, he gave instructions that the Indians of the area were to be warmly courted with trade and gestures of friendship.

The Spanish-Irish flavor of Louisiana now extended to Pensacola. Arturo O'Neill was named commander at Pensacola, and the Code O'Reilly, the basic civil law of Louisiana, was promulgated as the legal code for the inhabitants of West Florida.

Honors were showered on Gálvez. Pensacola Bay was rechristened, by order of the king, the Bahia de Santa Maria de Gálvez, and the victor, named governor of West Florida as well as Louisiana, was raised to the titled nobility as a *conde* (count). He was given as a crest for his coat of arms a depiction of the brig *Gálveztown*, and he received "*Yo Solo*" as his motto. The crest and motto would have been handed down to his sons and grandsons if he had left male heirs, but he did not; Bernardo de Gálvez alone bore the motto "*Yo Solo*."

The Natchez Rebellion

Plans for an assault on Jamaica were underway at this time, and Gálvez intended to go straight to Havana to begin preparations for it, but events in Natchez took him to New Orleans and some hard decisions.

Many of the residents of Natchez had been restive under Spanish rule, and General John Campbell worked from Pensacola to make use of them. His agents persuaded them to revolt, and he himself sent commissions in the British army to many of them so that the revolt would have the legal semblance of a regular military operation. All the origins of the revolt are not clear. American agents and sympathizers were among the dissidents, seeing the possibility of working with the British against the Spanish and then taking over the revolt and securing Natchez for the United States.

In any case, the rebels were fortunate in their leader—or perhaps the caliber of the leader demonstrated the quality of the rebels in general. This man was John Blommart, a native of Geneva, Switzerland, and apparently a respected Natchez resident. He was commissioned a British captain by Campbell, his commission arriving on April 20, 1781, two days before the Natchez rising.

On the twenty-second, Blommart and his two hundred men, including settlers and Indians, gathered and moved on Fort Panmure. The Spanish commander, Dellavillebeuvre, had been warned of the rebellion by an informant and was prepared for the attack. When Blommart demanded that the fort surrender, Dellavillebeuvre ordered the rebels to disperse. They refused and fired on the fort, wounding one of the Spanish defenders, who later died.

Unable to take the fort, the rebels tried a ruse. They intercepted a messenger from the Spaniards' informant and substituted one of their own men, who told Dellavillebeuvre that the fort had been undermined and that the Spaniards should surrender. Dellavillebeuvre followed this advice, and the Spanish flag came down.

Blommart then had the task of keeping order among his supporters and setting up responsible civil government for Natchez. The first problem came right away: which flag should be triumphantly raised over the conquered fort? The American faction that had worked with Blommart wanted to hoist the Stars and Stripes. He quashed this idea, and the British flag went up.

There was also the problem of what to do with the Spanish prisoners. Some of Blommart's followers wanted to send them to Pensacola under the kind of conditions and guard that made it unlikely that they would ever get there. But Blommart sent them to Spanish Baton Rouge under a responsible guard, and they arrived safely. The more bloodthirsty, power-hungry rebels in Natchez were effectively brought under Blommart's control, and Anthony Hutchins, a respected citizen who had been chief magistrate before Gálvez's men took Natchez, was put in charge of civil affairs.

Then came the news that Pensacola had surrendered to Gálvez. This was a thunderbolt. The Natchez rebels had counted on Pensacola staying in British hands, and on a British naval attack from Pensacola against New Orleans. They found themselves, instead, holding the only British post on the Mississippi or the Gulf. There was no possibility that they could hold out indefinitely.

When word reached Natchez that a detachment of Spanish troops was on its way from New Orleans, many of the rebels sought refuge with friendly Indians, or simply went into the wilderness, where many of them died. The rebel leaders put up no resistance. General Campbell, who was Gálvez's prisoner at Pensacola when the Natchez rebels surrendered, at first denied any responsibility for their actions. But when the terms of their capitulation were shown to him, and these included mention of the commissions he had provided, he admitted his part. Anthony Hutchins blamed the instigation to rebellion on a pro-American faction and said that Campbell had been duped. But it is impossible to believe that he was unaware of what he was doing.

When Gálvez reached New Orleans from Pensacola, he learned details of the rebellion and had to decide what to do with the captive rebels. His choices were characteristically statesman-like. Only the leaders were imprisoned, and they were eventually released. No one was executed, despite the fact that the rebels had broken their parole not to raise arms against the Spanish, that the Spanish flag had been fired upon, and that a Spanish life had been lost. In view of the amnesty, it was tragic that so many who had participated in the rebellion fled to their deaths in the forest, in panic over the expected Spanish retaliation.

With the Mississippi safely under Spanish control, Gálvez departed for Havana, leaving his deputy, Estevan Miró, to continue his moderate policy.

The James Colbert Story

The leaders of the Natchez rebellion were still in prison a year later when James Colbert, a picaresque hero, set out to right what he saw as the wrongs done by the Spanish.

Of the men who led the Indians in West Florida, all except Alexander Cameron and James Colbert eventually went over to the Spanish after the fall of Pensacola. Colbert remained permanently and intensely anti-Spanish. Sixty years old in 1782, living with the Indians, as he had for years, Colbert had also gathered about him a troop of Loyalist refugees from Georgia, the Carolinas, and the Cumberland region, together with tramps, vagabonds, small-scale soldiers of fortune, and eccentric misfits who had gravitated to the frontier. Reminiscent of Robin Hood in the greenwood, Colbert lived with his men in the Mississippi Valley forest and kept informed of the movements of boats up and down the river.

Colbert was strongly sympathetic to the Natchez rebels and was determined to free them. He was also not averse to garnering loot from the river. When he was informed, in early April, of the approach of a river boat from the south, carrying a rich cargo and passengers who included Señora Cruzat, wife of the Spanish commander at St. Louis, with her four sons, he decided to strike. On May 2, 1782, the vessel's commander was lured to the riverbank by a ruse, and he and his crew and passengers found themselves looking into the barrels of about forty muskets and rifles. The cargo—which included forty-five hundred pesos for government expenses in Spanish Illinois—was unloaded and moved overland, along with the passengers and crew, to Colbert's camp.

It is easy to imagine some of Señora Cruzat's feelings in this situation, especially since Colbert seemed to have only loose command over his often insubordinate followers. When the men reached camp they divided the loot from the boat, and then about two hundred Chickasaws were called in to share in the distribution of gunpowder and brandy.

Colbert planned to hold his high-ranking prisoners hostage for the release of Blommart and the other Natchez leaders. He also had plans to blockade Fort Panmure at Natchez and, if he failed to capture it, to do what damage he could to it. However, fearing Spanish retaliation, he seems to have become uneasy about holding his hostages indefinitely. He finally allowed Señora Cruzat to give him her note for four hundred pesos, for which price he sold the seized boat back to the hostages. He had nine of them sign a parole promising to consider themselves prisoners of war, ready to go to British territory on demand, until they should be exchanged for John Blommart and eight of the other Natchez rebel leaders. Then, on May 22, he released the hostages and they headed back to New Orleans. The Spaniards, of course, agreed to no such exchange, and the British made no demands on Colbert's paroled prisoners.

Estevan Miró, in command in Louisiana in Gálvez's absence, decided that an expedition of reprisal against Colbert was impractical. It almost certainly was, for that woods-wise man, aided by his intelligence network, could surely have melted into the forest at will. Instead of wasting effort on Colbert, Miró decided to go to Natchez and strengthen its defenses.

At the same time, he sent to Gálvez an analysis of the current Mississippi defenses and the need for changes in them. Baton Rouge and Manchac had been built on the east bank by the British to defend against the Spanish across the river, and, with the Spanish holding both banks of the river, there was no longer any need for them. Gálveztown provided better defense against threats to New Orleans than Manchac could. On the other hand there was a need for two new forts, Miró felt, between Natchez and the Illinois River, to protect river traffic from attacks like Colbert's. Miró wanted one of the forts built at Chickasaw Bluffs, near where Colbert had captured the boat carrying Señora Cruzat.

Gálvez after Pensacola

The proposed Spanish attack on Jamaica, for which Gálvez was making preparations after the capture of Pensacola, was abandoned. What happened to him during the brief remainder of the war is not clear, but he spent some time in the Bahamas. In 1784 he was named captain general of Cuba.

He succeeded his father as viceroy of New Spain in 1785, and took up his post in Mexico. Gálvez was as popular as viceroy there as he had been as governor in Louisiana. But his tenure lasted only a year. An epidemic of fever broke out in 1786, and the viceroy was one of its last victims. He was about thirty-eight years old. Gálvez left several daughters, including a little girl born a few days after his death. In an outpouring of tribute to her father, the child was showered with christening gifts of gold, pearl, and gems from the city officials of Vera Cruz, the Spanish leaders of Mexico and all New Spain, the church, and the royal family.

The spectacular and romantic career of Bernardo de Gálvez has been almost forgotten in the country where he won his great victories. The effects of his conquests on the future of the United States are not clear—U.S. boundaries would probably have ended up the same if Gálvez had not fought. But as the accomplishments of a great soldier and leader of men, fighting on the western frontier of the world war that was the American Revolution, his exploits shine bright.

V

NEUTRAL RIGHTS
AND THE DUTCH

11

The Empress and Armed Neutrality

The war had grown out of the power inherent in seaborne trade in the eighteenth century. The war, as it lasted and grew, pulling in France and then Spain, threw old trading patterns into new configurations, enriching some nations and threatening others. As inexorably as the wind pushed the sails of the all-important ships, their holds packed with powder, shot, cloth, hemp, and pitch, just as surely all the maritime nations of Europe were drawn into the war in some fashion. Those that were luckiest and most wisely led managed to evade the actual fighting and the outpouring of money, men, and ships that went with it.

Catherine

Because of the extraordinary leadership Russia, on the eastern edge of Europe, enjoyed at the time, that nation played a key role in organizing the neutral maritime states during the war. Empress Catherine II was then a woman of fifty and at the peak of her considerable intellectual and administrative powers. She directed her own foreign policy, always with the help of able military men and statesmen, and had recently completed a successful war with Turkey. This was the conflict that started over the uprising of the Confederation of Bar in Poland, in which young Pulaski fought. Vergennes, for France's sake, encouraged Turkey to attack Russia during this conflict, and the Turks soon regretted their acquiescence. They were driven out of the Crimea, and Russia's way lay open to the Black Sea coastline that Peter the Great had dreamed of and worked for. Vergennes, sharply set back, had lost Turkey as a useful client state in

163

Europe, and saw that he would have to build bridges to Russia.

At this point, the American Revolution broke out. Russia was at first considered to be pro-British. Catherine herself had earlier been influenced by British diplomats, and as an absolute monarch she might have been expected to support George III. The two rulers also had the tie of common German origins, for Catherine was German-born, daughter of a poor and obscure prince of Anhalt-Zerbst.

Catherine, however, had little sympathy for "Frère Georges," as she called him. She had followed the American protests and British parliamentary actions closely, and had nothing but scorn for the way the British government had bungled matters. From the beginning of the war she predicted that Britain would lose the colonies. Brother George soon had a chance to test her sentiments, for it was she whom the British first approached about hiring twenty thousand troops to help put down the rebellion. Catherine declined.

When France entered the war, Catherine felt the British would be well advised to make terms and cut their losses. This did not mean that she had any liking for the American cause. It indicated her realistic view of the situation. When she told the British ambassador that George III should give the colonies their independence and end the war, he asked her how she would feel about giving up the colonies if she were in George's situation. The empress replied with customary directness, "I'd rather lose my head!"

Not pro-British, not pro-American, Catherine was also not pro-French. France's entry into the war created the possibility that Britain would be crushed, rather than merely weakened, by a long colonial war. A triumphant France, dominant in Europe, would be a danger to Russia and Catherine.

Britain and France then began a fierce struggle for Catherine's favor. The British government had sent to St. Petersburg the man considered its ablest young diplomat, Sir James Harris. Harris was energetic and reputed to be brilliant, but he was apparently not sensitive in perceiving Catherine's own great ability, her cool diplomatic aims, and her sense of humor. He was also shocked by the loose morals of her court; Catherine herself took new lovers with great frequency. Relying heavily on the pro-British sentiments of Prince Potemkin, Catherine's former lover and valued advisor, Sir James pushed for a Russo-British alliance, or at least a Russian ultimatum to France. He was bound to be disappointed.

The new French ambassador who arrived in St. Petersburg in 1779 was Charles-Olivier de Saint-Georges, marquis de Vérac. Vergennes had given him sensible instructions. All France wanted was that Russia remain neutral and work to protect the rights of neutrals on the high seas. Because France needed the supplies that neutral ships could bring, while Britain had a large merchant fleet of its own and a large navy to protect it, these seemingly modest aims were very important to France. Neutral rights and French needs coincided.

What Catherine decided upon was a policy of strict neutrality, and she stuck to it. Her other aim was to act as a mediator when the two sides should be ready to end the war, a role that would bring prestige to her and to Russia.

Neutral Rights

Just what the rights of neutrals were was not at all clear. As in most matters of international law, the needs of the various nations determined the legal positions they took.

It was agreed that ships of warring nations had the right to seize war-related contraband goods under any circumstances, and that neutral nations had some right to carry on their ordinary non-contraband trade, since they, after all, were not involved in the war. The main questions were, first, which goods were contraband, and, second, were enemy-owned goods carried in a neutral ship protected by the fact that the ship was owned by a neutral?

Traditionally, contraband meant weapons and ammunition. By the eighteenth century, however, statesmen had come to realize that cloth for uniforms, timber for ships, and even salted fish for rations were extremely important matériel for fighting a war. A whole group of treaties had appeared, each defining contraband in a specific way for the particular countries adhering to that treaty.

As for the issue of neutral ships, the traditional doctrine held that all neutral goods were safe from seizure on a belligerent ship, but that all goods belonging to a belligerent could be seized if found on a neutral ship. In other words, the destination of the goods, not the ownership of the vessel, determined whether or not they could be seized. This was a poor doctrine for neutral seafaring nations like the Dutch, who made their living by serving the trading needs of other countries—and especially of goods-hungry belligerent countries—rather than by selling their own products. It was a fine doctrine for a strong belligerent nation like Great Britain, a nation that could carry and protect its own supplies without using neutral bottoms, and that had the navy to enforce the doctrine by seizing supplies destined for its enemies from the neutral ships that carried them.

The traditional doctrine was under challenge from a newer doctrine by the 1770s, a doctrine that was good for neutrals —"Free ships, free goods."

The League of Armed Neutrality

Britain stood behind and enforced the doctrine that enemy goods on neutral ships were fair game. It also, naturally enough, interpreted contraband very broadly to include naval stores such as timber, hemp, and pitch, and British captains seized these at will.

France, badly needing the transporting services of neutrals, took the opposite position. Louis XVI issued a decree on July 26, 1778, affirming the "free ships, free goods" doctrine. The neutral nations enthusiastically agreed.

Strangely, however, the next phase of this diplomatic ballet found some neutrals considering action against the United States, France's ally. In the same month in which the French decree appeared, an American privateer attacked eight unprotected British merchant vessels loaded with Russian goods in the North Sea, sinking, capturing, or stripping all of them. The neutral Russian government was not happy. Russia had a relatively small merchant fleet and depended on other countries, whether neutral or belligerent, to carry its products. Timber and other products of Russia's forests were in great demand in wartime, and Russia wanted to sell them freely to all buyers.

After the incident of the American privateer, therefore, Catherine proposed to Denmark that Russia and Denmark patrol the North Sea shipping lanes to protect merchant ships against privateers. In practice this meant protecting British supplies against American privateers.

The Danish foreign minister, A.P. Bernstorff, might seem at first glance an appropriate person to draw up an agreement on controlling American privateers, for he was strongly hostile to the idea of American independence and critical of the "poison" of pro-American sentiment that had spread widely through Denmark—"even into the village schools."* Engravings of Franklin were popular art in Denmark as well as in France, and Bernstorff undoubtedly detested them. However, what Bernstorff did was to draw up, in scholarly fashion, a proposal for a firm alliance that was much broader than Catherine's ideas. It incorporated the major points of the rights-of-neutrals, "free ships, free goods" doctrine that had been developing in international law during the past hundred years. If enforced, it would have been good for Scandinavian shipping. Perhaps Bernstorff did not realize that this kind of alliance would also be useful to the Americans and their French allies and would anger Britain.

Catherine and her canny foreign minister, Nikita Panin, certainly knew this was not what they wanted. Panin, an aging, obese, pleasure-loving man who was nevertheless highly capable and effective, strongly supported Catherine in her determination to remain untainted by partisanship in the war, in anticipation of the role she planned for herself as mediator. An agreement on patrolling for American privateers was one thing; an alliance challenging Britain's legal position and lining up neutral nations against Britain was another. Catherine and Panin turned their thumbs down. Bernstorff's proposal was shelved.

Just as a U.S. privateer had paradoxically stimulated Bernstorff's proposal, acts by Spain paradoxically brought the armed neutrality idea to its climax. When Spain entered the war in June 1779, the Spanish government proclaimed that it would follow the same traditional doctrine under which Britain was operating, with the difference that neutral goods on enemy ships could also be seized. In other words, for Spain, "free ships, free goods" did not apply, but "unfree ships, unfree goods" did. Spain, with a large navy and large merchant fleet, decided to have the best of both doctrines.

Wise Vergennes, who had worked skillfully to bring Spain into the war, was appalled at the idea of the Spanish seizing neutral shipping. He had been pushing the idea of a league of armed neutrals for a year, since Bernstorff first proposed it. He knew

*Quotation from Bernstorff in Bemis, *Diplomacy of the American Revolution*, p. 113n.

that what was good for the neutrals was good for France. The Spanish leadership, however, was concentrating on seizing Gibraltar, the great Spanish motive for entering the war. Gibraltar was under siege, and Spain was determined that no supplies get to the fortress, whatever doctrine had to be applied. A third issue of neutral rights (in addition to a definition of contraband and the right of a neutral flag to protect belligerent goods) became important at this point—the matter of what constituted a blockade. The neutral position was that if a port was to be blockaded, there had to be a real, palpable line of ships blockading it. It was not enough to declare the port blockaded and then feel free to fall upon any merchant ship in the area that one might fortuitously encounter.

Spain, however, quickly began putting the Spanish position into action. A Dutch ship with a Russian cargo, suspected of being destined for Gibraltar, was seized and its cargo sold at auction. A Russian merchant ship was treated likewise, and several other neutral ships met the same fate.

Catherine made what appeared to be a lightning response, although actually her concern for neutral shipping had been growing steadily for months. Even though Russia had few merchant ships, the neutral vessels that carried Russian products, including the naval stores then bringing such good prices, must be protected.

Catherine ordered Panin to draw up a declaration embodying the neutral nations' position on neutral rights, to present it as the official position of the Russian Empire, to address it to Spain, France, and Great Britain, and to invite the neutral European nations to join in solemn agreements with Russia, pledging to uphold the rights of neutrals stated in the declaration. Panin used Bernstorff's earlier proposal, almost word for word.

The empress had thus taken a step away from Britain and toward France. She had not done anything partisan, however, and she had assumed a position of leadership among the neutral nations of Europe.

The Declaration of Armed Neutrality was issued at St. Petersburg on March 10, 1780 (February 28, according to the Russian calendar of the time). Because of the Spanish acts that precipitated it, it was not immediately clear which governments should be unhappy about the declaration. Potemkin, who was friendly with Sir James Harris, assured him that the declaration was aimed at Spain. When Vergennes heard of it, however, he knew that his own purposes for Russia had been fulfilled. France quickly accepted the Declaration of Armed Neutrality, and under Vergennes's prodding, Spain did too. Great Britain did not.

Of the neutrals, Denmark signed a convention with Russia and became a member of the League of Armed Neutrality on July 9, and Sweden did likewise on August 1. The Netherlands, Prussia, Portugal, and Austria also joined.

The four principles to which the neutrals agreed were that neutral ships could sail freely from port to port and along the coastlines of belligerent nations; that goods belonging to belligerent nations, except contraband, were free and safe from seizure on neutral ships; that contraband was to be narrowly defined and was not to include naval stores; and that a blockaded port must be in reality closed off by blockading ships to an extent that made it obviously dangerous to enter. Panin took the points from Bernstorff's 1778 proposal, but they had not been original with Bernstorff either. They had grown out of the hard experience of neutral shippers and captains in wartime and had been polished by European jurists and diplomats for a hundred years.

The League of Armed Neutrality was, on paper at least, good for the neutrals, good for France and the United States, and bad for Britain. In practice it did not work perfectly in aid of the Americans and French, and at least one of the neutrals—the Netherlands — suffered badly. Bernstorff, who had become even more pro-British, sabotaged Denmark's participation by making a quid pro quo with Britain by which Denmark gave up shipping naval stores and Britain declared salt fish, a major Danish export, not to be contraband. Spanish officials and Panin were outraged by this deal and were able to retaliate in ways that forced Bernstorff out of office. However, neither Sweden nor Denmark did much to enforce the league.

12

The Netherlands and the Coasts of Africa

The United Provinces of the Netherlands was a republic, a rare kind of state in eighteenth-century Europe. It had a hereditary ruler, the stadholder, who at this time was Willem V, a grandson of George II of England and a devoted Anglophile. He was apparently unappealing personally, and he drank too much. His titular position carried little power, since the country was actually ruled by the States General, a legislative body made up of representatives of each of the seven provinces. Every decision of the States General had to be unanimous—an unfortunately cumbersome requirement—and what power the stadholder had came through his ability to persuade one of the provinces to vote his way, thus effectively exerting a veto on the majority in the States General.

The Netherlands had a well-developed party system, political leaders being divided into supporters of the stadholder, who were generally conservative and pro-British, and the opposition, who were called Patriots and were generally pro-French and anti-British. The Patriots tended to be wealthy middle-class merchants, bankers, and tradesmen, while the stadholder's party was made up largely of aristocrats and was generally supported by the peasants.

The little Netherlands was highly urbanized for its day, with its wealth and power in trade, and especially in banking and other financial services. In contrast to its earlier great maritime days, it had only a small navy and a much reduced, though still sizable, merchant marine. The cities of the United Provinces, including Rotterdam, Harlem, Leyden, and especially Amsterdam, were the real centers of power, and there the middle-class businessmen ruled.

170

The American Revolution brought the Netherlands a great upsurge in trade, especially with the rebelling colonies and especially through St. Eustatia. It also brought the accompanying problem of confrontation with Great Britain.

Able Sir Joseph Yorke, the British ambassador to the Netherlands, closely observed Dutch trade with Britain's enemy from the beginning and made repeated protests. When the *Andrew Doria*'s American flag drew a salute at St. Eustatia, the British complained. In February 1777 the British government successfully demanded that the salute be disavowed, that the offending governor of St. Eustatia be removed, and that the embargo on contraband munitions be enforced in the West Indies.

Not stopping with words, the British began halting and searching Dutch ships near St. Eustatia. Those carrying munitions, or the cloth so badly needed for American uniforms, were seized. But the Dutch businessmen went on shipping goods to America, and the governor of St. Eustatia was eventually reinstated.

When France entered the war, British pressure on the Dutch increased. By the terms of a seventeenth-century treaty, Britain and the United Provinces had agreed to aid each other in case of attack. But although France was at war with England, the treaty was not invoked. The Netherlands government, on the other hand, did invoke a joint maritime treaty of the seventeenth century which called for a "free ships, free goods" policy and which defined contraband strictly, excluding naval stores. In spite of this, the British went right ahead treating naval stores on Dutch vessels as contraband. They paid for them, however, an approach that simply forced the Dutch to sell to Britain instead of to Britain's enemies.

The unwieldy States General rejected the British position but was unable to prevent the seizure of scores of Dutch ships. In October 1778 alone, forty-two vessels were taken. The Dutch merchant fleet was rapidly diminishing.

Meanwhile, pro-French and pro-American propaganda was being spread across the United Provinces. Before the Declaration of Independence the Americans had hired an effective agent, Charles William Frederick Dumas, a Dutchman of French ancestry, who was a friend of Benjamin Franklin. Dumas listened, reported, and, as tension between the Netherlands and Britain increased, distributed pro-American pamphlets. The French were also winning support through their friends in the

Patriot party. The French ambassador, the duc de la Vauguyon, assiduously cultivated the Patriots and also worked on the eagerness of the traders of Amsterdam for more and more war profits, a lust that required defying Britain.

Finally the British government made a decision. In July 1779 Ambassador Yorke formally asked the Netherlands to give military aid to England under the terms of the treaty of alliance. The Netherlands government delayed replying throughout the summer, fall, and winter, despite British prodding. In September 1779, Governor de Graff returned to St. Eustatia, exonerated by the Dutch government for the salute to the U.S. flag for which the British had demanded his punishment. By March the Dutch still had done nothing, and the British government demanded for the third time that they honor the treaty of alliance and gave them three weeks to do so. When this ultimatum ran out, Britain still did not declare war, but announced that the Dutch would be treated just like other neutrals, with no attention paid to the maritime treaty and its "free ships, free goods" clause.

The States General took action then, but it was not useful. The members voted to build "adequate" naval armaments and to stand fast for neutral rights as they saw them. Meanwhile, Catherine II of Russia had issued her Declaration of Armed Neutrality, and the Netherlands was under pressure to join the League of Armed Neutrality. And in July, John Adams left Paris for Amsterdam, where he would make the case for America.

The Dutch did not have adequate time to build their "adequate" naval armaments. As they were building, British privateers were crushing the Dutch merchant fleet. Dutch maritime power was being snuffed out, and the country was drifting into a war that would be disastrous to Dutch international banking.

The Netherlands held off joining the League of Armed Neutrality as long as possible. The Dutch asked Catherine to guarantee all their colonial possessions—far-scattered islands in the East and West Indies—in return for a Dutch signature on the agreement. Catherine was much too realistic to do any such thing.

British seizures of Dutch ships continued, and the seizure of one American ship, the brigantine *Mercury*, had especially serious consequences for the Netherlands. Aboard was John Laurens of South Carolina, U.S. Commissioner to the Netherlands. When the ship was seized off Newfoundland in September 1780, some of Laurens's papers were captured with him, among them a draft treaty of alliance between the Netherlands and the United States, drawn up a year earlier. Neither of the agents who drafted it had any authority to negotiate such a treaty, and the paper had no legal value, but it was a handy weapon for the British to use against the hapless Dutch. Quickly the Dutch, desperate for allies, rushed to join the League of Armed Neutrality, without worrying about such conditions as the protection of the Indies. Even more quickly Great Britain declared war on the Netherlands, on December 21, 1780.

John Adams wrote in Amsterdam that on New Year's Eve there was singing in the streets, as Dutch patriotism rose in response to the British attack. Adams felt hopeful of securing his own goal of official Dutch recognition for the United States, and perhaps even a loan.

For the Netherlands, however, the last belligerent to join, the war was to bring only more military defeat and economic disaster. The British were prompt to take advantage of the chance to grab for the most strategic Dutch territories.

It would be hard to say which of the Dutch possessions was most important. There was St. Eustatia, the golden rock of the Caribbean, at once a sharp stone to be removed from the British lion's paw and a precious nugget to be captured for Britain's enrichment. There were Dutch ports on the Gold Coast of Africa. There was the Dutch Cape Colony at the southern tip of Africa, guardian of the sea route to India, where Britain's Second Empire was slowly taking shape. And there were Dutch settlements in India, Ceylon, and the East Indies. Ships of the British navy were soon moving in on most of them.

The Route to the East

In the eighteenth century it took from four to six months to make the long trip from the ports of western Europe to India and the East Indies, and supply bases along the route were of great importance to the trading nations that sent convoys regularly to the Indian Ocean. The first of these was the Cape Verde Islands, off the western hump of Africa. They belonged to Portugal, neutral in this war, but traditionally pro-British. Next on the route was the Cape of Good Hope, where the Dutch had maintained a colony for more than a hundred years. Off the east

The Route to India in the 18th century

coast of Africa France had bases on Madagascar. France also held Ile de France—which the Dutch who originally colonized and then abandoned it had named Mauritius—four hundred and fifty miles out to sea from Madagascar. Ile de France was of great importance to any nation that wanted firm control of the Indian Ocean. Essential to Ile de France, in turn, were food supplies from the Dutch Cape of Good Hope, since the island produced only some sugar cane and spices; it grew almost no staple foodstuffs.

The interests of the powerful British East India Company had long coveted the strategic Dutch Cape of Good Hope. Once the declaration of war with the Netherlands made it a legitimate prize, a naval expedition was sent out to take it.

Encounter at Porto Praia

The man sent to take the Cape was Commodore George Johnstone. He seems to have been a poor choice. There is some question as to whether he had ever before commanded a sizable ship, although he had been commodore on the Lisbon Station just before his selection to head the 1781 Cape expedition. In any case, he had not spent much time at sea as a captain.

Johnstone sailed from England on March 13, 1781, traveling with Vice Admiral Darby's fleet, which was heading for Gibraltar. Johnstone had one 74, one 64, and three 50s, plus eleven smaller armed vessels and a sizable number of troops for the planned assault on the Cape Colony. The British ships arrived at the Cape Verde Islands and put in at Porto Praia Bay to take on water and supplies.

The French, meanwhile, had sent five ships of the line—two 74s and three 64s—to keep Johnstone from getting to the Cape of Good Hope. They were on their way to the Far East, and they were commanded by a man who was to become known as one of Europe's great admirals, Pierre de Suffren de Saint Tropez, known as the Bailli de Suffren, his title in the Order of the Knights of Malta.

Suffren's name, even if Johnstone knew it, could not have been expected to strike terror to his heart at that time, but from what he knew of his own situation, if not from simple standard procedures and common sense, he should not have allowed his vessels to anchor wherever their captains chose, with no planned disposition for meeting a possible attack. This, however, is what he did. His own flagship, the *Romney*, 50, was surrounded by other British ships in such a way that she could not easily fire her guns. While the British were thus lying at anchor, with about fifteen hundred of their crews and troops ashore on various errands, including the pleasures of shore leave, Suffren's ships came into view.

The French had not expected the encounter. Suffren was putting into Porto Praia Bay for the same reason Johnstone had—to get fresh water for his ships. When he saw the opportunity, however, he immediately decided to attack.

Deciding to attack and clearly communicating the intention and the tactics to one's subordinates were two very different things in the eighteenth century, as battle after battle in this war alone makes clear. At Porto Praia, of Suffren's five ships two carried almost the entire battle against the English squadron, and one of those was not engaged at anything like her full firepower.

Suffren sailed into the bay, and brought his ship, *Héros*, 74, into the wind, which was coming from the shore. He anchored in position to engage the British 74, *Hero*, and commenced firing, all the while flying the signal flag for battle. Suffren's other 74, *Annibal*, followed him in and anchored in front of him, but her captain had thought the signal was an alert only and was not cleared for action. The *Annibal* never made her weight fully felt, and she also anchored so close to the *Héros* that the latter ship had to drop astern, and thus out of position to hit the *Hero*. The captain of the third French ship was killed outright by a lucky British shot as his ship came into position, and in the resulting confusion she drifted seaward. The other two French vessels did not manage to enter the bay, merely firing rounds as they passed its entrance. After less than an hour of fighting, Suffren slipped his cable and put to sea, with the badly damaged *Annibal* following.

Johnstone followed soon after, but he was hampered by the slowness of one of his ships, the *Isis*. He had ordered her to join the pursuit despite her captain's protest that she could not bear sail without repairs, and she promptly lost her fore topmast. The French slowly pulled farther ahead of the British as both fleets sailed before the steady northeast trade winds. Darkness caught Johnstone some distance to leeward of the island, and he had forgotten to arrange a rendezvous point with the transports he

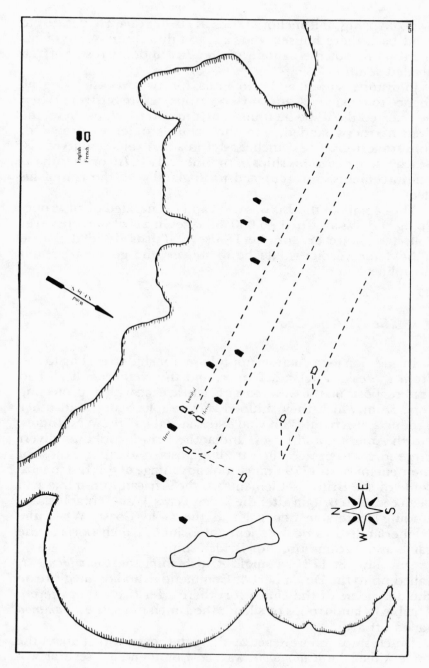

Battle of Porto Praia, April 16, 1781

was convoying, still anchored back at Porto Praia. He decided to head back there himself and, apparently venting some of his frustration, put the captain of the *Isis* under arrest. Suffren headed south.

Johnstone stayed at Porto Praia for two weeks, losing all chance to make the Cape of Good Hope before Suffren. When he reached the Cape he found Suffren and his ships there, the French troops landed, and the colony's defenses prepared. Johnstone took five Dutch East Indiamen (merchant vessels) nearby, sent two of his ships of the line and the *Isis* on to India as reinforcements, and returned to England with the rest of his fleet.

The captain of the *Isis* was tried and exonerated of all wrong-doing and was awarded £6,000 damages in a civil suit. He never collected, however, for the House of Lords decided that to uphold the verdict would be to subvert the good order and discipline of the navy.

The African Coast

In addition to the major supply bases for ships traveling to and from the east, England, France, and the Netherlands all had trading posts on the west coast of Africa, each with its protecting fort, from which they shipped slaves, gold, ivory, and other products of Africa. With vital issues at stake in the West Indies, North America, and far-off India, the British could not divert large forces to protect their trading posts or to capture those of their enemies. In 1779 France took advantage of this fact to seize some of the British settlements on the African hump that had been ceded to Britain after the Seven Years' War—notably slave-trading centers in Senegal and the Gold Coast. When the Netherlands became an enemy of Britain, Dutch ports in the same area became prey for British ships.

On May 28, 1781, a single British ship, the *Champion*, 32, sailed up to the Dutch port of Commendah and opened fire on the defenders of the Dutch fort there. Her fire was answered. Unable to land troops or silence the Dutch guns, the *Champion* sailed off again.

Dutch ships too were active along the coast, and at about the same time the *Champion* was at Commendah, several approached the British Gold Coast fort of Secondee. It fell to their attack.

The following winter and spring two British ships, the *Leander*, 50, commanded by Captain Thomas Shirley, and the *Alligator*, 14, under Commander John Frodsham, made an organized attempt to capture the Dutch forts on the Gold Coast. Elmina resisted an attack in mid-February 1782, but Captain Shirley managed to put some troops ashore near Mouree a few weeks later. With their help he captured a series of Dutch forts: Mouree on March 2, Commendah on March 6, Apam on March 16, Barracoe on March 23, and Accra on March 30. These lucrative points of access to slaves and ivory were a serious loss to the Dutch traders.

VI

AROUND THE
WORLD

13

The War in the Caribbean

Although it was the East Indies for which Columbus searched, the Indies that he found in the Caribbean had become by the eighteenth century as rich a treasure as he could have dreamed of. In the commercial value of their products the Caribbean islands were then the richest area of the world. Sugar, spices, cocoa, and coffee brought prices so high in relation to their weight that they were comparable to precious metals. British West Indian planters were proverbially rich, and Great Britain seriously considered giving up the chance to get all of Canada for two small West Indies islands after the Seven Years' War. During the Revolutionary War British leaders would have been very happy to acquire Martinique and Guadeloupe, or any of the other sugar islands.

For France's leaders, from the point of view of their country's interests, the West Indies was the significant theater of combat during the war, even though France made a major commitment on the North American continent and in its waters. Aside from weakening Britain through loss of its North American colonies, what France especially wanted from the war was a strengthening of its holdings in the Caribbean.

More than the wealth of West Indian products was at stake, too, for location gave the West Indian islands another value in the eighteenth century. Lying as they do, just where the trade winds deposit a ship that has caught them in her sails off northern Africa, the islands were considerably more accessible to Europe than North America was, and were natural trade centers and bases for naval forces and for merchant-ship refitting. The role of St. Eustatia, based on its special location as a neutral Dutch possession in the midst of French, British, and Spanish islands, and on its being a free port, has already been discussed (Chapter 3). St. Eustatia achieved this important status without even possessing a good harbor. Other islands, like Jamaica, Antigua, and Martinique, although they lacked St. Eustatia's unique attributes, did have fine harbors, and they were valuable assets to those who controlled them.

Eight of these islands changed hands during the American Revolutionary War, as naval forces of the European powers landed troops and fought naval battles in the nearby harbors and surrounding waters.

Dominica and St. Lucia

The islands of the Caribbean lie in a long curve that describes a slow southeastward diagonal from Cuba through Haiti, Puerto Rico, and the Leeward Islands, and then, at the Windward Islands, curves sharply almost straight south. It was at one or another of the Windward Islands that ships from Europe usually made land, and it was in this area that most Caribbean action of the Revolutionary War centered.

When France entered the war against Britain, the French held three islands, north to south, in the Windwards—Guadeloupe, Martinique, and St. Lucia. Martinique's good harbor, then called Fort Royal, was the main French naval base. St. Lucia, just to the south, protected Fort Royal from close British surveillance and British attack. St. Lucia was thus of special strategic importance to both sides.

There was a gap in the French line, however. Dominica, between Guadeloupe and Martinique, was British-held. As soon as war was declared, orders went out for a French force from Martinique to seize Dominica; they were expeditiously carried out in September 1778. The French surprised the small British garrison, and there was no significant resistance. The French had simply received their wartime orders before the British did.

The frustrated British commander in the area, Rear Admiral Samuel Barrington, was soon to have his own orders for an attack, and reinforcements to carry them out. A squadron of eight ships, including two 64-gun ships of the line, left New York on November 4 and joined Barrington at his main base, Barbados, on December 10, bringing five thousand troops.

As it happened, French Admiral d'Estaing also sailed from

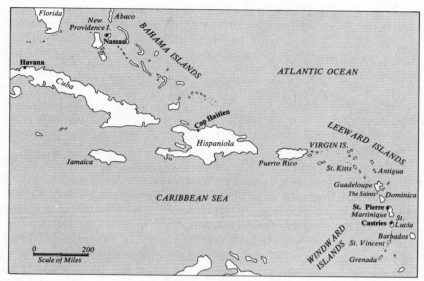

Florida
New Providence I.
Abaco
Nassau
BAHAMA ISLANDS
ATLANTIC OCEAN
Havana
Cuba
Cap Haïtien
Hispaniola
LEEWARD ISLANDS
VIRGIN IS.
Jamaica
Puerto Rico
St. Kitts
Antigua
Guadeloupe
The Saints
Dominica
CARIBBEAN SEA
St. Pierre
Martinique
St. Lucia
Castries
Barbados
St. Vincent
WINDWARD ISLANDS
Grenada
0   200
Scale of Miles

The West Indies

North America for the West Indies on November 4, leaving Boston after his unfortunate experiences with the weather, General Sullivan, and American officers in general in the Newport area. D'Estaing's fleet anchored at Fort Royal, Martinique, on December 9.

As soon as Barrington's reinforcements arrived, he set sail from Barbados for St. Lucia, about a hundred miles west. The British fleet anchored in Grand Cul de Sac inlet on the west side of St. Lucia on December 13, just three days after the British squadron from New York had arrived at Barbados. Barrington had moved fast.

Some of the troops landed at once and seized the high ground north of the inlet and the batteries protecting it. On the fourteenth, the rest of the troops landed.

The key to holding northern St. Lucia was a precipitous promontory, La Vigie, which stands at the north end of the bay (then called Carénage) that lies just north of the Cul de Sac inlet. By nightfall of December 14, the British had secured La Vigie and held all the shoreline from La Vigie through the southern end of the Cul de Sac. They also held the island's capital, Morne Fortuné, which they called Fort Charlotte. The French garrison had hastily withdrawn to the island's interior, leaving their powder and stores behind and their guns unspiked. If the British could hold La Vigie and keep their fleet in the waters off St. Lucia, shielding their transports with their warships, the French would lose St. Lucia.

Just as the French colors were struck at the governor's house in Morne Fortuné, late on the fourteenth, word came that a sail had been sighted. D'Estaing had arrived. He had, in fact, moved very fast himself, having learned only that morning that Barrington had sailed for St. Lucia.

During the night of December 14-15, Barrington perfected his plan of defense. D'Estaing outnumbered him, with twelve ships of the line and at least seven thousand troops. Barrington disposed his warships very carefully. He had four ships of the line and three 50-gun ships, plus three frigates. Placing the *Isis*, 50, at the north (windward) end of the inlet, he supported her with the three frigates, determined that no French vessel should slip between the shore and the northern hinge of his line to attack the transports in the inlet. His ships stretched southward and slightly outward from that point, with his flagship, the *Prince of Wales*, 74, holding the southernmost and most exposed position.

D'Estaing sailed his line past the British ships, north to south, on the morning of the fifteenth, each ship firing as she passed, but without effect. In the afternoon, he repeated the maneuver, again without effect. Apparently there was not a strong enough breeze at either time to allow d'Estaing's ships to close with the British, but still, he gave up easily, in a way that brings to mind his behavior off Newport.

Deciding to shift to an attack on the land defenses, d'Estaing anchored in a small bay north of the Carénage, and landed his seven thousand troops. Although generally tactically cautious—and often overcautious—d'Estaing was always personally brave. On the eighteenth, as later at Savannah, he abandoned tactical caution and displayed personal courage in leading a doomed assault against a formidable objective. The French charged the promontory of La Vigie three times, and finally had to withdraw, after losing forty-one officers and about eight hundred men killed and wounded. D'Estaing planned to try again by sea, but Barrington, leaving nothing undone, immediately strengthened the shore defenses at the flanks of his ships and warped his vessels even closer to shore. Ten days later, having found no good opportunity to attack, d'Estaing sailed away, and at the end of the month the French garrison surrendered the island.

The American naval writer Alfred Thayer Mahan called Barrington's victory at St. Lucia ". . . a success whose distinction should be measured, not by the greatness of the scale, but by the perfection of the workmanship, and by the energy of the execution in the face of great odds."*

Grenada

A few days after St. Lucia surrendered, Vice Admiral John Byron, having done very little in the north, arrived in the West Indies and, being senior to Barrington, relieved him as commander in chief of the station. Little happened in the West Indies during the next six months except that in mid-June d'Estaing, convoying French merchant vessels past British islands and part way to France, took the occasion to capture lightly held St. Vincent, just south of St. Lucia.

Then, on June 30, d'Estaing took his whole fleet—reinforced to twenty-five ships of the line, plus frigates—to British Grenada, southernmost of the Windwards, a pendant to the chain of tiny Grenadines. He anchored at Grenada on July 2 and landed troops that evening.

Capturing Grenada was no more trouble than taking St. Vincent had been. The garrison surrendered on the fourth, and there was no naval action involved. A lone British sloop, 12, and thirty well-laden merchant vessels were captured. The French fleet and convoy lay quietly in St. George's Harbor at Georgetown, on the southwestern tip of the island.

Then, at daybreak of the sixth, sails appeared. It was Byron with twenty-one ships of the line, a frigate, and twenty-eight transports carrying troops and equipment. D'Estaing had been warned of their approach during the night, and by 4:00 A.M. the French vessels were hastily forming a line of battle on the starboard tack; the wind, the prevailing trade wind, was northeast by east.

*In William Laird Clowes, *The Royal Navy*, Vol. 3, Ch. 31, p. 432.

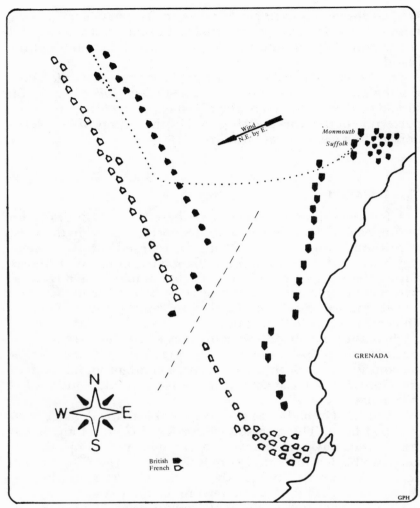

Battle of Grenada, July 6, 1779

The British, although they had sought out the French and were bound to be expecting an engagement, seem to have been in more confusion than their opponents. Mahan, in studying the Grenada engagement, could find no excuse for Byron's failure to have his line in order.

To Byron, bearing down from the north, the French ships, which were moving into a line of battle out of a cluster, in the usual French fashion, seemed to be in greater disorder than his own ships. The bunching of the French ships also deceived him as to their numbers; he thought he easily outnumbered them, whereas they actually slightly outnumbered him. Thinking he had an advantage, Byron ordered an attack on the group of ships at the French rear and hoisted the signal for a general chase to bring his ships closer. Leaving three ships to guard the convoy, he attempted to form a line as his fleet bore down on the French, who by this time had clearly formed their line. Three of the British ships, commanded by Barrington (by this time a vice admiral), were well ahead of the rest and came within range of the French first on a converging, nearly opposite, course such that they took fire from each French ship as it passed.

When Barrington's ships reached the French rear the order was given for the British line to wear in succession,* and fall in in line ahead to windward of and on the same tack as the French line. The three ships behind Barrington's van were to leeward of the rest of the line, and, like his, received fire from almost the entire French line as they came down on the opposite tack prior to wearing. They were so badly damaged that they could not keep up with the rest of the British line.

A hero of the action was Rear Admiral Joshua Rowley, who had been far astern and close to shore, guarding the convoy. He saw the isolation of Barrington's ships, which were still in the van on the new tack, and cut across the intervening water and through the British line, running straight before the wind, to take up a position in support of Barrington. His *Suffolk*, 74, was joined by Captain Robert Fanshawe's *Monmouth*, 64, a conspicuous "little black ship," whose gallantry was reportedly toasted by French officers after the battle.

The two fleets proceeded on parallel courses, exchanging broadsides as they went, until about noon. Then d'Estaing dropped off to join some of his ships that had fallen to leeward. Since Byron held his course, the two fleets diverged, and about an hour later passed out of range. Two hours later d'Estaing tacked and headed toward the three damaged British vessels, and a fourth which also had been forced to drop behind. Byron

*The first ship turned away from the wind until it came directly across her stern and her sails swung over to the other side. Then she turned toward the wind on the desired tack. Each successive ship did the same when she reached the point where the first ship had worn.

also tacked, still out of range. Seeing the danger he was in, the captain of one of the crippled British ships headed off before the wind for far-off Jamaica. The others held a course to windward of the French fleet, taking fire from the enemy ships as they came within range. But d'Estaing made no attempt to head them off, to the dismay of the commander of the *Fantasque*, Vice Admiral Suffren, who wrote of d'Estaing, "Had our admiral's seamanship equalled his courage, we would not have allowed four dismasted ships to escape."*

The battle off Grenada has been called the most disastrous British naval defeat since 1690, when the French mauled a combined British and Dutch fleet. Casualties on both sides were heavy at Grenada, with the French suffering the heavier casualties and the British suffering crippling damage to their ships.

There were reasons for these differences in damage aside from Byron's having attacked with ill-advised haste and in some disorder. The British had become accustomed to superior numbers in naval battles, and their tactics reflected that fact. They customarily, as in this battle, sought and held the weather gauge, that is, entered battle with the wind behind them, in a position for aggressive action; the French customarily sought the leeward position, good for withdrawing when need be. The British ships, heeled toward the enemy, pounded away at their hulls, causing heavy casualties and sometimes sinking ships. The French, striving more for crippling their enemy and escaping, fired on the rise or when heeled away from enemy ships, and aimed for the spars and rigging, often rending sails and bringing down masts.

Two-thirds of the British casualties of the Grenada battle were on the six ships that were isolated and exposed because of Byron's mismanagement before the battle and poor judgment in opening the action when unready. He left Grenada to the French, of course, and went to the island of St. Kitts for repairs, which took him a long time, as materials were not immediately available.†

D'Estaing had effectively protected Grenada, but he has been given little credit for his behavior toward the end of the battle. It seems certain that the French could have captured or sunk three ships, and probably two more. D'Estaing's almost apathetic

*Mahan in Clowes, *The Royal Navy*, Vol. 3, Ch. 31, p. 439.
†Byron has had his defenders; the judgment given here is based on Mahan's analysis.

handling of the situation left these ships in British hands to fight again.

The Battle off Martinique

In March 1780 the Leeward Islands Station got a new commander in chief — the noted Admiral Sir George Brydges Rodney. Rodney had captured several Caribbean islands for Britain during the Seven Years' War and he came to the West Indies straight from his victories off the Spanish and Portuguese coasts. He arrived on the Leeward Islands Station in a blaze of glory.

At almost exactly the same time, a new French commander arrived. He was Rear Admiral Louis Urbain de Bouënic, comte de Guichen. He, too, had been a successful captain in the Seven Years' War. As soon as de Guichen reached Martinique he began planning to attack one of the British islands, working with the marquis de Bouillé, governor of Martinique. Settling on Barbados or St. Lucia, de Guichen embarked three thousand troops on April 13 — troops that would eventually fight at Yorktown — and set sail, first heading north to accompany a convoy for Santo Domingo past the British.

Rodney's lookouts, always alert to French moves from their vantage point of St. Lucia, noted de Guichen's departure, and Rodney took out his entire fleet, twenty ships of the line, including two 90-gun vessels. The French were sighted on April 16 — twenty-two or twenty-three ships of the line and a 50-gun vessel — beating up against the east by north wind toward the channel between Martinique and Dominica. After a general chase to catch up with them, Rodney formed his line of battle on a parallel northwest course as darkness fell.

Rodney's plan was to attack only a part of the French line with a line more compact then theirs, rather than using the traditional coterminous line with each ship firing at her opposite number. With this slightly unconventional tactic, Rodney hoped to bring off a decisive victory.

What happened the next day was a classic case of communications failure, an especially graphic example of the kind of confusion that occurred in many naval battles when every order had to be signaled by flag. Because Rodney's captains were new to him, and because he tended to keep himself

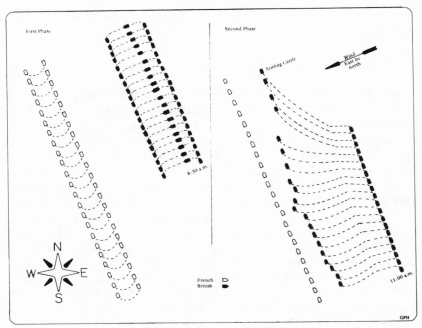

Battle of Martinique, April 17, 1780

aloof, the communications problem was further complicated.

Early on the 17th de Guichen reversed his course and headed south-southeast on the port tack. Soon thereafter Rodney signaled to his captains to close the intervals between ships, with intention of concentrating the fire of his compact line on the enemy rear. At that time the two lines were sailing on parallel, but opposite, courses, out of range of each other. As usual the British held the weather gauge, and they kept it throughout the battle.

At 8:30, when the more compact British line was opposite the French rear, in preparation for attack Rodney gave the signal for "line abreast," that is, each of his ships was to turn toward the enemy immediately, so that the line of ships would draw closer to the French. This was done. The *Stirling Castle*, commanded by Captain Robert Carkett, which had been the leading British ship, was now at the right of the British line, headed for the last French ship. The former rear British ship was headed a few ships forward of the center of the French line.

De Guichen saw what was happening, however, and he had his

ships wear together, reversing the direction of his line, so that the former lead ships were heading toward the threatened rear. Rodney countered by heading up on the opposite course from the French, who were now heading north by west. Sailing on a parallel course out of range, Rodney was moving his concentrated line toward the new French rear. Shortly after 10:00 A.M., he ordered his ships to wear together. The two fleets thus came on parallel courses, both heading north by west, and the compact British line, having progressed toward the French rear, was concentrated opposite the last of the enemy ships.

Rodney ordered his ships to steer to port at 11:00, in order to reduce the distance from the enemy line and bring the French ships within range. At 11:50 each ship was ordered to "bear down, steer for her opposite in the enemy's line, agreeable to the 21st article of the Additional Fighting Instructions." This article ordered that "every ship in the squadron is to steer for the ship of the enemy which, from the disposition of the two squadrons, it must be his lot to engage. . . . ."* Rodney, who had made his general tactical intentions clear early in the morning, thought there could be no doubt as to what was to be done. Each ship was to steer straight for the closest enemy ship and engage her. Because of the firmly shortened British line, this meant that each French ship would be receiving fire from more than one Britisher.

However, Captain Carkett and a number of other officers, including the two rear admirals present, misunderstood the orders. While Rodney's own flagship, the *Sandwich*, 90, closed and fought hard and successfully against three French vessels, Carkett headed the *Stirling Castle* toward his opposite number in the enemy line, the first ship of the French van. He thus stretched out his distance from the next British ship far, far beyond the prescribed two cables, took an inordinately long time to close with his adversary, and violated Rodney's plan for a mass attack. At least six other ships in the British van followed Carkett's lead, and Rodney thus had far less concentration than he would have had if he had never contracted his line in the first place.

After more than four hours of fighting, the French broke off the battle with indecisive results; as usual, they had sustained the heavier casualties, but the British ships were more heavily dam-

*Michael Lewis, *The Navy of Britain*, p. 513.

aged. Rodney had missed what he always considered to be the greatest opportunity of his career for decisive victory.

Furious with many of his subordinates and eager to catch the French, Rodney ordered repairs made at sea, chased de Guichen to Guadeloupe, where the Frenchman put into port, and then returned to St. Lucia, where he maintained a watch for the French fleet to return to Martinique. De Guichen may also have repaired some damage at sea, with help from St. Eustatia. He carried out more repairs at Guadeloupe, and then sailed out to attack St. Lucia, the British watchdog of the Windward Islands. The French already had left the British too long undisturbed there, free to harass them.

De Guichen sailed around Martinique, and approached St. Lucia from the northeast on May 9, as Rodney, whose lookouts had reported that the French ships were off Martinique, was preparing to leave to meet him. Thereupon there followed almost two weeks of maneuvering. Most of the time the two fleets were out of range. Twice a change of wind resulted in an engagement involving parts of both fleets. But neither was decisive, and both fleets suffered some damage and casualties. Finally Rodney put in at Barbados, and de Guichen took his ships to Fort Royal in Martinique. Both fleets were long overdue for rest and repair.

Rodney spent some of the next weeks writing angry reports on the action off Martinique. Five captains whom he judged to have followed orders well were given his official praise. The unfortunate Carkett was singled out for particular disapprobation. Rear Admirals Hyde Parker and Joshua Rowley were criticized for inattention to signals. Since Rowley was the same officer who had shown such courage and initiative at Grenada, it is hard to believe that the fault at Martinique was all in slow-witted subordinates or even in eighteenth-century doctrinal rigidity. In April 1780, Rodney did not seem to know how to bring out the best in his subordinates.

De Guichen, who had avoided decisive action in the battle off Martinique, as was his intention, had managed to inflict enough damage on the British ships to keep them in port for some time. However, about six of his own were also kept out of action for several weeks. He himself, worn by the strain of the preceding weeks and the loss of a son in one of the engagements, asked to be replaced by someone better qualified than he to handle so large a fleet. It would be months, of course, before he could expect a reply from France.

When word of the maneuvering of de Guichen and Rodney in the West Indies reached King Charles III of Spain, he decided to send men and ships to the West Indies to join de Guichen, protect Spanish colonies, and perhaps expand Spanish holdings at the expense of the British. On April 28 Admiral Don José Solano sailed from Cadiz with twelve ships of the line and twelve thousand soldiers.

A British vessel that spotted the Spanish fleet hurried to take the news to Rodney, who put to sea on June 7, hoping to intercept it east of Martinique. But Solano had spotted the informer and passed north of Guadeloupe to approach Martinique from the west. De Guichen with fifteen ships met him near Guadeloupe on June 9, and together they returned to Fort Royal.

Conditions aboard the crowded Spanish transports had been so miserable that when they at last dropped anchor most of the men were ill. It is estimated that as many as five thousand men died from illness. Because of the depletion of his force, Solano refused to cooperate with de Guichen and instead insisted that de Guichen convoy his vessels to the Bahama Channel so that they could proceed in safety to Havana.

The French admiral had received orders to return to France in the fall, and decided it was time to go. There was a large convoy making up at Cap François in Haiti, and he would escort it home; he could take the Spaniards almost to Cuba on the way to pick up his convoy.

On July 5, 1780, the Spanish and French fleets and transports weighed anchor in Fort Royal. De Guichen escorted Don Solano's ships to the eastern end of Cuba and then proceeded to Haiti. There he found messages from Lafayette and the French minister to the United States urging him to come north and participate with Washington in a joint land and sea operation. But de Guichen sailed instead for Cadiz on August 16, taking nineteen ships of the line and ninety-six merchant vessels with him.

Seizing the Golden Rock

Since first arriving in the Caribbean, Admiral Rodney had

coveted the supposedly neutral Dutch island of St. Eustatia. Not only was it rich, it was overtly helping England's enemies. Rodney claimed that when de Guichen's fleet could not get back to Fort Royal after the bloody battle off Martinique, supplies and workmen were sent from St. Eustatia to make repairs on his vessels at sea. On the other hand, in late 1780, after his return from New York, when Rodney himself needed cordage to repair the rigging of his ships that had been damaged by the severe autumn hurricanes, the merchants of St. Eustatia told him they had none. This was not true, as he soon found out.

When Britain finally declared war on the Netherlands on December 21, 1780, a fast ship immediately left England with orders for Rodney. On January 27 they were handed to him at St. Lucia. He was to seize all Dutch possessions in the Caribbean.

Three days later Rodney sailed for St. Eustatia. On February 3 he approached the island. He had with him a dozen ships of the line, having left six others to watch four French ships lying at anchor at Fort Royal.

At St. Eustatia there was no battle, no resistance. The Dutch did not even know war had been declared. Rodney reported that the attack "was as sudden as a clap of thunder." With sketchy fortifications, a garrison of only fifty or sixty men, one frigate, 38, and five smaller American vessels, there was little the defenders could have done in any case. As it was, Governor de Graff surrendered unconditionally within an hour. The neighboring islands were also taken, and a convoy of twenty-three well-laden merchant vessels that had sailed three days earlier was pursued and captured. To complete the haul, the Dutch flag was kept flying over the port for some time, and as each new merchant captain, ignorant that the Netherlands was at war, brought his ship into harbor, he was relieved of her by the occupying British.

The booty was all Rodney had dreamed of. He seized 130 merchant ships in the harbor. Every warehouse was packed with goods, and the beach was reported covered with barrels of tobacco and sugar. The total value of goods seized was estimated at more than £3,000,000. Rodney must have felt both triumph and chagrin when he learned that several thousand tons of cordage were on hand—and the merchants had told him they had none!

When the news of the capture reached London, the guns of

half percent. Lady Rodney wrote the admiral that her house was like a fair, with every friend and acquaintance crowding in to congratulate her, and that at court "the attention and notice I received from their majesties were sufficient to turn my poor brain."* Rodney was raised to the peerage, and a handsome commemorative medal was struck in honor of "the glorious 3rd February 1781 when St. George punished the Dutch &c. &c."† In the Netherlands, John Adams wrote, there was also celebration—at the Stadholder's court. Pro-British and hostile to the Amsterdam merchants and traders, the courtiers were overjoyed at the fall of St. Eustatia.‡

Rodney spent three months on St. Eustatia, and his behavior there aroused controversy. He was furious with its leaders and merchants, and especially with the British merchants who lived and traded there. He wanted vengeance. He would have liked to make the island "a mere desert." He also had heavy personal debts, and the wealth of St. Eustatia was tempting.

Immediately after the surrender the admiral decreed that all residents of the island—military or civilian, Dutch, British, American, or neutral—were to be treated as prisoners of war. All property was to be confiscated for the British crown without respect to the nationality of its owners or the nature of the property. A carpenter's tools were to be seized just as gunpowder destined for the rebels was. The warehouses of Statia's "lower town" were to be destroyed or unroofed, for Rodney felt they were comparable to fortifications; if they ever fell again into enemy hands, they could be turned against the British.

The French merchants were treated somewhat better than other nationals; they were sent to French islands and were allowed to take their household goods and house slaves with them. The Dutch, British, and Americans, however, lost everything, including the business records that might later have allowed them to file claims for compensation. The Jews on the island were treated most harshly of all. The 101 men of the community were deported without their wives and children, and were personally searched before they left so that no coin might elude the British. Ironically, one of these men was a refugee

*J. Franklin Jameson, "St. Eustatius in the American Revolution," p. 701.
†Photograph in Clowes, *The Royal Navy*, Vol. 3, p. 480.
‡*The Works of John Adams*, ed. Charles Francis Adams, Vol. 7, p. 523.

Loyalist from Newport who had twice earlier lost all his property to the Americans.

It is not clear how much of this loot Rodney took for himself, but it seems likely that, as Horace Walpole put it, "Admiral Rodney has a little overgilt his own statue." He certainly aroused much indignation in Europe and stirred up a hornet's nest of powerful West Indiamen in London. Ignorant of the law involved, he had violated an act of Parliament by imprisoning masters and mates of American merchant vessels, and he was devastatingly attacked by Edmund Burke for violating universally accepted international law by confiscating private property in a captured place and by imprisoning noncombatants. Perhaps even more damaging was the charge that England's enemies actually benefited from Rodney's actions, since at the grand auction at which goods from Europe seized on Statia were sold they brought far less than their actual value. Despite the precautions Rodney attempted to take, most of these goods ended up in American, French, or Spanish hands—probably at a lower cost than if they had been bought from the merchants of St. Eustatia. Most damaging of all was the accusation that by dallying three months on Statia to deal with all the financial and administrative matters involved there, Rodney had sacrificed opportunities to seek out and defeat the French. It was during those months that Admiral de Grasse, who had just come out from France to command the station, managed to slip around the tip of Martinique and join the rest of the French fleet at Fort Royal. This was the spring of 1781, and as it turned out, his safe arrival was crucial to de Grasse's appearance off the Virginia Capes in the fall, and to the allies at Yorktown.

In the end Rodney himself profited little from the rape of Statia. Not only was his hero's image tarnished, but much of the richest produce of the Indies seized on Statia was captured by the French when Admiral La Motte-Picquet attacked the convoy carrying it, west of the Scilly Islands. A contemporary newspaper estimated that Rodney and General Vaughan, commander of the army troops that took Statia, personally lost £300,000 by La Motte-Picquet's seizures.

As for Statia itself, Rodney succeeded in insuring that it would never again be what it had been. It did not stay in British hands, however. He thought he had left it adequately defended and garrisoned, but before the war's end the French easily retook it.

The peace treaty made it Dutch again, and so it remains in the twentieth century.

Two Failures and a Quick Conquest

Not every amphibious landing in the West Indies gained a conquest. When Rodney returned to the West Indies from North America in December 1780 to a hurricane-ravaged fleet, he was given reports that the fortifications of St. Vincent, taken from England by d'Estaing in June 1779, had been destroyed by the devastating October storms. It was not hard to believe, for Rodney could see how Barbados looked after the winds. "The most beautiful island in the world has the appearance of a country laid waste by fire and sword."*

He planned to seize St. Vincent, and landed troops there on December 15. It turned out, however, that the report was wrong; the fortifications were intact. The troops reembarked, and the fleet sailed back to St. Lucia.

De Grasse, newly arrived in the West Indies in April 1781, hoped to seize St. Lucia, temporarily unprotected by British ships. Rodney was then counting his loot at St. Eustatia; his second in command, Rear Admiral Sir Samuel Hood, outnumbered by de Grasse in an action off Martinique in late April, had been forced to withdraw toward St. Eustatia.

De Grasse sailed to St. Lucia with almost all his fleet and landed twelve hundred troops at the northwest tip of the island, the spot closest to Martinique. The defending batteries and fortifications were too strong, however, and the French had to give up. The British continued to watch Martinique from St. Lucia throughout the war.

At the same time that he had attacked St. Lucia, de Grasse had sent two ships of the line and thirteen hundred troops to Tobago, which lies well to the south, near Trinidad and the South American coast. Coincidentally, at about the same time Rodney finally sailed from St. Eustatia with his fleet and put in at Barbados for water. When de Grasse, back in disappointment from the St. Lucia venture, learned that Rodney had sailed from

*Quoted by Mahan in Clowes, *The Royal Navy*, Vol. 3, Ch. 31, p. 479.

St. Eustatia, he became concerned about his two vulnerable ships at Tobago; and sailed on May 25 with the rest of his fleet to reinforce them. Rodney, upon reaching Barbados, heard of the attempt on Tobago, and he, in turn, sent a contingent of six ships of the line to reinforce that island. They were too late, and too few. They encountered the whole French fleet on its way to the same island and necessarily declined battle. Rodney then headed for Tobago with his own entire fleet, but when he arrived off the island on June 4 he learned that the garrison had surrendered to the French on the second. The French had been a jump ahead all the way.

De Grasse's next move was to the Chesapeake.

St. Kitts and Nevis

When the year 1782 opened, American leaders knew the war was basically over for them. The great victory of Yorktown had been celebrated, Lafayette had sailed back to France, and in London, Lord North's government was tottering. Soon Parliament would ask King George to make peace with the colonies. None of this, however, affected the determination of each European power to have the war's end find it in the strongest position possible and, particularly, in control of the most profitable islands of the West Indies. There was no thought of winding down hostilities between the British, French, and Spanish.

De Grasse, triumphant after Yorktown, and Governor de Bouillé set their sights on another British island. They still wanted Barbados, a major British base, and the French fleet sailed from Martinique to take it in December. Barbados lies to windward of Martinique, however, and the French could not beat successfully against the strong northeasterly trade winds. They had to give up.

De Grasse sailed out again on January 5, to the northwest this time, and anchored in Basse Terre Roads, off St. Kitts, on January 11. He landed a formidable force, eight thousand troops, and the British garrison quickly retired to the stronghold of Brimstone Hill, at the northwest end of the island. The island's residents surrendered to the French. The little nearby island of Nevis surrendered on the twentieth. Only the Brimstone Hill fortifications on St. Kitts remained to be cleared.

Admiral Hood had learned what the French were up to on January 11 and had sailed immediately for St. Kitts. He put in on the twenty-first at Antigua, less than fifty miles to windward of the island. There he took on supplies and men, assembling a landing force of twenty-four hundred.

Hood was a fine tactician and careful to communicate his intentions clearly to his subordinates. He set sail for Basse Terre at 5:00 P.M. on January 23, intending to sail around the southern tip of Nevis and up to Basse Terre Roads by daylight. The roadstead lies east-west, and Hood's intelligence reports told him that the French ships lay in such a way that he could get the weather gauge of the easternmost ships and attack them before the ships to the west could come up to support them. This plan went awry when two British ships, including the leading ship of the line, collided. The repairs delayed the fleet, and the French sighted it at daybreak before it had reached the southern tip of Nevis.

De Grasse put to sea and by dark was standing to southward, approaching the British. Hood went about, so that his ships also stood to southward, and at daybreak of the twenty-fifth the French saw them thus and assumed they were in retreat. Hood, however, had a new and elegant plan. He slipped between the island and the French and usurped their anchorage there. As Lord Robert Manners, captain of one of Hood's ships, described the action, "The taking possession of this road was well judged, well conducted, and well executed. . . . The van and centre divisions [were] brought to an anchor under the fire of the rear, which was engaged with the enemy's centre; and then the centre, being at an anchor and properly placed, covered us while we anchored, making, I think, the most masterly manoeuvre I ever saw."*

French land forces were still besieging the British defenders on Brimstone Hill, however, and de Grasse could not abandon them. Twice on the twenty-sixth he sailed his fleet past the British, with each ship firing in tun. His flagship, the mighty 104-gun *Ville de Paris*,† on which he had conferred with Washington off Yorktown, was held the longest before the British in the first engagement, and the firing was so heavy that for a

---

*Quoted in G. J. Marcus, *A Naval History of England*, Vol. 1, p. 446.
†Sometimes given as 100 guns and sometimes as 110.

while watchers on shore could see nothing of the ships involved except de Grasse's white flag at the main-topgallant masthead, floating over the clouds of smoke, and occasional glimpses of the pennants of nearby ships.

The British were not dislodged, but the troops Hood had with him were not enough to give much help to the British garrison on the island. De Grasse waited offshore, sometimes exchanging distant shots with the British ships, and the battle was fought out on land. The British surrendered the island on February 12, and Hood's fleet was consequently endangered by shore guns. On the night of February 13, leaving lights burning on buoys tied to

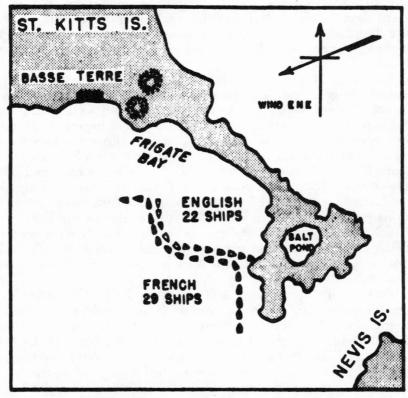

British Maneuver at St. Kitts, January 26, 1782

their anchors, the British crews cut their cables, and the ships slipped out to sea before de Grasse could enter the harbor.

Hood could not save St. Kitts, but his skillful handling of his fleet gained valuable time. While Hood and de Grasse maneuvered, Rodney arrived from England, whither his gout and his Statia booty had taken him, and brought with him enough ships to give Britain the stronger position in the Caribbean.

The Saints

For 1782, the French and Spanish planned an expedition to seize the British island of Jamaica, over fifteen hundred miles from Martinique, but close to Spanish Cuba and to half-French, half-Spanish Hispaniola. Cap François, Haiti, would be the departure point for the assault on Jamaica. This was the operation Bernardo de Gálvez was busy planning in late 1781 and early 1782.

A great convoy of transports to supply this enterprise had been assembled at Brest late in 1781 and then dispersed by a British fleet under Admiral Kempenfelt off Ushant. The French gathered another convoy as soon as possible and got it safely past the British Isles.

Admiral Rodney not only knew of the French plans to seize Jamaica but also was aware of the imminent arrival of the convoy. However, he positioned his own ships so close to the eastern side of Martinique that the French transports and two ships of the line were able to pass north of them. They arrived safely at Fort Royal on March 20, 1782.

Even though the convoy reached Martinique, Admiral de Grasse was left with the highly difficult job of getting out of Fort Royal, under the eyes of the British on St. Lucia, and safely to Cap François. With his reinforcements, he had 35 ships of the line, and Rodney had 36. De Grasse had 150 unarmed ships to protect, for he was escorting not only the supply ships intended for the Jamaica operation but also the trade ships for France.

The French admiral decided to keep as close to friendly shores as possible. If he followed the inner curve of the Windwards and Leewards, he would pass Dominica, Guadeloupe, and St. Kitts— all in French hands—and then the Spanish island of Puerto Rico.

De Grasse set sail on the morning of April 8, 1782. Rodney,

waiting at St. Kitts, soon knew it, and by noon he too had put to sea, with all his fleet; by 2:30 in the afternoon his lookouts had sighted the French. Here St. Lucia, and its conquest at the beginning of the war by Barrington, served Britain well. There was no way the big French fleet—no faster than the slowest ship in its convoy—could get a significant head start on the watchful British, based so close to Martinique.

De Grasse did not want battle; he wanted to get his 150 transports safely to Haiti. When it became clear, on the following morning, that the British were gaining on him, he sent the transports temporarily to Guadeloupe, where they arrived safely. His intention was to take his fleet through the channel between Dominica and Guadeloupe—the channel where the islands called Les Saintes lie—as quickly as possible, beating against the wind and drawing the British away from the transports. He would go back for the transports after he had evaded the British.

On April 9, however, de Grasse saw an opportunity he could not resist. The British van, eight ships under Admiral Hood, had moved well ahead of the rest of the British fleet. It was vulnerable, and de Grasse felt he had to attack it. However, he sent only half his vessels to do the job. They passed the line of the British van twice, firing as they went, but did no serious damage, largely because they kept a cautious distance from the enemy. They feared the new British carronades, short-barreled guns that were reputed to be deadly at close quarters.

De Grasse soon began to pull well ahead of the British again. Even though the British ships were coppered, and the French apparently were not, the well-designed French ships were still faster, and the distance increased during the next two days. But one of the French ships, the *Zélé*, was twice damaged in collisions, the second time with de Grasse's own *Ville de Paris*, and early on the twelfth de Grasse sent the *Zélé* off, towed by a frigate, toward Guadeloupe. Rodney detached four ships to pursue them and thus baited a trap for de Grasse.

De Grasse took the bait. He bore down toward his limping vessels with the *Ville de Paris*, on the port tack but running free, and ordered the rest of the fleet to follow. Rodney, meanwhile, had established an orderly line and was preparing for battle. When he was ready to move to the attack, he called back the pursuing vessels.

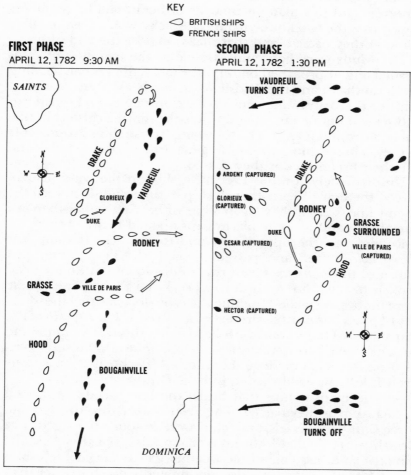

KEY

◁ BRITISH SHIPS
◀ FRENCH SHIPS

FIRST PHASE
APRIL 12, 1782 9:30 AM

SAINTS

DRAKE

VAUDREUIL

GLORIEUX

DUKE

RODNEY

GRASSE   VILLE DE PARIS

HOOD

BOUGAINVILLE

DOMINICA

SECOND PHASE
APRIL 12, 1782 1:30 PM

VAUDREUIL
TURNS OFF

ARDENT (CAPTURED)

GLORIEUX
(CAPTURED)

DRAKE

RODNEY

GRASSE
SURROUNDED

DUKE

CESAR (CAPTURED)

VILLE DE PARIS
(CAPTURED)

HOOD

HECTOR (CAPTURED)

BOUGAINVILLE
TURNS OFF

Battle of the Saints

205

The French line was not in good order. De Grasse was not ready for battle, and he held the weather gauge, which made escape impossible. He did not have much wind of any kind, however, and this made maneuver difficult. Still he doubtless hoped that the two lines, on opposite tacks, would pass parallel, firing as they passed, and that that would be the end of it.

The winds were light and variable as the two lines of ships formed and approached on opposite tacks, the French heading south southeast and the British north northeast. Before the first ships of the British line could get within range the French van had passed out of range, and it was the ninth British ship that opened fire at 8:00 A.M. The following British ships dropped off as they came within gunshot range in order to pass parallel and fire their broadsides as they passed.

Unfortunately for the French, a shift in the wind at 9:15 forced the bow of each French ship to turn slightly toward the enemy line, so that they lay in a line of bearing rather than in a line ahead, and in some places gaps opened between them.

Rodney saw the opportunity and took it. His flagship, the *Formidable*, luffed and passed through the French line, just astern of the *Glorieux*. Five British ships followed. Rodney had broken his own line in order to break the French line. These were innovative tactics, flouting the rigid doctrine that the integrity of one's line must be preserved at all costs. The captain of the ship ahead of the *Formidable* followed the admiral's example and cut a new hole in the enemy line. A captain several vessels astern of Rodney, Commodore Edmund Affleck, also broke the French line, probably acting independently.

All the British ships that broke the line raked the nearest French ship as they passed. The French were thus divided into three clumps of vessels, and many were seriously damaged. The British were divided into three groups also, but they held the initiative and had gained the weather gauge. De Grasse's ships had suffered heavy casualties, undoubtedly much heavier than the British, and three of them were dismasted.

The three disabled ships were captured, then another French ship, and finally, near sunset, the *Ville de Paris*, with de Grasse aboard. But most of the French ships escaped to Cap François, where the transports diverted to Guadeloupe on the ninth had already arrived. Six ships went all the way to Curaçao and finally reached Cap François in May.

Rodney did not attempt to follow up his victory with a determined pursuit; after cruising near Guadeloupe until April 17, most of the time becalmed, he went to Jamaica. He was strongly criticized for not pursuing. Hood, to whom de Grasse surrendered and who later captured four other vessels when he was sent on April 17 to search for the French, believed the British could have taken twenty ships and virtually removed the French navy from the Caribbean. Rodney, no longer a vigorous man, and pained with gout, answered Hood's reproaches with, "Come, we have done very handsomely as it is."*

This was the last significant action in the Caribbean. Admiral Hugh Pigot relieved Rodney on July 10, and twelve days later Rodney sailed for home. The French and Spanish abandoned the idea of attacking Jamaica. De Grasse returned to England as a prisoner aboard the *Sandwich*, his critical victory off the Chesapeake clouded by his loss at The Saints.

*Quoted by Mahan in Clowes, *The Royal Navy*, Vol. 3, p. 537.

14

Britain Fights in European Waters

To most of those living in Europe or the British Isles the war was distant. It affected those involved in trade overseas or in diplomacy, but only people in the busy ports saw much to remind them that somewhere a war was going on in earnest. With only a few miles separating England from the Continent, however, the British and the French kept a large part of their fleets close to home. And on a few occasions fleet met fleet not far from the shores of the belligerent nations.

First Battle at Sea

The beginning of the war between France and England came at sea. As soon as the treaties between France and the United States were signed in February 1778, it was clear that there would be war, but there were no formal declarations. In April, Admiral d'Estaing's fleet sailed from Toulon for America, to cooperate with Washington.

In hopes of misleading the British as to d'Estaing's destination, the French government leaked word that the ships were being transferred to Brest, to join the main French fleet. The deception was successful. When no word of d'Estaing's whereabouts had been received in London by June, Admiral Augustus Keppel was sent to sea with instructions to cruise in the area of Brest and prevent the two fleets from joining. With twenty-one ships of the line, four frigates, and three smaller vessels, Keppel sailed on June 15, prepared to fight if necessary. There had thus far been no encounters between French and British forces.

On June 17, 1778, Keppel's watch sighted four French vessels:

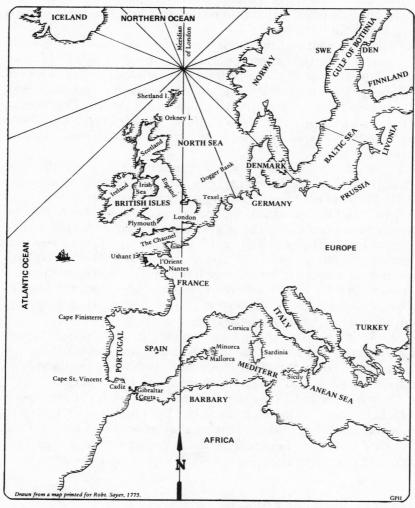

ICELAND NORTHERN OCEAN

Meridian of London

SWE DEN

GULF OF BOTHNIA

NORWAY

FINNLAND

Shetland I.

Orkney I.

NORTH SEA

BALTIC SEA

LIVONIA

Scotland

Dogger Bank

DENMARK

Ireland Irish England
Sea

BRITISH ISLES

Texel

GERMANY

PRUSSIA

London

Plymouth

EUROPE

The Channel

Ushant I. l'Orient
Nantes

FRANCE

ATLANTIC OCEAN

ITALY

TURKEY

Cape Finisterre

Corsica

PORTUGAL

Minorca

Sardinia

SPAIN

Mallorca

Cape St. Vincent Cadiz Gibraltar
Ceuta

MEDITERR

Sicily

ANEAN SEA

BARBARY

AFRICA

N

Drawn from a map printed for Robt. Sayer, 1775.

GPH

The Coasts of Europe

209

two frigates, the *Licorne* and the *Belle Poule*; a corvette, the *Hirondelle*; and a lugger, the *Coureur*. Keppel ordered a general chase and directed his commanders to catch the French ships and bring them to him.

Late in the afternoon the British frigate *Milford* caught the *Licorne*, which tried to escape and halted only when fired at by one of the British 74s. The *Milford* shepherded her prize close to Keppel's flagship, the *Victory*, where she stayed until morning, when her captain attempted to slip away. Again, fire from a British ship stopped the *Licorne*. Her captain fired a broadside into the British ship *America* that wounded four men. Then he struck his colors.

Shortly after the *Licorne* was apprehended by the *Milford*, at about 6:00 P.M., the British frigate *Arethusa* caught up with the *Belle Poule*. The French commander refused to be taken to Keppel, and the *Arethusa* opened fire. In a light breeze the two frigates fought a fierce battle at close range for from two to five hours, depending on whether the British or the French report is correct. Finally they broke off, and the *Belle Poule* withdrew toward the French coast. Almost half her men had been killed or wounded (102 of 230), and the vessel had been badly damaged. The *Arethusa* had been severely damaged in masts and rigging, but only 44 of her 198 men were casualties.

While these two ships were engaged, the French lugger *Coureur* was overtaken by the British cutter *Alert*. She too refused to go to the British admiral and was promptly fired upon. An hour and a half later her commander struck.

Only the *Hirondelle* seems to have escaped in this engagement, which, except for those on the ships that participated, is important primarily because the king of France later said that this was the date when war began. There was no formal declaration for another year, and the king's statement is as true as any.

The Battle of Ushant

Admiral Keppel returned to Spithead after this little encounter. On July 9 he set forth again, with thirty ships of the line. This time there was no question. England was at war with France, and Keppel was looking for French ships to fight. His departure had been preceded the day before by the departure of a French fleet from Brest, under the command of Lieutenant

General* le Comte d'Orvilliers. D'Orvilliers had thirty-two ships of the line—twenty-nine of them fit for combat—and orders to stay at sea for a month. What he should do while there was not very clear, and he interpreted his orders to mean that he should avoid action unless the circumstances were clearly in his favor.

Two weeks later, on the afternoon of July 23, the fleets sighted each other. Although initially to leeward, the French commander managed to work all but two of his ships to windward, northwest of the British, during the night, even though it meant that Keppel was between him and Brest. The two laggards apparently returned to Brest, reducing the French fleet to twenty-seven effective ships. For three days Keppel tried in vain to get within range, until the morning of July 27 found the two fleets about a hundred miles off the Breton Island of Ushant (Isle d'Ouessant), six to ten miles apart, both on the port tack and heading northwest.

The two fleets maneuvered until they were on roughly parallel courses on opposite tacks, neither line well ordered. The leading British ships came in range of the fourth ship of the French line, the first three having passed out of range, and the Frenchman, to windward, opened fire. The two lines passed each other slowly, firing broadsides. The British line was in confusion by the time the French line had passed and the smoke had cleared. D'Orvilliers, seeing the condition of the enemy, wore his fleet and headed back to pass them again, this time to leeward, so that he could fire at the rigging of the British ships with the guns on his lowest windward decks. Keppel, recognizing his intent, called his ships to form a line of battle. But before the two fleets came within range darkness fell. Sunrise found them about fifteen to twenty miles apart. Keppel's ships had taken considerable punishment from the French guns, and he did not attempt to pursue, but returned to Plymouth. D'Orvilliers's ships were in better shape, but he made no attempt to renew the battle or try to pursue the departing British ships. It was almost a year before the French and British met again in their home waters.

Events ashore after this battle illustrated the friction between supporters and opponents of Lord North's ministry that hampered the British navy and Admiralty during the war.

Even before the battle, there had been bad feeling between

*Lieutenant-Général des Armées Navales, equivalent to Rear Admiral.

Keppel and Vice Admiral Hugh Palliser, who commanded Keppel's rear division. Late in the action, when Keppel was trying to form a line of battle before dark, Palliser failed to respond to the admiral's signal, and then ignored a message sent to him by frigate. Keppel blamed him for throwing away a final chance at British victory, and Palliser in turn claimed that earlier in the battle, when Keppel had carried out a movement that took his flagship away from the French, he was actually fleeing in the face of the enemy.

Significantly, Keppel was an opponent of the war with America and had refused to serve against the Americans. Like many naval officers at the time, he owed his high command to earlier Whig ministries; Lord North was no friend of his. Palliser, on the other hand, was a supporter of the North ministry. Soon after the battle, English gentlemen began taking sides for one admiral or the other in coffeehouse arguments, and by October the affair had broken into the press. Palliser, a member of the Board of Admiralty, managed to have Keppel court-martialed, and although no formal charges were made against Palliser, the Admiralty carried out an investigation into his conduct and lightly reprimanded him.

After a trial that filled the newspapers for five weeks in early 1783, Keppel was completely exonerated. Antigovernment crowds cheered, lit bonfires, wrecked and looted Palliser's house, and wrenched the great gate of the Admiralty from its hinges. Up and down England, innkeepers hauled down their old signboards and hoisted new ones emblazoned "Admiral Keppel."

The split in public opinion, and within the navy and Admiralty, that broke into the open in the Keppel-Palliser case was always in the background and more than once affected naval operations during the war. Together with the slack period in shipbuilding and ship maintenance that preceded the war, and with the ineptitude of several key Admiralty officials, it was a burden to Britain's fighting admirals.

The Invasion Fiasco

The French were inspired at this time, as many have been before and since, by the proximity of the British Isles to the northern coast of France. In the spring of 1779, while French diplomatic efforts focused on getting Spain into the war, French military efforts focused on an invasion of England. A force of fifty thousand men was assembled at Le Havre and St. Malo under the command of the comte de Vaux, and four hundred vessels were assembled to transport them. Plans were made, troops were drilled, and agreement was reached with Spain to join the two fleets in an enormous naval expedition across the Channel. Rochambeau was one of the commanders, and Lafayette was intent on participating. Even John Paul Jones was to play a part.

There was no concealing the preparations going on in France, and fear gripped residents of the south of England. All horses and cattle were driven inland from the coasts, and many people departed from the threatened area. The entrance to Plymouth Harbor, which seemed the likely objective, was closed with booms and sunken vessels.

On June 4, just before Spain's declaration of war, but almost two months after the signature of the secret Spanish-French alliance, Admiral d'Orvilliers took his fleet of thirty ships of the line out of Brest in anticipation of a British attempt to blockade the port as soon as Spain's declaration was made. D'Orvilliers sailed south to rendezvous with the Spanish fleet. For six weeks the French fleet waited, cruising back and forth off Cape Finisterre, eating up their provisions and wearing down ships and men. At length, on July 23, thirty-four Spanish vessels appeared. D'Orvilliers's first job was to supply them with French signals so that they could communicate. They had plenty of time to practice them, for the Spanish ships were slow, and it took three weeks to arrive in sight of the Lizard, at the southwest tip of England.

A British fleet of thirty-five ships under Admiral Sir Charles Hardy had put to sea on June 16 to keep an eye out for the French. But Hardy was cruising southwest of the Scilly Islands, and the two fleets did not see each other as the French and Spanish turned up into the English Channel. On August 16 the combined fleet anchored off Plymouth, where the next day the British ship *Ardent*, 64, with a crew of five hundred, of whom four hundred were impressed landsmen, appeared. Her captain, Philip Boteler, mistook the fleet for British, and discovered his error only when a large frigate fired a broadside at him.

Although the *Ardent* was apparently the only naval vessel captured by the allied fleet, a more valuable victory was won on

August 9, when a huge British convoy bound for the East and West Indies ran into the great combined fleet. Fifty-five merchantmen were captured, along with 2,865 members of their crews and cargoes worth a million and a half pounds. The captures of the *Ardent* and these merchant vessels were the only accomplishments of the invasion armada.

When D'Orvilliers sailed from Brest, the French government's plan had been to seize the Isle of Wight and Spithead in order to secure a base close to the coast of England and an anchorage for the fleet. Now, however, he found that plans had changed. The landing was to be made in Cornwall, near Falmouth, where there was no adequate anchorage at all. D'Orvilliers protested, but nature intervened to settle the issue. A strong wind came up from the east and blew so hard for several days that most of the fleet was blown out of the Channel. Having heard that the British Channel Fleet was off Scilly, d'Orvilliers decided to try to force an engagement at sea. Hardy was not sighted until August 29, however, when he was already back in the Channel. He easily eluded his pursuers and returned safely to Spithead.

By this time the French ships were very low on provisions, having been at sea since early June, and in both the French and Spanish fleets scurvy, smallpox, and typhus were rampant. Orders finally came to return to Brest, and the combined fleet anchored there on September 14. The Spanish government promptly recalled its ships, in order to devote its efforts to taking Gibraltar. The invasion plan was abandoned. It had been an expensive and fruitless exercise. What the outcome of it might have been cannot be known, but its failure resulted in the release of men and their capable commander, Rochambeau, to be sent to help the Americans win their fight.

La Motte-Picquet's Bonanza

During the next two years, except for the dramatic exploits of John Paul Jones, the chief action in European waters was the preying, by privateers and naval vessels, on the merchant shipping of their enemies. One of the largest hauls was made by French Admiral La Motte-Picquet, who happened to be cruising near the entrance to the English Channel with six ships of the line and a few frigates on May 2, 1781, when the convoy bringing the spoils from St. Eustatia appeared. La Motte-Picquet succeeded in driving off the naval escort and capturing twenty-two of the thirty merchant vessels before a fleet of eight British ships put an end to his fun. He sailed triumphantly to Brest, with two thirds of the booty Rodney had shipped to England.

The Dogger Bank

The Dutch navy had theoretically joined the war against England in December 1780, but it made very little difference. Although the Dutch merchant fleet was—before the Netherlands stumbled into the war—still a fine instrument of trade, there were only twenty ships of the line in the Dutch navy, and they were generally old and in bad repair. Besides this, they could not get out of the English Channel to join forces with the French and Spanish; the British Channel Fleet would not let them.

There were many minor actions between British and Dutch ships in or near the North Sea, most of them British victories. The one significant battle that involved the Dutch occurred on August 5, 1781. Vice Admiral Hyde Parker, one of the officers scolded by Rodney for inattention to signals during the battle off Martinique, was back in the North Sea. With nineteen ships, five of them ships of the line, he was accompanying a convoy from the Baltic—undoubtedly one carrying much-needed naval stores for England—when he encountered a Dutch squadron, also convoying merchant ships and apparently headed toward the Baltic. The Dutch, with seventeen ships, of which three were ships of the line, were southwest of the British, and the courses of the two fleets were such that they were bound to meet. They were near the Dogger Bank, a shoal lying roughly in the center of the North Sea triangle between England, the Low Countries, and Denmark. Both sides had old, ailing ships, and some of the British vessels mounted fewer than their standard number of guns; they were considered too much weakened by decay to carry such a heavy load.

Parker sent his convoy and poorest ships off to England and prepared with seven ships to do battle with the Dutch commander, Rear Admiral Johan Arnold Zoutman. Zoutman likewise prepared, putting his convoy to his lee and ranging his line, also of seven ships, between his convoy and the British. Parker sought the battle in a most aggressive way, ordering the signal for line abreast—that is, closing the enemy—at 6:10 in the morning. His ships quickly approached the Dutch, running almost directly before the wind. The maneuver was carried out so fast that there was little time for the British sailors to prepare for firing, and the Dutch, if they themselves had been quick, could have fired first with deadly effect. Zoutman was apparently as deliberate as Parker was impetuous, however, and he waited to hoist his own battle signal until he saw the red British combat signal—the British called it "the bloody flag"—flying on Parker's flagship, the *Fortitude*.

The British had one minor problem. And it may indicate that Parker did indeed have the blind adherence to the doctrine of the line that seemed to cause him trouble off Martinique. Parker intended that his flagship should engage Zoutman's flagship as the two lines sailed on parallel courses, and his own ship was directly in the center of the line, where an admiral's flagship was usually placed (primarily so that the admiral's orders could be readily communicated by signals to the rest of the line in both directions). Zoutman's flagship, however, was fifth in his line of seven. Parker engaged her all the same, and the lines thus overlapped. For a while the rear British ship had no enemy to fight, while the second and third British ships faced three enemy ships. This situation was eventually corrected, and the action continued hotly for three hours. The Dutch then made for home, following their convoy, which had been sent toward the coast in the middle of the battle.

The battle was not a great victory for anyone. The British ships were too badly damaged to pursue the Dutch. Still, the Dutch convoy had been heading out, and it had to return home. Britain was keeping the Dutch merchant fleet off the seas.

Parker was undoubtedly bitter about his treatment by Rodney after the Martinique battle and disappointed at the lackluster results of his own battle, which he attributed largely to the old age, slowness, and paucity of the ships the Admiralty had given him. He was abrupt in discussing the Dogger Bank action with George III. "I wish your Majesty better ships and younger officers," he is reported to have said. "For myself, I am now too old for service."*

*As quoted by Mahan in Clowes, Vol. 3, p. 508.

Kempenfelt off Ushant

The so-called Second Battle of Ushant, fought three years after the first, was not really a battle, but it had a good deal of impact on the naval operations of 1782 in the West Indies. The French convoy carrying supplies for the Caribbean campaign of 1782, the one that was intended to capture Jamaica, left Brest in December of 1781. It was of crucial importance, and it was assumed that the British would send out a force to intercept it—as indeed they did. Admiral de Guichen was therefore assigned to escort the convoy clear of the Bay of Biscay, and was given twenty-one ships of the line to do the job.* Five of them were to continue to the West Indies with the convoy, and two were to sail out to the East Indies.

Watching for de Guichen was British Rear Admiral Richard Kempenfelt, to windward of the convoy with eleven or twelve ships of the line, one 50-gun vessel, and a few frigates. De Guichen should have been able to sail safely past this relatively small force, but when the two fleets came in sight of one another, on December 12, about a hundred and fifty miles southwest of Ushant, the French admiral had let his warships get out ahead of the convoy and, worse than that, to leeward of it, leaving the unarmed merchantmen vulnerable. Kempenfelt quickly saw the situation. Ignoring the warships, he headed for the transports, easily capturing fifteen before sunset, and sent them, with their valuable cargoes, off to England. De Guichen, with the wind against his naval ships, could do nothing to rescue them. Kempenfelt's fleet was still in sight when the sun rose the next morning, but it soon disappeared. Kempenfelt had no desire to risk his small fleet against de Guichen.

The convoy continued on its way toward the West Indies, but more trouble soon struck. Only a few days after the encounter with Kempenfelt, a severe storm arose, scattering the ships far and wide and severely damaging many. When the storm cleared, only two ships of the line and two transports were in shape to continue their journey to the West Indies. The rest eventually straggled back to Brest.

Although the French convoy operation had been disrupted, there was criticism of the Admiralty in Parliament for not having

*G. J. Marcus, *A Naval History of England*, Vol. 1, p. 432. Mahan has nineteen of the line.

given Kempenfelt a force adequate to his assignment. An opportunity for decisive victory had again been missed. Since Kempenfelt was popular with the Admiralty, there was no question of his having been slighted for political reasons. The administration in the Admiralty had simply failed to concentrate its forces for an important objective.

15

Carrying the War to Britain

The U.S. Navy had no great fleets with which to fight the British at sea. Seldom did more than two or three of the converted merchant ships or newly constructed frigates authorized by Congress sail or fight together. Never did they participate in the great battles the French fought off the North American coast. They protected American shipping and coastal towns as best they could, and looked for prizes, both naval vessels and merchantmen. Some of them pursued their quest far out into the Atlantic and to the shores of England itself.

Commerce Raiders

Capturing British merchant ships was a profitable occupation, and it attracted not only the few ships of the U.S. Navy, but hordes of privateers—fast vessels, privately owned, sometimes officially supported, and sufficiently well armed to challenge and capture slower and weaker merchant ships and to escape from their naval escorts. All nations spawned privateers. America had about two thousand sailing under its new flag. A few of them were based in France and sailed in British waters from time to time, some of them at least encouraged by the U.S. commissioners in France. With French, Dutch, Spanish, British, and American privateers swarming over the Atlantic, no merchantman's captain could sail with confidence that his ship would reach her destination unmolested.

What happened when ships were captured marked the difference between a U.S. privateer and a U.S. naval vessel. The privateers disposed of their prizes as they pleased, usually by selling the ship and the cargo. Proceeds were distributed among the crew in proportionate shares corresponding to the established order of rank. Many a young lad was attracted to a life at sea by tales of great profits from a richly laden British vessel. The prospect of capturing a prize or two helped make up for the misery that life could be aboard eighteenth-century sailing ships. It also attracted boys away from service in the navy, however, for Congress, having decided that the navy could help pay for the war, took part of the proceeds of all prizes taken by naval vessels, and the share that finally came to the ordinary seaman was likely to be rather small.

The Reprisal

One of the ships that found profit in the waters close to Britain, where merchantmen arrived from both east and west, was the U.S. naval brig *Reprisal*, commanded by Captain Lambert Wickes. After taking Benjamin Franklin to St. Nazaire late in 1776, Wickes cruised about in the English Channel. In January he returned to St. Nazaire with five prizes. He sold them, divided the money among his crew, and fitted out a schooner, the *Dolphin*. In May 1777 he was ready to go out again, this time with the *Dolphin* and the brig *Lexington*, as well as the *Reprisal*. They had fine luck off the Irish coast, where they captured eighteen vessels. Late in June, however, the three ships were spotted by a British 74-gun ship of the line, which pursued the *Reprisal*. Wickes managed to evade her and return safely to St. Nazaire. But since France was still neutral, the British government protested his use of French ports, and he was ordered to leave. He finally sailed for home on September 14, eluded the British ships that were waiting outside the harbor, and then ran into a gale off the coast of Newfoundland that destroyed the *Reprisal* with all hands.

The number and boldness of the privateers increased as the years passed. But none of their exploits were more dramatic than those of a Scotsman who wore the uniform of the U.S. Navy—another foreign-born volunteer who wrote a chapter of psychological warfare as well as one of courage and suspense on and off the coasts of the British Isles.

John Paul to John Paul Jones

John Paul was born in Galloway in 1747 and grew up near the waters that were to see some of his exploits in a foreign uniform thirty years later. He was not yet fourteen years old when, proud of the humble rank of ship's boy, he shipped aboard the brig *Friendship* out of Whitehaven bound for Barbados and Virginia. His oldest brother had preceded him across the Atlantic and was a tailor in Fredericksburg, Virginia, when Paul's ship took him there on the first of at least three such trips. Meeting his brother's friends and making his own, Paul established emotional ties that later would draw him to cast in his lot with the colonies when they needed men with experience in command at sea.

John Paul was a small man, with strong, alert features, well dressed and well mannered, attractive to and attracted by women. He was a hard worker and not an easy man to work for, demanding as much from his men as from himself, and not given to showing affection for his crews. Their feeling for him was not improved by his violent temper, and while he had devoted friends he had no less persistent enemies.

A little more than seven years after he shipped out of Whitehaven, John Paul, aged twenty-one, was given command of his first ship, the *John*. He was master of the *Betsy*, a large, square-rigged merchantman, in 1773, when an incident at Tobago put an end to his career as a merchant skipper. Forced to defend himself against a mutinous seaman, Paul ran him through with his sword. Whether wisely or not, he took the advice of some friends on Tobago and left the island hurriedly and secretly rather than risk trial or reprisal. Where he went is not clear, and when he next turned up, in Philadelphia in the fall of 1775, he was calling himself John Paul Jones. On December 7 of that year he accepted a commission as lieutenant in the Continental Navy.

After a first cruise on the ship *Alfred*, 30, on an expedition that raided Nassau in the Bahamas in 1776, Jones was given command of the sloop *Providence*, 12, and then of the *Alfred*. With both ships he captured numerous prizes and successfully avoided being captured by British warships. But already the new U.S. Navy was rent by politics and jealousy, and in January 1777 Jones was relieved of command of the *Alfred* with promises of a fleet but no immediate prospect of a new command. It was not until July 1 that he was sent to Portsmouth, New Hampshire, to take command of the new sloop of war *Ranger*, newly launched and being fitted out. His orders were to take her to France, where it was understood the commissioners were to procure a new frigate for him to command.

The Ranger

John Paul Jones's new command was 110 feet overall, her three masts were square rigged, and she was designed to carry twenty 9-pounder guns. Jones considered her too light for twenty, and carried only eighteen. On first sight he was delighted with his new ship, but he soon learned that her masts were too long and too heavy, and her sails were not only made of cheap cloth but were too large for her size. It was November 1 before Jones finally set sail, with 10 officers and 140 men, among them a French Canadian, a Swede, a few Irishmen, and two free blacks. On December 11 the *Ranger* arrived at Paimboeuf, the port of Nantes, bringing with her two fruit ships she had captured on the way.

Jones set off five days later for Paris, happy at the prospect of being rid of the *Ranger*, which had proved to be underballasted and oversparred, and confident that he would be taking command of the 154-foot ship *L'Indien*, which was being built in Amsterdam for the U.S. Navy.

Unfortunately, the situation had changed since Jones had left Portsmouth. The American commissioners in France, unable to persuade the neutral Dutch government, which was under pressure from the British, to let them take possession of *L'Indien*, had sold her to the French government.

Jones's visit to Paris won him the friendship of Benjamin Franklin and the enmity of Arthur Lee, and introduced him to the pleasures and intrigues of life in Paris, but try as he would he could not persuade the French government to give him *L'Indien*. So he went back to the *Ranger* at the end of January, with orders from the commissioners to "proceed with her in the manner you shall judge best for distressing the Enemies of the United States, by sea or otherwise, consistent with the laws of war, and the terms of your commission."

On February 13, 1778, one week after the treaty of alliance between France and the United States was signed, the *Ranger* weighed anchor. She stopped at Quiberon Bay and Cameret— long enough to have extensive alterations made—and finally at

Brest, where the French fleet of Lieutenant General le Comte d'Orvilliers was anchored. A Swedish officer, Lieutenant Jean Meiher, joined her there and took command of the marine guard.

The French frigate *Fortunée* and a tender escorted the *Ranger* past the waiting British outside the harbor of Brest on April 10, when Jones set off, intent on raiding an English port. He was imbued with the idea of taking a hostage for whom the British Government might exchange some of the many American seamen who were languishing in British prisons. Capturing two ships as she went, the *Ranger* headed generally north, into the Irish sea. Off the Isle of Man she met up with a revenue cutter, the *Hussar*, which escaped, after receiving one hit in the stern and two holes in the mainsail. Jones proceeded to capture and sink a coasting schooner, and then a sloop, near the entrance to the Firth of Clyde, before turning about and heading back to the Irish Sea. After an abortive attempt to capture the British sloop of war *Drake*, which was anchored in the Belfast Lough, he decided to make for the familiar harbor of Whitehaven and attack the town itself.

With forty men in two ship's boats, Jones headed for the shore at Whitehaven just after midnight on April 23, against an ebbing tide. It took three hours to reach the beach, where the plan was to spike the guns of the defending batteries on each side of the harbor and set fire to as much of the abundant coastwise shipping in the harbor as possible. While Jones and the crew of his boat were spiking the guns, however, those from the other boat were drinking in the nearest pub. One of these, an Irishman, turned traitor and dashed from house to house, warning people that there were pirates ashore, about to burn their houses and ships. The inhabitants swarmed toward the beach, and Jones and the rest of his men were forced to flee. But they left a fire burning merrily on the collier *Thompson*.

As the *Ranger* stood in closer to pick up the boats, confusion reigned ashore. The fire was soon put out, and little physical damage had been done. But psychologically the effect was enormous. Where would this brigand—who had been identified by someone who had known him as a young man as John Paul, now called Jones—strike next? Before the day was out the question was answered.

As soon as he was back aboard the *Ranger* Jones headed for his

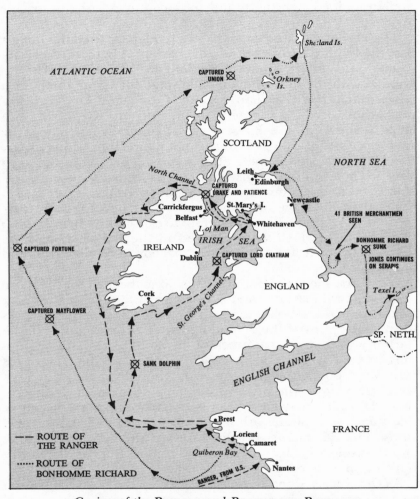

Cruises of the RANGER and BONHOMME RICHARD

next objective, St. Mary's Isle in Kirkcudbright Bay, about twenty miles away. He had conceived the idea that the Earl of Selkirk, whose home was on the island, would be a good hostage to offer in exchange for American prisoners. It was only ten o'clock that same morning when the *Ranger* reached the entrance to the bay. Jones climbed into a boat with two officers and a dozen men and was rowed to the island. As the group walked up the path toward the earl's grand house, they met a gardener, who informed them that the earl was away. Jones was in favor of abandoning the whole project, since its purpose was already defeated, but his companions begged to be allowed to proceed to the house and demand the family silver. He knew that there was grumbling among his crew over the Whitehaven project, which seemed futile to men whose objective was prize money, and recognized that another complete disappointment here might result in mutiny. So although asking for the family silver smacked of piracy, he sanctioned it, and the officers and a few of the men proceeded to the house. Lady Selkirk was gracious and compliant, and the silver was borne proudly back to the *Ranger*. But Jones was not at all happy about this adventure. He paid the crew the value of the silver from his own pocket—and after the war returned it to its rightful owners.

Jones's next objective was to take the *Drake*, which had been on his mind ever since his first attempt failed, although it was definitely not the sort of target his near-mutinous crew would have chosen. At daybreak the next morning the *Drake* was sighted emerging from Belfast Lough. Word of the presence of the "privateer" in the area had reached her captain, but he was taken in as the *Ranger*, disguised as a merchant vessel, came in sight, and he sent his gig with a crew to look her over. When the gig came within hailing distance Jones invited the officer in charge to come aboard. Only when he was on the *Ranger*'s deck was he informed that he was a prisoner of Captain John Paul Jones of the United States Navy. The unhappy crew of the *Ranger* were impressed with this performance, and they abandoned thoughts of mutiny at the prospect of engaging the *Drake*.

Jones's tactics were to lure the *Drake* into open water, then maneuver close enough to hail before abandoning his disguise, hoisting the U.S. flag, and opening fire. The *Drake* responded nobly to the *Ranger*'s broadside, but in an hour of close fighting her captain was killed and the second in command mortally wounded. The next senior officer surrendered, and Jones had a prize. He took her in tow, for her spars had been badly damaged, casting her off long enough the next day to capture the brigantine *Patience*. Then, with a jury rig and a prize crew aboard the *Drake*, Jones headed north, rounded the tip of Ireland, and went back to France. He sailed happily into Brest on May 8, 1778, twenty-eight days after he had left.

On the Beach

The months that followed this dramatic adventure were months of frustration for John Paul Jones, with one disappointment after another in his search for a new command. *L'Indien*, he found on his return, was still at Amsterdam and almost ready to sail. But, alas, she was French property, and still being held by the nonbelligerent Dutch. In spite of Franklin's assurances to Jones that she would be given to him, assurances that persuaded him to leave the *Ranger*, the Dutch refused to release *L'Indien* until they too entered the war. When the French government finally got her free she was sold to the duc de Montmorency-Luxembourg, and leased by him to Alexander Gillon of the South Carolina navy. Under his incompetent command she finally sailed for America in the summer of 1781. A lot had happened to John Paul Jones by that time.

Jones had turned down the offer of lesser ships and seen his hopes of commanding a U.S. fleet disappear. He scorned the suggestion of Franklin and others whom he badgered for a command that he give up and go home to try his luck with the Congress. He watched from the sidelines as the French and British fleets fought to a draw off Ushant. And although his raid on Whitehaven and capture of the *Drake* were well publicized and much applauded at home, no official recognition of his exploits came to raise his spirits.

The Bonhomme Richard

At last, on November 10, 1778, an Irish merchant at Lorient, one of numerous people Jones had begged to find him a ship he could convert to a warship, recommended to him *Le Duc de Duras*, a nine-hundred-ton vessel built in 1766 for the French East Indies trade. It was almost a month before Jones gave up hope of getting something else and went to Lorient to look her over, and two more months before he finally received word that the French king would buy her and give her to him to command, under the American flag. As Jones set about fitting *Le Duc* out for sea, he changed her name to *Bonhomme Richard*, in honor of Benjamin Franklin, whose *Poor Richard's Almanac* was well known in France as *Les Maximes du Bonhomme Richard*.

Lafayette returned to France at about this time, seeking men and ships for the American cause and hoping to find something for himself to do close to home. His efforts for the former mission contributed to the decision to dispatch Rochambeau and de Grasse to America. His efforts for the latter developed into a scheme for an amphibious operation against Liverpool. At Franklin's suggestion Jones was brought into the plan as commander of the fleet, and the two officers began to make preparations with great enthusiasm. Unfortunately word of the project reached Liverpool, where the frightened inhabitants promptly demanded more protection from the British government. Increased defenses meant the need for a bigger attacking force, and the French government couldn't or wouldn't countenance that. So the plan was abandoned.

Meanwhile, apparently with some help from Lafayette, John Paul Jones had not only been fitting out the *Bonhomme Richard*, he had been assembling a squadron. Largest among its ships was the brand new American frigate *Alliance*, on which Lafayette had returned to France. She was a good ship, with twenty-eight 12-pounders and eight 9-pounders, but she was commanded by a man who was at best odd and who some think was insane. Pierre Landais had served in the French navy until 1775, and after two years on the beach had gone to America in command of a supply ship, provided by Silas Deane with a recommendation to the Congress for a commission in the U.S. Navy. Landais had returned as captain of the *Alliance*.

Also assigned by the French government to Jones's command were the former privateer *Pallas*, a frigate with thirty-two guns, commanded by Capitaine de Brulot Cottineau de Kerloguen; the brig *Vengeance*, commanded by Lieutenant de Vaisseau Ricot; and a fast cutter, *Le Cerf*, that had formerly belonged to George III's navy. She carried eighteen guns and was commanded by Enseigne de Vaisseau Varage. The French commanders of these three vessels were all given commissions in the U.S. Navy upon joining Jones's squadron.

This was the time when the French were assembling a large fleet and troops for a joint operation with the Spanish to invade England. To support this project, John Paul Jones was ordered to take his squadron to Scotland or northern England to create a diversion that would attract British forces from the south. When the invasion project was ultimately aborted, Jones was off on what his final orders had reduced to a voyage around the British Isles and back to the Texel in Holland, attacking British commerce as opportunity offered.

On June 19 Jones's squadron set forth to escort some French ships in the Bay of Biscay. On this brief cruise Jones found, when he tried to challenge some British warships to fight, that the *Bonhomme Richard* was not as fast as he had hoped. More significantly, however, Captain Landais showed his insubordination by refusing to yield the right of way to the *Bonhomme Richard*. The result was a collision and damage to both ships. While repairs were being made, Jones revamped his crew, removing some English prisoners who had volunteered to serve but who proved to have mutinous intentions. His crew as finally constituted was made up of 380 men, of whom 79 were Americans, many of whom had been released from English prisons. The remainder offer an outstanding example of the involvement of men from other countries in America's fight for independence. They included 59 English volunteers, some French volunteers, Portuguese and Dutch sailors transferred from the French cutter *L'Epervier*, Irishmen (including a few officers), Scots, Swedes, Norwegians, Swiss, Italians, East Indians, and 137 French marines.

Two French privateers, the *Monsieur* and the *Granville*, joined the squadron, which assembled on August 10, 1779, at Ile de Groix and finally sailed on its fateful expedition four days later. The first vessel encountered was neutral, bound for Madeira from London. Commodore Jones graciously entertained her captain and supercargo—the officer in charge of her cargo— aboard his flagship and sent her on her way. The *Monsieur* captured a vessel on the eighteenth, and promptly deserted with her prize. Three days later a brigantine, the *Mayflower*, carrying provisions to London from Liverpool, was easily taken and sent off to Lorient with a prize crew.

Heading west of Ireland on August 23, Jones as easily took the brig *Fortune*, using two armed boats in a flat calm. She too was sent back to France. From that point on the voyage became more complicated. The first in a series of unfortunate incidents was the desertion by the coxswain and the Irish crew of the commodore's barge. They had been ordered to tow the *Richard* when, while becalmed, she was carried by the current too close to a rocky island off the southwest coast of Ireland. Cutting the towline at 10:30 P.M., the deserters headed for shore, soon pursued by another boat with three officers and men, which proceeded to get lost in the darkness and fog. That boat finally landed, and her crew was captured. The following day Jones sent the *Cerf* to look for them both, and she too disappeared. Never able to catch up, she returned to Lorient. By the evening of the twenty-fifth, Jones gave up looking for them all and headed north, his ship's sails reefed in a gale of wind. During the night Landais set off on an independent course in the *Alliance*, the *Granville* departed for good with a prize she had captured, and the *Pallas* lay to to repair her tiller. So on the morning of August 26 only the *Vengeance* and the *Bonhomme Richard* remained together.

While word of Jones's proximity spread through Ireland and England, he and his two vessels sailed four hundred and fifty miles in four days, taking advantage of good winds and bright days. Off the northwest corner of Scotland on September 1 the *Richard* captured the British ship *Union*, carrying clothing for the British army in Canada. Shortly thereafter the *Alliance* appeared, the area having been designated earlier as a point of rendezvous should the squadron become separated. She too had a prize, the *Betsey*. Both ships were sent by Landais, with prize crews from his own vessel, to Bergen, Norway, in spite of Jones's orders to send them to a French port. The *Vengeance* had her turn the following day, capturing an Irish brigantine. In the meantime the *Pallas* had appeared.

By this time the squadron was approaching the Shetland Islands. The ships cruised in that area for two or three days, the *Alliance* taking some small prizes and then departing again on an independent course, while the *Bonhomme Richard*, *Pallas*, and *Vengeance* headed south, well off the east coast of Scotland. The next land they sighted was near the Firth of Forth. After taking two colliers, Jones conceived the idea of sailing into the Firth, landing at Leith, seaport of Edinburgh, and demanding a ransom as an alternative to sacking the city. The captains of the *Pallas* and the *Vengeance* were far from enthusiastic, but they finally agreed to go along.

Beating up the Firth of Forth on September 16, with a pilot he had retained from a yacht encountered on the way in, John Paul Jones was intent on carrying out a detailed plan of action including landing parties and an ultimatum. Watchers on shore had already identified him, and word of the approach of the notorious Jones had terrified many and called out all local defense units, which amounted to more noise than substance. On September 17 the three vessels approached within a mile of Kirkcaldy, across the bay from Leith, but even as the townspeople there trembled the ships came about on the starboard tack and headed for Leith. The wind was freshening all the time, and before they came within cannon shot of their objective, it had become a gale. Jones could only shorten sail and run before it out of the Firth, reluctantly abandoning his project.

The little squadron headed down the coast, sighted occasionally from the shore, and spreading terror and alerting defenders as it went. Jones wanted very much to attack Newcastle, but the other captains would not cooperate, and that project too was abandoned. Various prizes were taken as the ships proceeded south. The *Bonhomme Richard* and the *Vengeance* sailed as far as the mouth of the Humber, where on September 22 Jones captured two pilots and tried in vain to lure some ships out of the river to fight, not daring to enter the estuary in a light and variable wind. The *Pallas* meanwhile was chasing prizes off Flamborough Head, and Jones turned north to join her. During the night Landais and the *Alliance* showed up once again.

The following afternoon, as the four vessels approached Flamborough Head, forty-one ships appeared to the north northeast, a convoy of ships from the Baltic escorted by the frigate *Serapis*, 44, commanded by Captain Richard Pearson, and the sloop of war *Countess of Scarborough*, 20, commanded by Captain Thomas Piercy. Both Captains Pearson and Jones decided to engage, John Paul Jones with the intention of trying to take some of the convoy after the battle, Pearson protecting his convoy by diverting the enemy while the merchantmen took shelter under the guns of Scarborough Castle.

Jones signaled a general chase to his three other ships and put all sail on the *Bonhomme Richard*. Just as the sun was setting, at 6:00 P.M., he hoisted the signal to form a line of battle. The three other ships ignored it. The *Alliance*, which had been leading, fell off, the *Pallas*, astern of the *Richard*, turned away, and the *Vengeance* continued on her own course. With the wind southwest by south, and the *Richard* to windward of the *Serapis*, both ships headed west on the port tack. Jones was flying a British flag—a legitimate ruse—as he moved in closer.

When they reached pistol range Captain Pearson, having opened his gunports, challenged, "What ship is that?" "The *Princess Royal*!" was the answer, as Jones sought time to ready for action. "Where from?" came the next question. This time the answer was the striking of the British colors, hoisting of a big American ensign, and the order to fire a broadside. The *Serapis*'s response was almost simultaneous. One or two broadsides later, two of the old 18-pounders Jones had mounted below decks in the gunroom exploded, rendering the others unserviceable, killing many of the gunners, and blowing a hole in the deck above. As the furious exchange continued, Jones, well aware that he was outgunned, attempted to grapple on to the *Serapis* and board, maneuvering up to her starboard quarter. The attempt failed. Then as Pearson tried to cross the *Richard*'s bow and rake her, Jones ran his bow into his enemy's stern. Seeing the *Richard* in this highly unfavorable position—her deck a mass of rigging, splinters, wounded men, and blood, and with no flag visible—it is little wonder that Pearson called out, "Has your ship struck?"

Struck she had, the stern of the *Serapis*. But her colors? Never! "I have not yet begun to fight!" yelled Jones, as he backed his topsails to get clear of the other vessel and moved into position again upwind from the *Serapis*. Pearson dropped back to get broadside to the *Richard*. Jones, taking advantage of a fair puff of wind, moved ahead and then bore off to try to cross his enemy's bow and rake her. But he was too close. The jibboom of the *Serapis* caught in the shrouds of the *Richard*'s mizzenmast, and the wind caused both vessels to pivot so that they lay side by side, bow to stern, headed north and south. To secure the position still further, a fluke of the *Serapis*'s starboard anchor hooked the side of the *Richard*. There they stayed, with the muzzles of their guns touching each other's sides.

For Jones the unique position was an advantage, for he was outgunned and knew he could win only by cutting up the rigging of the *Serapis* and disabling her crew with muskets and hand grenades. Pearson tried in vain to separate the vessels, in order to bring his broadside to bear. Those who tried to cut the lines that held them—Jones had ordered grappling hooks set to cement the relationship—were picked off by the accurate fire of the *Richard*'s French marines. Pearson's attempt to separate them by dropping an anchor and using the force of wind and tide merely fixed them with the *Serapis*'s bow and the *Richard*'s stern firmly into the wind.

The British 18-pound guns continued to fire into the *Richard*, in spite of problems of loading at such close quarters. They silenced the American's 12-pounders, leaving Jones with only three 9-pounders on the quarterdeck. The French marines and assorted gunners high in the *Richard*'s spars and rigging kept up such murderous fire that few men stayed alive on the deck of the *Serapis*. Many others were killed by grenades thrown through the hatches.

Both ships were afire, but the fighting continued. In vain Jones hoped for help from his other ships. The *Vengeance* merely sailed around and watched, the *Pallas* was fighting, and defeating, the *Countess of Scarborough*, and the eccentric Landais was sailing back and forth in the *Alliance*, occasionally firing a broadside at the *Bonhomme Richard*. She was now filling so fast through the many breaches in her hull that the prisoners she had picked up were released to man the pumps.

At last a grenade dropped down a hatch on the *Serapis* touched off an explosion of powder cartridges, and the *Richard*'s 9-pounders, aimed at the enemy's mainmast with double-headed shot, began to weaken it. Pearson made an abortive attempt to put a boarding party on the *Richard*, but his men were driven back to their own vessel. Although Jones's men were ready to give up, Jones refused, and he was rewarded. Just after 10:30 Captain Pearson, realizing that his mainmast was about to go, tore down the ensign he had nailed to the staff. An American officer boarded the *Serapis* and escorted Pearson back aboard the *Bonhomme Richard*. In proper fashion he handed his sword to Commodore Jones, who promptly handed it back. Then the two went to Jones's cabin to drink a glass of wine.

At the end of the battle, which had lasted almost three hours and a half, each ship was a shambles. Jones had lost about a hundred and fifty men, Pearson about a hundred and twenty. A few sails could still be set on the *Serapis*'s foremast and what remained of the mizzen, but the *Bonhomme Richard* was so riddled with holes that the most desperate efforts to keep her afloat proved insufficient. Regretfully, John Paul Jones moved his flag to the *Serapis*, transferred the wounded and the crew to other vessels, and watched his ship disappear into the waters of the North Sea at 11:00 A.M. on September 25.

While British ships put to sea and searched in vain for Jones and his squadron, the *Serapis, Alliance, Countess of Scarborough, Pallas*, and *Vengeance* sailed straight to the Texel, as Jones had been ordered when he left France. This proved embarrassing to the Dutch, who were still neutral and were under pressure from the British government to treat Jones as a pirate and seize his prizes. The Danish government did just that, turning over to the British the three vessels that Landais had sent to Bergen. Months passed while Jones tried to get his prisoners, of whom he had 504, including 26 British officers, exchanged for Americans and to have repairs made to his ships.

Word of the victory of the *Bonhomme Richard* delighted Americans at home and their friends abroad. In Paris, where Jones promptly sent an official report to the commissioners, it was the talk of the town.

The Alliance

Jones left his prize, *Serapis*, and transferred to the *Alliance*, having shipped Landais off to be relieved of command by Franklin. On the morning of December 27 he finally sailed from the Texel with a fair wind and eluded the British ships that had been lying in wait for him. Boiling along with an east wind that reached gale force, he covered the first seventy miles in seven hours, continued on through the English Channel, and arrived off Ushant by midnight of December 31. Then the *Alliance* headed south, searching for British shipping with very little success. She put in at Corunna in Spain for some repairs and provisions in mid-January, and after crossing the Bay of Biscay finally sailed into Lorient on February 19.

The Congressional Board of Admiralty was anxious to have the *Alliance* back home, and Jones found a letter from Franklin waiting for him, urging him to leave as soon as possible, with sixteen thousand stand of arms that Lafayette had obtained and a hundred and twenty bales of uniform cloth. But his departure was delayed while more work was done on the *Alliance*, and Jones went to Paris to enjoy its delights, admired and feted everywhere as a hero. He was already well known and popular there, but now, in the words of John Adams, "the cry of Versailles and the clamour of Paris became as loud in the favour of Monsieur Jones as of Monsieur Franklin, and the inclination of the ladies to embrace him almost as fashionable and as strong."* While enjoying the pleasures of Paris, however, Jones worked during his stay there at trying to get the French government to sell the prizes he had captured so that he could distribute the money among his crew.

During Jones's absence Landais went to Lorient, where with the help of Arthur Lee he stirred up support for himself and antagonism to Jones among the *Alliance*'s crew. Two days after Jones returned to the port, without the prize money, Landais seized the ship while Jones was still ashore. Jones ultimately gave up the attempt to recapture his own command, and Landais sailed for America at the end of June. His actions on that voyage were so irrational that his officers, led by Lee, who was aboard as a passenger, forced him to give up the command. He was later court-martialed and dismissed from the navy.

The Ariel

After a long wait ashore, Jones was finally given command of the sloop *Ariel*. She had been loaned by the French government, one of whose frigates had captured her from the British off the Carolinas. Jones was to carry to America some of the goods that had not fitted aboard the *Alliance*. With a nucleus of survivors of the *Bonhomme Richard*, some Americans, English prisoners, and a French marine guard, and carrying eleven thousand muskets, uniforms for ten thousand men, a hundred and twenty bales of cloth and eight hundred barrels of powder, the *Ariel* finally sailed from Lorient on September 5, 1780, delayed over a month at Groix roads, sitting out bad weather. When she finally put to sea, on October 7, the *Ariel* ran into a very heavy storm and was so badly damaged that Jones ordered the foremast and main-mast cut away; the mizzen was carried away. Anchored to wind-ward of a reef, Jones rode out the storm in his battered vessel until the wind finally abated at midnight on October 11. With a jury rig she sailed back to Groix the next morning. Jones was

*Samuel E. Morison, *John Paul Jones*, p. 250.

applauded for surviving the storm, which had wrecked vessels and drowned men all along the coast of Brittany.

Another two months passed while the *Ariel's* repairs were made. On December 18 she sailed again. Two months later Jones finally dropped anchor at Philadelphia, having almost captured a British privateer, the *Triumph*, on the way. The *Triumph's* captain, having been taken by surprise and engaged at pistol range, struck his colors, then sailed off, too rapidly to be caught, while Jones was preparing to lower a boat and board.

This ended John Paul Jones's active career in the U.S. Navy. Although Congress gave him command of the ship of the line *America*, under construction at Portsmouth in June 1781, she was far from ready for sea. The battle at Yorktown came and went as he waited. Jones, upon learning of the preparations for the crucial battle, asked to serve on Lafayette's staff, but unfortunately his request did not reach Lafayette, who would have granted it, until after the battle.

The *America* was approaching completion in September 1782, when Congress, hard pressed for money to complete her, presented her to the French king to replace a ship of the line, *Le Magnifique*, which had been lost in August on a rock in Boston Harbor.

Disappointed in his hopes for a major command, Jones decided to seek the experience with fleet maneuver he had always hoped for by sailing as a passenger with the fleet of French Lieutenant General le Marquis de Vaudreuil. The ships set sail on Christmas Eve of 1782, and they were at Puerto Cabello, Venezuela, when word of the signing of the Treaty of Paris arrived.

The career of John Paul Jones thus not only touches on many of the international aspects of the American Revolution but clearly reveals the lack of organization and planning of its naval aspects. Frustrating as it was to him to spend month after month trying to get to sea in command of a good ship or an expedition, in retrospect the more striking aspect is the gross negligence of the Americans and French in wasting so much of this imaginative and highly competent sailor's time on the land.

16

On the Other Side of the Earth

While British and French armies were fighting in North America, and British and French fleets were fighting naval battles in the Caribbean, forces of the two nations were also fighting half a world away. They were fighting for power and territory, and for trading rights and all-important seaports for the merchant ships that carried spices and tea to Europe, including the tea that found its destiny in the waters of Boston Harbor.

The war in and near India, so far off, so intricately enmeshed with exotic Asian peoples and issues, sometimes seemed entirely unrelated to the rest of the war. But it was related. Frenchmen fought Englishmen on the coast of Coromandel and off Trincomalee as they did in North America and off the Virginia capes. But in India they also fought dark-skinned men who knew nothing of North America nor the war there of which theirs was a distant part.

It is hard for a modern occidental to gain an accurate impression of this oriental part of the war of American independence. Governments, arms, and men in India were utterly alien, not only to the ways and thoughts of twentieth century America but also to those of eighteenth-century Europe. Armies, with or without a nucleus of Europeans, often comprised tens of thousands of Indian cavalry and foot soldiers, all bringing with them widely varying customs, capabilities, and motivations— and also bringing their families and camp followers. The fighting men were often only a tenth of the horde; the trailing collection of humanity included traders and the wives and children of soldiers as well as officers. Usually they lived off the land they swarmed over. Baggage, which meant tents and furniture and other amenities of home in addition to the necessities of war, was carried in bullock-drawn carts; officers were carried in litters. Much of the fighting was done by mercenaries, the sepoys, drawn from all over India and trained in something vaguely approaching European tactics. European methods had been superimposed on people who had been warring for centuries. Both had been changed in the process.

India in the Late Eighteenth Century

India was not a nation in the eighteenth century, but a land of rival potentates. The decay of the Mogul Empire had resulted in chaotic struggles for power among the Indian states and principalities. Europeans, who had been trading there since the sixteenth century, vied with one another for the support, and the territory, of the warring factions.

Portuguese ships had led the way around the Cape of Good Hope to India, and for a long time the Portuguese had almost a monopoly on the trade they found there. But they were followed by Dutch, English, French, and Danish merchants, who found the four to six-month trip to the East lucrative. By the middle of the eighteenth century the Portuguese and the Dutch had been replaced as the chief traders in India by the British and the British East India Company. Chartered by Queen Elizabeth I in 1600, the British East India Company both represented the British government in India and was itself the government of the areas it controlled. It had its own army and it controlled enclaves around a number of ports, of which the most important were Calcutta, Madras, and Bombay.

Chief rival of the British in India for trading rights and the support of the native rulers in mid-century was the French Compagnie des Indes Orientales, whose principal post was Pondicherry, on the Coromandel coast in southeast India, between the British posts at Madras and Fort St. David. Founded in 1664, the Compagnie had become strong enough by the mid-eighteenth century so that British and French fought in India in the War of the Austrian Succession and again in the Seven Years' War. As in North America, Europe, and the Caribbean, the Seven Years' War set the stage in India for the war spawned by the American Revolution. Unlike the wars elsewhere, those in India involved large native forces with their own objectives, as well as the two European powers.

The Peninsula of India

The Seven Years' War

The first confrontation between English and French forces in the Seven Years' War was in Bengal, where the French controlled the port of Chandernagore, and the East India Company had a thriving trading post and town at Calcutta and Fort William. Siraj-ad-daula, nawab of Bengal, captured Calcutta in June 1756, before news of the war reached India. Six months later, Robert Clive, who had been responsible for the establishment of British domination in the Carnatic, in southern India, supported by five warships under the command of Vice Admiral Charles Watson, retook Calcutta and then marched on the French fort at Chandernagore. With Watson's fleet controlling traffic on the river, the fort held out under heavy bombardment for only a week. On June 23, 1757, with about three thousand men, including the 39th Foot, the first British army troops to be sent to India, Clive soundly defeated the nawab, who had amassed at Plassey fifty thousand men, including a detachment of French troops and some European artillery officers, most of whom were also French. This established British control over all of Bengal.

Meanwhile, while Clive and most of the British troops were in Bengal, in the Carnatic a French force of both army and Compagnie troops commanded by the Irish-French comte de Lally (baron de Tollendal), who had recently arrived from France, had laid siege to Fort St. David and captured it. But a siege at Madras failed when British reinforcements arrived by sea. And at Wandiwash the French were soundly defeated by a British force commanded by Major Eyre Coote, who thereupon, in May 1760, besieged Lally, who had withdrawn to Pondicherry. With food and supplies gone, and lacking seapower to support him, Lally surrendered on January 15, 1761. Since the other French forts in India had all been taken, this marked the end of the French presence in India until 1763, when the Treaty of Paris restored all the forts to France. But the most important, Pondicherry, had been reduced to rubble. Lally meanwhile had been charged with treachery, and when allowed by his British captors after two years' imprisonment to return to Paris to clear his name he was found guilty and beheaded.

Hyder Ali

The most powerful Indian leader in the 1760s and 1770s, and most bothersome to the British, was Hyder Ali, who was undisputed head, although not the titular sovereign for most of the period, of Mysore, a state in southwest India. Son of an army officer and man of property in Mysore, Hyder claimed descent from Mohammed. He stood about five foot five, was fat but spry, and wore an immense turban. His big face was clean-shaven and otherwise distinguished by his small nose. He controlled huge territories, but whether because of a learning problem or, as one of his biographers put it, "his impetuous character, impatient of every restraint," he never learned to read.*

Hyder rose rapidly to an army command through a combination of ability and influence, and was in and out of favor with the *dulaway* (prime minister) of Mysore, who dominated the weak rajah. At length the dulaway's jealousy led him to send Hyder a cordial invitation that was in fact a trap to assassinate him. Since Hyder kept a paid spy at court, one Kendeh Rao, he learned what was going on. He seized the dulaway, whom he thenceforth confined, with a generous pension, and he forced the terrified rajah to make him dulaway, with the prestigious title of *bahadur*.

The timid rajah subsequently conspired with the Marathas, his traditional enemies, to seize Hyder, and sent an army against him under the command of—of all people—Kendeh Rao, Hyder's quondam spy! Hyder tricked Kendeh Rao and took over his deserting troops. Kendeh Rao he confined in an iron cage until he died. The rajah remained nominal ruler of Mysore until late in Hyder's regime, when Hyder took the title for himself.

Hyder Ali was wise in judging men, fatherly toward his subjects, impartial in administering justice, encouraging of agriculture and science, strict in military discipline, and pitiless toward his enemies, especially the English, who inspired him with both hate and terror.

The First Mysore War

Since early in the eighteenth century Mysore had threatened English power in India. While the Carnatic and Bengal were

---

*Langlais in *Biographie Universelle*, 1967 edition, Vol. 20, pp. 245ff.

torn by war, Hyder annexed Bednore, Sunda, Sera, Canara, Guti, and other petty states. He made an alliance with Lally in 1760 and sent some troops to help the French at Pondicherry. But when no feasible plan could be agreed on, they returned to Mysore.

In 1766 Clive consolidated alliances with the Nizam of Hyderabad (which gave the East India Company control of about eighty miles of coast north of the Carnatic) and with the powerful confederacy of the Marathas, largely for protection against Hyder. But with bribes and influence Hyder won over these fickle allies (who soon deserted him too), fought his way to Madras, and dictated terms of a peace treaty which included a promise by the British to aid him if he should be attacked by any other power. This ended what the British called the First Mysore War.

Notwithstanding this treaty, when the Marathas attacked Mysore in 1771 the British did not help Hyder, and so, eight years later, with the British facing a rebellion in America, Hyder got the Nizam and the Marathas to join him against them.

British vs. French Again

In 1773 a move was made in London to bring the British East India Company, which was in fact representing Britain in India, under government control. As part of this plan, a governor general was appointed, senior to the formerly independent governors of Bombay, Madras, and Calcutta. Named to the post was Warren Hastings, an old hand in India, who had first gone there in 1750 as a minor official of the company and had been governor of Bengal since 1772. He was a good choice for the new post and proved able to contend with fractious members of his council as well as with the complex problems of defending and extending British interests in India.

When word reached India on July 7, 1778, that the French were again at war with Britain, Hastings immediately ordered the seizure of French possessions and sent troops from Calcutta to Madras to carry out the order. France had reoccupied the trading centers restored to them by the Treaty of Paris and tried to rebuild the trade and influence French representatives in India had formerly enjoyed. Small garrisons were stationed at all French ports. Pondicherry had regained much of its importance and was again the principal French port. But it was not fully equipped to maintain a fleet, and the French warships assigned to protect shipping to the East were based thousands of miles away on Ile de France. The French presence in India was by no means dead, and Hastings was determined that the war that had its beginning in the American Revolution should not give France an opportunity to diminish the British influence that had been increasing rapidly since the Seven Years' War.

Chandernagore was lightly protected, and British forces promptly took it from its French defenders. On the west coast of India British troops based at Bombay quickly occupied French Mahé. But Mahé was within the jurisdiction of Hyder Ali, and its seizure gave the leader of Mysore an excuse for supporting the French and attempting to drive the British from the Carnatic.

Pondicherry was the primary target for the British, and preparations to attack it began as soon as Hastings issued his order. From Madras Major General Sir Hector Munro, with East India Company troops, native troops, and British army troops, moved down the coast and arrived outside Pondicherry on August 8, 1778. His movements were coordinated with those of the British East India Squadron, commanded by Commodore Sir Edward Vernon. As the troops appeared on land, Vernon's two ships of the line and three frigates approached by sea and anchored to blockade the port. Shortly thereafter a French squadron appeared. Commanded by a Captain Tronjoly, it had one ship of the line, two frigates, and two smaller armed vessels. Vernon sailed out and chased the French ships, and on July 10 there was a desultory engagement that was not decisive and didn't do a great deal of damage to either. Tronjoly subsequently sailed into Pondicherry, but when Vernon reappeared he decided not to risk further action. He set sail for Ile de France, leaving the seas around India to the British. Pondicherry, cut off on land and sea, once again surrendered, on October 15, 1778.

To protect British interests in India, in the spring of 1779 a fleet of six ships of the line was sent from Britain to India, under command of Rear Admiral Sir Edward Hughes. Although at the same time a few ships were sent from France to Ile de France, and Commodore le Comte Thomas d'Orves was sent out to command them, they did not proceed to the Far East until 1781.

The Second Mysore War

While the British held control of the waters around India, on land British armies were busy fighting the Indian allies of France. In July 1780, Hyder Ali, still smarting under the British refusal to help him nine years earlier, and eager to support the French and to eliminate British influence in the Carnatic, descended from the hills onto the coastal plan with eighty thousand to a hundred thousand men and a hundred guns. He proceeded to attack British garrisons in interior towns, seized Arcot, the capital of the Carnatic, and eventually retook Pondicherry. The main British force was split between Madras, where Sir Hector Munro was in overall command, and Guntur, farther north. Hyder sent his son Tipu Sahib to attack the force at Guntur, which was commanded by a Colonel Baillie. Overwhelmed by the much larger force, lacking artillery ammunition, and poorly led, Baillie's force was almost completely wiped out before Munro could arrive from Madras to help. Sir Hector could then only return as rapidly as possible to Madras. In three weeks Hyder had taken most of the British posts in the Carnatic. At this critical juncture Hastings sent General Sir Eyre Coote down from Calcutta to confront the emergency.

Tall, eagle-eyed, and hawk-nosed, Irish-born General Coote, with the 39th Foot, had played a vital part in Clive's victory at Plassey in 1757, won a decisive victory over the French at Wandiwash in 1760, and commanded the land forces which participated in the capture of Pondicherry. Now fifty-three, he was in poor health, but his military capacity was still outstanding, and his sense of duty sent him, grumbling and bad-tempered, to the Carnatic.

Assembling an army of seventy-five hundred men and fifty-two guns at Madras, Coote proceeded to relieve the British forts that Hyder's men were besieging and retake the ones they had occupied. One after another fell into his hands—Chingleput, Carangooly, Wandiwash, and then Permacoil. Late in January 1781 comte d'Orves and the French squadron finally appeared off Fort St. George near Madras. Coote, hearing of this and knowing that Hughes and the British fleet were wintering at Bombay, feared that the French might try to land troops. But d'Orves was short of supplies and of spare parts for his vessels, and he was carrying no troops. So he avoided combat. He anchored for a time at Pondicherry, and although Hyder Ali begged him to put a force ashore, he refused and soon sailed back to Ile de France.

Coote by this time was himself short of supplies. He moved into Fort St. David at Cuddalore (Goudelour) on February 9, 1781, and waited there for five dismal months for enough supplies to maintain his army. Grain finally came by sea from Madras, but beef and mutton were scarce, and sickness at Fort St. David was widespread. Tipu Sahib attacked the position in June but was repulsed. Then Coote tried in vain to relieve Thiagar, which was under siege by some of Hyder's troops. At last Hughes returned from the Malabar Coast, bringing with him supplies and two battalions of men, which gave Coote enough force to challenge Hyder.

Porto Novo

When Coote finally moved out of Fort St. David late in June, he tried unsuccessfully to capture Chillumbrum and then went to Porto Novo, just south of Cuddalore, where supply ships from Madras landed provisions for his army. He knew that Hyder Ali, with a large force, was between him and Cuddalore, but because the Mysorean cavalry was constantly patrolling outside the British camp it was impossible to scout the area to determine where and how the force was deployed.

At five in the morning of June 1, 1781, Coote formed his men, eighty-five hundred of them, each supplied with four days' rations (mostly rice), and started north for Cuddalore, prepared for battle. Delegating two regiments of cavalry and a battalion of sepoys with three 6- and four 3-pounders to protect his large baggage train, he sent them ahead, along the seacoast, between the road the army was traveling and the sea, to keep them away from the coming battle. The rest of the force marched out onto the plain, astride the road in two lines. The first, with two regiments of native cavalry, three European and five sepoy infantry battalions, and thirty guns, was commanded by Sir Hector Munro. The second line, commanded by Major General James Stuart, had four sepoy battalions and twenty-six guns.

When the army had proceeded for about a mile the enemy was sighted, and Coote called a halt, while he and his staff reconnoitered. The British troops were just within range and sight of the enemy as they waited, but their supply of ammunition was low,

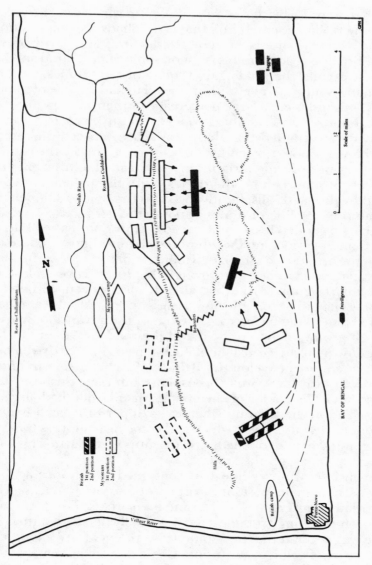

Road to Chillumbram

Road to Cuddalore

Nullah River

N

Myscorean camp

Redoubts

Vellaur River

Baggage

Intelligence

BAY OF BENGAL

Hills

British camp

Porto Novo

British
1st position
2nd position

Mysoreans
1st position
2nd position

0   1   2   3   4
Scale of miles

GPH

Battle of Porto Novo, July 1, 1781

and they were forbidden to return the fire which was showered upon them. Coote soon found that Hyder had taken his position behind a line of redoubts west of, overlooking, and partly across the Cuddalore road, with his right on some high ground and his left just beyond the road against a line of sand dunes that ran north and south, parallel with the sea. He had a force of about sixty thousand men, a large percentage of them cavalry, including six hundred and twenty Europeans, mostly French officers.

Having ascertained that there was space between the dunes and the sea, Coote turned his lines into columns by the simple expedient of ordering a right face. He headed to his right and then left around behind the dunes. With his movements concealed by the sand hills, he advanced his first line to an opening he found in the line of dunes opposite the left rear of Hyder's line. He positioned his second line to occupy dominating hills at his left and overlooking the left of the enemy's line of redoubts. When the artillery was in place, Coote again formed his first line for battle and marched out through the dunes, covered by fire from Stuart's guns. Hyder had already hastily been shifting his infantry and guns from the now useless line of redoubts and had formed a new line facing east in front of the advancing British, on high ground between them and the road. Waves of cavalry swept down on the British line. Each time they were driven off. In an attempt to envelop the British left, Hyder sent infantry and cavalry to attack Stuart's positions, but the British resisted stubbornly. The leader of the attack, Meer Sahib, had already been killed in the fighting when the skipper of a small British schooner, the *Intelligence*, which had come near shore, saw what was going on and opened fire to support Stuart. This was enough to break up the attack.

Meanwhile Munro's line had continued to advance against Hyder's new main position, in spite of repeated attacks. The Mysorean infantry line wavered and then broke. Hyder Ali, who had been watching from nearby, was finally persuaded that the battle was lost and that he should leave the field. All about him his army was fleeing in confusion. Coote moved his men into the vacated positions, rested his army for two days, and then proceeded to Cuddalore.

In mid-July Coote again took to the field, capturing Wandiwash, enlarging his force to twelve thousand by adding, at Madras, a detachment of sepoys that had come by land from Bengal, and then taking a series of forts, including Tripassore

(August 22), Polilur (August 27), and Sholinghur (September 27). In October, on the other side of the world, Yorktown surrendered, but that British loss had no immediate effect on the war in the East.

The victories in India restored English confidence there, but they were not decisive victories. Coote had made no real progress toward driving Hyder out of the Carnatic, and he had made no real territorial gains. He was a sick and weary man, and in the fall he returned to Calcutta.

Hastings and the Marathas

While Hyder Ali and the French had been occupying British attention in southern and eastern India, Governor Hastings in Calcutta had been contending with the Marathas, who had been fighting the British off and on for many years. After two treaties between the British government at Bombay and the peshwa (chief minister) of the Marathas had been annulled or ignored, in 1778 the government of the Marathas at Poona had enlisted the services of a French adventurer, the chevalier de St. Lubin, and promised the French, who were at war with the British by this time, a port on the west coast of India in return for their support. Thereafter the Marathas defeated British-led forces from Bombay and in 1779 dictated the humiliating Treaty of Wadgaon. By its terms the British government in Bombay withdrew its troops from Maratha territory and gave up the territory it had gained since 1773.

Hastings promptly repudiated the Treaty of Wadgaon and sent troops from Calcutta all the way across central India to strengthen the Bombay forces. One by one they captured Maratha cities. In May 1782 a new treaty was signed with the Marathas, the Treaty of Salbai. Although it merely restored the *status quo ante bellum*, this treaty gave the British twenty years of peace with the Marathas and permitted them to concentrate their efforts against the French and the forces of Mysore.

Action in Western India

With peace in the north, Hastings, with the support of the government at Madras, put pressure on the British government in Bombay to mount an expedition against Hyder Ali's western provinces, and draw Hyder away from the Carnatic. Fresh British troops were sent by sea to Calicut on the southwest coast of India, where they were joined by troops marching south from Bombay. When this combined force invaded Mysore from the west, Hyder Ali was forced to detach troops from his force at Cuddalore and elsewhere in the Carnatic and send them across southern India. Led by Hyder's son, Tipu Sahib, the Mysoreans drove the invaders out.

Early in 1783 the Bombay government organized another attack from the west, this time under the command of an East India Company officer, Brigadier General Richard Mathews. This force attacked the city of Mangalore on the Malabar coast about four hundred and fifty miles south of Bombay, and the province of Bednur, which lay behind it. The attack was helped by a disloyal Mysorean commander, Aiyaz Khan, who surrendered the provincial capital on condition of being allowed to serve there under the British. Mangalore was quickly captured, and soon thereafter Bednur was occupied. Again Tipu, taking a major part of the army from the Carnatic, hastened to the area. Finding the invaders widely dispersed, he easily defeated Mathews and captured him and most of his troops. Only Mangalore remained in British hands.

With the Mysorean forces mostly in the west, there appeared to be an opportunity to attack in the Carnatic. Coote had returned to Calcutta in the fall of 1782, and his place as commander in chief in the Madras area had been taken by Major General James Stuart, who had commanded the second column at Porto Novo and lost a leg later in the year at Polilur. In 1783 he had little ambition or enterprise, but he summoned his energies and assembled a force to attempt to retake Cuddalore from the French and Mysoreans, who had taken it in April 1782. But in the meantime a real threat to British control of the Indian Ocean had arrived off the coast in February.

17

Suffren Challenges British Seapower

The new force in Indian waters was Vice Admiral Suffren, the French seaman for whom Napoleon later longed when he found no living Frenchman strong enough to pit against Nelson.

Suffren's reputation is based on his battles off India, even though he did not win any clear-cut victories there. What was striking about Suffren were his vigor, energy, and aggressiveness. His style was very different from the customary French approach—so clearly demonstrated in the war's Caribbean operations—of avoiding the weather gauge, firing at the enemy's rigging, and always keeping an escape route open.

The French Fleet Arrives

After Suffren's encounter with British Admiral Johnstone at Porto Praia, and his successful forestalling of Johnstone at the Cape of Good Hope, he had sailed on to Ile de France, convoying troops and supply ships for India and a shipload of presents for Hyder Ali from the French king. He arrived in October 1781, a week after the surrender of Yorktown, joining the command of the comte d'Orves. On December 7 the fleet set sail for India.

It was a long trip from Ile de France to India, and for Suffren not uneventful. On January 18, 1782, the French fleet encountered the British ship *Hannibal*, 50, which was on her way to India. The winds were light and she could not elude the larger vessels of the French fleet. Her captain fought gallantly but ultimately struck her colors. Three weeks later the comte d'Orves died, and Suffren succeeded to command of the fleet,

249

which comprised three 74s, seven 64s, two 50s, three frigates, and three corvettes.

While the French ships were sailing east, Admiral Hughes, having learned of the Dutch entry into the war, had sent the frigate *Seahorse*, 24, to blockade the important Dutch port of Trincomalee on the island of Ceylon. Aware that a French fleet was on its way to the east, he decided to take possession of Trincomalee, lest the comte d'Orves, whom of course he expected to be in command, decide to use this desirable harbor and its facilities as a base for his fleet; French Pondicherry had never been sufficiently rebuilt to support such a force. On January 4 Hughes and his fleet sailed into the harbor of Trin-comalee. He proceeded to land five hundred sepoys, a battalion of sailors, and a detachment of marines. The Dutch garrison resisted strenuously, but one of the two forts fell to the marines on January 5, and the other was finally taken by the sailors and marines on January 11.

Leaving a small garrison in Trincomalee, Hughes returned to Madras, where, on February 15, lookouts reported the approach of Suffren's fleet. Suffren had come to reconnoiter the situation. Noting the size of Hughes's fleet—two 74s, one 68, five 64s, and one 50, plus two frigates—and the shore batteries that protected it, he canvassed his captains as to whether to attack. All but one were opposed. The prospect cannot have been very attractive after over two months at sea, and with a large convoy to protect. Suffren followed the view of the majority and headed south for Pondicherry, which was in the friendly possession of Hyder Ali. Hughes put to sea after dark and followed.

Suffren had turned away after his first view of the enemy, but, unlike the comte d'Orves on his earlier visit, he had come to India to fight. He intended to use his fleet to expand French power in India. In pursuit of that aim, his primary objective was to seize a naval base, Trincomalee or Negapatam, that was adequate to support his fleet, and before he could achieve that objective, he had to defeat the British fleet that protected those bases. In the next year and a half, he managed to engage Hughes five times in major battles. For the sake of convenience each is generally known by the name of the place on the coast nearest to the spot where it was fought. The first of them takes the name of a small, otherwise undistinguished town south of Madras.

Sadras

During the night of February 16-17, Suffren's warships became separated from the slower transports they were convoying, and when the sun came up Hughes sighted the French ships of the line twelve miles east of his own fleet, and the transports about nine miles southwest. It was a sad day for Suffren, for Hughes, with a fair wind, headed at once for the French transports and captured six of them, including the one bearing King Louis XVI's gifts for Hyder Ali. With prize crews aboard they headed back to Madras. It was sundown before Suffren managed to catch up with the British ships, and he had to wait for daylight before he could engage them.

The morning of February 17 found the two fleets six miles apart, with the French to windward, northeast of the British. The wind out of the north northeast was light and puffy, and Hughes put his ships in line on the port tack, heading east. He was well acquainted with conditions in the area, and he expected that as usual the wind would move into the east and give him a windward position. But this time it did not, and Suffren, running before it, closed on the British and then headed up on a parallel course, still to windward, his van abreast of the British flagship, in the center of the British line. In order to concentrate his fire on the last five ships of the British line, Suffren planned to send three of his ships around the British rear, so that the last three of the British ships would come under fire from both sides, while the first four British ships received no fire at all and could not tack to come to the rescue of the rest. But his orders were not carried out. Only two French captains headed to leeward of the British, and consequently only two of the British received fire from both sides. The other ships did not close to pistol range from windward as ordered. Their fire was thus less accurate, and the results less damaging than Suffren had hoped. After two hours of fighting, the wind swung around into the southeast, and both lines tacked. At last the British van could join the action. By this time, however, it was getting dark, and the fight was soon broken off. Suffren went on to Pondicherry, where his remaining transports were waiting for him. Hughes proceeded to Trincomalee. There he repaired his vessels before returning to Madras early in March.

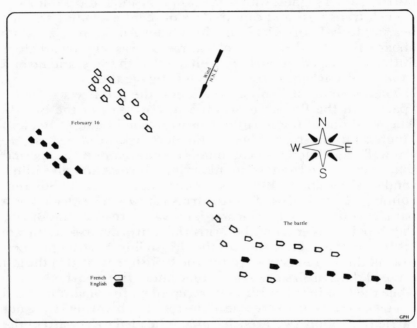

Battle of Sadras, February 17, 1782

252

Hyder Ali Takes Cuddalore

Suffren had brought with him not only a fleet to challenge the supremacy of British seapower in the India Ocean but also soldiers to assist Hyder Ali on land. Still far from being beaten, although he had lost some positions and prestige, Hyder in the winter of 1782 laid siege to British-held Cuddalore. On March 22 Suffren landed two thousand troops as reinforcements for him. With little prospect of relief by sea now that Suffren was close by, on April 4 the commander at Cuddalore surrendered.

Providien

There were two ships on the way from England to reinforce Hughes's fleet, and he planned to await their arrival at Madras. But he had hardly anchored there before he learned that Suffren, after dropping off his troops, had sailed south. Fearful that the French might be heading for Trincomalee, which was in fact Suffren's objective, Hughes loaded some reinforcements to take to the garrison there and put to sea on March 29. The next day the two new ships joined his fleet.

Suffren meanwhile had been cruising in hopes of intercepting the British reinforcements. Finally abandoning the search, he headed toward Ceylon, and on April 8 the two fleets sighted one another, sailing south in a light northeast breeze. Hughes, intent on delivering his troops to Trincomalee, continued on his course for three days, as Suffren gradually closed the gap between them. Finally, as they approached the coast of Ceylon on April 12, Hughes formed his ships in line of battle on the starboard tack, headed west, and Suffren, to windward, headed on a parallel course. At about noon, Suffren ordered his twelve ships to bear down together toward the eleven ships of the British line, with the last one directed to go to leeward of the last of the British.

As the French ships came within range the British commenced firing, causing the ships at both ends of the French line to luff up in order to fire broadsides instead of closing as Suffren had ordered. Suffren's flagship, the *Héros*, and three others continued down to within pistol shot of the British center. A very hot and bloody battle followed, with the ships in the center pounding each other and those at the end firing at much longer range.

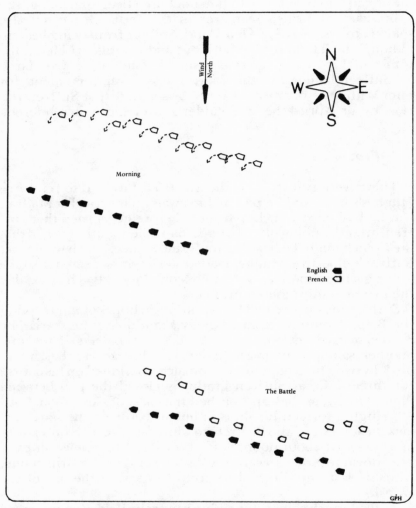

Battle of Providien, April 12, 1782

After three hours Hughes wore his ships, which by then were so close to the beach that he feared running aground. Suffren in turn followed. As darkness fell Hughes anchored in fifteen fathom of water. About five miles away Suffren too anchored his battered ships. Both sides had had 137 men killed. The British had 430 wounded, while the French counted 357.

The two fleets remained at anchor until April 19, while they jury rigged their damaged ships. Then Suffren hoisted sail and set off for Dutch-held Batacalo, about sixty miles south of Trincomalee. There he received provisions from the Dutch and watched for convoys coming from Europe. With the help of a few prizes, he was able to equip his ships for six months more, thus enabling them to remain in the area rather than returning to Ile de France for refitting, as he had, in fact, been ordered to do. Hughes, whose ships had suffered much greater damage, remained at anchor three days longer and then moved into the harbor of Trincomalee, where he stayed for the next two months in order to complete his repairs.

Negapatam

With repairs made, Hughes set sail on June 23 for Negapatam, south of Cuddalore, formerly a major port of the Dutch East India Company. Like Trincomalee, it had been seized by British forces at the earliest opportunity. Suffren meanwhile had been paying a brief visit to Cuddalore. Learning that more ships were on the way from England, and that Hughes was at Negapatam, Suffren headed there, hoping to engage Hughes before his fleet was reinforced by the new arrivals.

As soon as the French ships hove in sight on the afternoon of July 5, Hughes put to sea. The following morning, having headed south during the night, he was in the windward position as the two lines sailed south southeast on the starboard tack. A squall the previous afternoon had so badly damaged one of the French ships that she had dropped out, and both commanders had eleven ships in their lines. Again the ships in the center had the worst of it as the two fleets poured fire on each other for two hours. The French *Brillant*, fourth in the line, lost her mainmast and dropped off to leeward of the French line. Suddenly the wind backed into the southeast, causing both lines to fall off in order to keep the wind in their sails. Most of the ships fell away

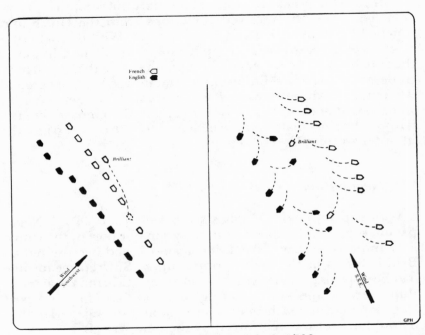

Battle of Negapatam, July 6, 1782

from the center, the British to starboard and the French to port. But four British vessels and two French, one of them the *Brillant,* turned toward one another and were soon engaged in a fierce battle between the two lines. Suffren turned and went to the rescue of the *Brillant,* which was being badly battered by the last two ships of the British line. The other French ship, the *Sévère,* on the orders of her captain, struck her colors to the British *Sultan.* But the crew, in spite of this demonstrated intention of surrender, continued to fire at the *Sultan,* which had hove to in order to take the prize. Instead of surrendering as she had indicated, the *Sévère* dropped off to rejoin the French fleet. After the battle Suffren relieved her captain and sent him home. All of the ships had been damaged, and Hughes broke off in the early afternoon and headed toward shore. He remained anchored there until July 18, when his fleet was finally in condition to sail to Madras.

Suffren had returned to Cuddalore the morning after the battle. After repairing his ships in the open roadstead by cannibalizing his frigates and smaller vessels and his English prizes, and even taking timbers from houses on shore, Suffren conferred with Hyder Ali and then put to sea again, this time headed for Batacalo to meet a convoy bringing six hundred troops, supplies, and two ships of the line. He arrived on the ninth and waited until the twenty-first, when the ships appeared. Two days after they came he was ready for sea again, his objective the capture of Trincomalee, which would give him facilities he needed for maintaining his ships. Hughes had left a small garrison at Trincomalee, and although he feared that Suffren might try to capture it, he dallied at Madras, not sailing until the day before Suffren's convoy arrived at Batacalo. So it was that when Suffren, with his fleet increased to fourteen ships of the line, sailed into the harbor of Trincomalee on August 25, he was able to land troops and guns without much opposition. The garrison surrendered on August 31; and when Hughes, his fleet increased to twelve by a newly arrived ship, got to Trincomalee two days later he found the harbor full of French vessels.

Suffren had already taken most of his men and guns back aboard, leaving ashore a garrison large enough to hold the port. Early on the morning after the British sails were sighted, he stood out of the harbor to challenge Hughes.

Trincomalee

Hughes was to leeward, some distance away, heading east southeast, and Suffren spent the morning trying to get into position to attack, as the British ships, in line of battle, repeatedly changed course to draw Suffren farther to leeward of Trincomalee. The wind, which had been strong from the southwest, dropped off. Suffren's line, fifteen ships, since he included a vessel with thirty-six guns, was poorly ordered, and when, at 2:30 P.M., as he drew close to the British, he gave the signal to bear down and attack, confusion resulted. Seven of the French ships ended up in a group ahead of the enemy's van and too far to windward to fire effectively. Suffren again, as he had at Sadras, had ordered two ships to take positions to leeward of the British rear, but their captains, afraid to get to leeward of the British line, instead attacked the last British ship from windward. When the one ahead came to her rescue, the French ships were driven off. Three of the French ships, including Suffren's *Héros*, carried the major share of the battle. They alone came within close range of the center of the British line, and the ships ahead and astern in the British line were able to fire on them as well as on those opposite. The *Héros* and the other seventy-four lost their mainmasts and mizzenmasts, and the *Héros* lost her foretopmast as well. The third, a 64, lost only a topmast. Suffren ordered the seven ships out in front towed around, since the air was too light for them to tack, and when the wind shifted suddenly to east southeast they were finally able to move in closer. But it was already late, and the fighting was broken off at about 7:00 P.M. It was the seventh of September before the French fleet returned to Trincomalee. Disaster awaited them, for the *Orient*, 74, ran aground on a bar at the entrance to the harbor and could not be saved. All in all, it had not been the best of Suffren's engagements.

Cuddalore—The Finale

Hughes went back to Madras. It was late in the season. The southwest monsoon would soon yield to the northeast monsoon, which races across the Indian Ocean in the fall and winter, and which, in the eighteenth century, made the east coast harbors unsafe for ships and made naval battles and naval support for

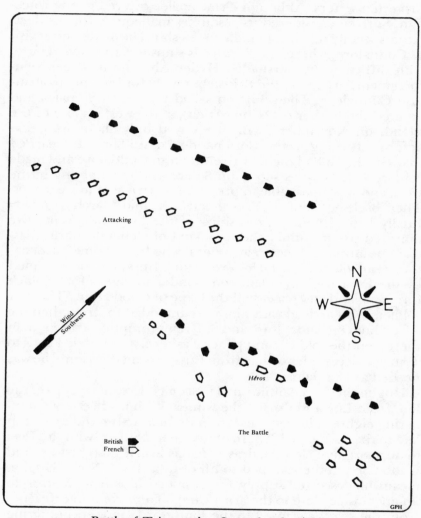

Attacking

Wind
Southwest

Héros

The Battle

British
French

GPH

Battle of Trincomalee, September 3, 1782

land battles impossible. As he had in previous winters, Hughes headed for Bombay on October 17, to spend the winter in its protected waters. Although Trincomalee offered good protection, Suffren considered its resources inadequate for his fleet. After speedily repairing his damaged ships, he made a brief visit to Cuddalore, where another of his ships was wrecked. There, with difficulty, he persuaded Hyder Ali, who had seen reinforcements arrive for the British but none for him, not to abandon Cuddalore. Then Suffren sailed for Dutch Sumatra and entered the harbor of Achin (Atjen), at the western end of the island, on November 2. But he stayed only about six weeks before returning to the Coromandel coast. There he learned that Hyder Ali had died. Suffren went to Cuddalore and made contact with Hyder's son Tipu Sahib, who was fighting in the west, and was at last able to promise the arrival of more troops. Then back he went to Trincomalee. In mid-March a convoy finally brought him three ships of the line and twenty-five hundred troops, under the command of General Charles Castelau de Bussy, a once great general who by this time was sixty-four years old and suffering from gout. Bussy had been named by the French government commander in chief of all French forces on land and sea east of the Cape of Good Hope. The new soldiers who arrived with him were intended to strengthen the Allied hold on Cuddalore, and Suffren promptly escorted them there, put the soldiers and general ashore, and hurried back to Trincomalee, under orders from Bussy to wait there until he was needed at Cuddalore.

Hughes in the meantime had welcomed five more ships of the line from England during the winter. With his fleet now numbering eighteen he returned from Bombay to the Indian Ocean late in the spring of 1783. In May General Stuart, with this fleet to support him, left Madras with his army, marched around Cuddalore, and encamped south of it, at Porto Novo. Hughes meanwhile escorted supply and support ships from Madras to an anchorage close to the army camp. To prevent interference from the sea, he cruised to the southward, and, encountering nothing, returned and anchored off Porto Novo.

Word of the threat to Cuddalore reached Suffren at Trincomalee on June 10, and he sailed at once. Two days later he sighted the anchored ships of the British fleet. Hughes spotted the approaching French ships and promptly weighed anchor, sending the supply ships posthaste to Madras. Neither comman-

der was eager to fight, and with Hughes away from the coast
Suffren was able to sail unmolested to Cuddalore. There he
embarked twelve hundred men to replace the casualties suffered from battle and disease and bring his ships to full strength.
Then he went out to challenge Hughes. Although he was outnumbered fifteen to eighteen, Suffren hoped to damage the
British ships so that they would have to leave the area to be
repaired, thereby forcing the unprotected British troops at
Porto Novo to surrender or withdraw.

Hughes had put to sea again, and the two fleets maneuvered
for two days in light and variable winds, each trying to get a
favorable position. When the wind finally settled down in the
west on the afternoon of June 20, the British were formed in line
on the port tack, heading north, with the French sailing a parallel course. This time Suffren straightened his line before bearing
down to attack at about 4:00 P.M. It was a classic battle, with each
ship engaging her opposite number as both lines headed generally north. Just before 7:00 the action was broken off. Both fleets
had suffered many casualties—the British 99 killed and 434
wounded, and the French 102 killed. This time, however, damage to the ships was less. Still, neither commander had much
interest in renewing the fight the next day. Hughes was short on
water and had over eleven hundred men down with scurvy. He
returned to Madras, leaving Stuart with no naval support, and
no supplies, since the supply ships had left before the battle
began.

Suffren went to Cuddalore, where he had unquestioned control of the sea. This spelled ruin for British hopes of a combined
naval and land action.

Three days before Hughes returned to Madras, word had
arrived here of the Preliminary Articles of Peace, signed at Paris
five months before. Hughes at once dispatched the frigate
Medea to Cuddalore to carry the news to British and French
alike. Since there was no longer a state of war between the two
nations in Europe, the hostilities in India were halted.

What had Suffren accomplished? For himself, a reputation as
a great naval hero, in spite of the fact that he had fought no
decisive battles, his instructions were not always followed, and
his plans were at times better than their execution. With no
adequate base of support, he had fought five battles with a
British fleet and inflicted more damage than he had suffered.
He had kept the waters of the Indian Ocean open for convoys,

had supported his country's Mysorean allies, and had secured the important base at Trincomalee. By taking Trincomalee from Britain (it is indicative of the non-allied status of the French and Dutch that he did not turn it back to them), he frustrated any thoughts the British may have had of using it as a stepping-stone to other Dutch possessions in the islands of the East Indies. While he had not destroyed British strength in India, he had increased France's claims to a portion of Indian territory.

VII

IN THE CAPITALS
OF EUROPE

18

The Powers and the Peace

From the beginning of the Revolutionary War, and throughout its course, world capitals simmered with plans, threats, and bribes as men tried to wrest national political gains from the conflict. Long Island, Trenton, Saratoga, Charleston, and Yorktown meant defeat or victory for Americans, but in European diplomatic circles they were points on a graph that marked the rise and fall of the rebellion's political value and determined the gambling odds of the hour.

The attempts of the European powers to deal with the Revolutionary War through diplomacy are often thought of as peace efforts or mediation efforts, but this approach puts the often frantic activity out of focus. For each country, termination of the war was one factor in a complicated equation expressing what that country valued most. A rock, a river, a place to dry fish, the humbling of a powerful adversary, the suppression of rebellious subjects, the avoidance of national bankruptcy—these were some of the things that mattered.

What the European Powers Wanted

Spain's war aims were clear—Gibraltar, first and always, and then, exclusive navigation rights on the Mississippi River, the return of Florida, and control of the Gulf of Mexico. France's primary aim was to weaken British power by securing independence for the American colonies. As the war stretched on, and as French debts piled up, American independence began to seem less important to the French king and his ministers. Even the knowledge that France's honor demanded it, since it was written into the Franco-American treaty, could not keep it an absolute. Strengthening France's position in the economically important islands of the West Indies and in distant India was a vital part of the whole picture of French-English rivalry, and participation in the fight for American independence was hardly more important as a French war aim.

France never sought to recover Canada from Britain, but French leaders generally preferred that it not be handed to the United States, a transfer that would have made the new nation a colossus, too strong for the French to contemplate. Some powerful Frenchmen hoped to recover territory in India and Africa that had fallen to England in earlier wars and to develop a new imperial effort based on trade. These were not the interests of Vergennes, but he had to listen to them.

France had one economic aim that conflicted with those of its American ally. It seems insignificant now, but it caused the American peace commissioners weeks of work and worry. When the French yielded Canada to Britain after the Seven Years' War, they kept rights to fish the waters off Nova Scotia and Newfoundland, and two tiny islands to serve as bases for their fishing fleet. The British, of course, also had rights to fish in that lucrative area. But did the Americans retain rights once they declared themselves independent of Britain? The French did not want them to. Sharing the fisheries with the British was enough, members of the French ministry believed. Since most of the U.S. fishermen lived in New England, the fisheries up north were a much worried bone of contention not only in Paris but between New England's representatives in the Continental Congress and France's ministers to the United States.

Britain's aim of keeping all the colonies as colonies was stubbornly maintained by George III. If he had been more flexible, he would probably have responded favorably to one of the numerous offers and feelers that came from the capitals of Europe, some through proper diplomats and some through unsavory double agents. Most of these offers were based on one idea, expressed in the Latin legal phrase *uti possidetis*. This meant that each side would keep what it possessed at the time of the truce, which to many Europeans seemed a reasonable compromise. If these proposals had been carried out, the United States would have kept New England and whatever else it held at the time, while Britain kept New York, Georgia, parts of the Carolinas, and various other parcels of land, depending on the particular year and month the truce was signed. The United States would have been a collection of patches and enclaves strung along the eastern seaboard of North America. Such fragmentation would have been disastrous for the new country, and was unthinkable to American leaders. It was also and always unacceptable to George III and Lord North, for converse reasons. Even after Yorktown they were unwilling to yield independence to any of the colonies, even one or two.

Men with Messages

All during the Revolution, and especially after France entered the war in 1779, agents and couriers crisscrossed Europe constantly. From London to Amsterdam to Paris to Madrid to Turin to Geneva they went, the stagecoaches carrying many a set of peace terms for the perusal of ministers and monarchs. There was, for example, the English banker Thomas Walpole, a cousin of the British opposition leader Horace Walpole. In the summer of 1780, Thomas Walpole made peace overtures in Paris, acting entirely on his own. There was also the English stock speculator and paid British agent Paul Wentworth, who tried to talk terms in Paris in 1780 and the Netherlands in 1782, and sent messages to Britain in 1780 from the incredibly successful double agent Edward Bancroft, the friend and assistant of Benjamin Franklin. Another double agent was William Wardlow, who worked, when he was working for Britain, for Lord George Germain, Secretary of State for the American Department, the man who was actually running the war for George III and Lord North. Wardlow carried out missions for Germain off and on throughout the war.

Then there was Viscount Mountstuart, whose father, Lord Bute, was George III's close friend and the man he had chosen to head his first ministry when he came to the throne. A different kind of messenger from the scroungy double agents who did much of the work, Mountstuart was Britain's envoy to the court of Sardinia. Contacted in 1780 by French director of finances Necker through the viscount's old Swiss tutor, Mountstuart carried suggestions for peace terms from Necker to George III. Since they contained a proposal for independence for some of the colonies, specifically those of New England, George promptly rejected them. (It is significant that the proposals came from Necker and not from Vergennes, who would not have been likely to suggest colonial status for any of the United States at that time.)

A surprising French agent was Louis-Valentin Goezmann, the very judge who had blatantly extorted a bribe from Caron de Beaumarchais. It was against Goezmann that Beaumarchais's famous series of pamphlets, the pamphlets Voltaire praised, were written. Goezmann had lost his judicial post as a result of Beaumarchais's fight for justice, and to support himself he had turned to the same kind of secret-diplomacy chores that Beaumarchais himself carried out on his road back to respectability. In 1781, Goezmann was in London, calling himself Goezmann de Thurne, posing as a German and sending information to Paris. Most of Goezmann's work was simple spying, not transmission of peace offers, although he sent a good deal of bad advice to Vergennes on what he felt the peace terms should be. Just after Yorktown the discredited North ministry considered using Goezmann to take its desperate—and unacceptable—peace offer to France, but settled instead on an experienced, though hard-drinking and indiscreet, agent named Nathaniel Parker Forth.

One of the most interesting and mysterious agents called himself by the aristocratic name of Montagu Fox; it is still not known who he really was. Fox arrived in The Hague in the summer of 1780, claiming to be an antigovernment Englishman who was ready to lead an uprising of miners in Cornwall, if the French government, which he approached through its ambassador to the Netherlands, would only give him four thousand muskets. Fox also produced, from time to time, various documents that purportedly showed treasonous antigovernment activities by such leading British opposition figures as Lord Shelburne. Some of these have survived and have been proved to be forgeries. Other Fox documents now appear to have been carefully constructed to sow discord between France and Spain. In short, if Montagu Fox had been a secret agent of the North government on a "dirty tricks" assignment, he would have acted much as he did. Vergennes was so nervous about Spain's loyalty to the Franco-Spanish alliance, however, and wanted so much to know just what was going on between the Spanish government and a certain pair of British agents in Madrid that he allowed himself to be strung along by Fox.

Hussey and Cumberland in Madrid

The two British agents and their activities in Madrid may be looked at more closely as an example of the kind of dealings that were going on throughout the war. Father Thomas Hussey was an Irish Catholic priest, educated in Seville, who was, unknown to the British government, a paid agent of the Spanish government when he was in London. Unknown to the Spanish government, however, when he was in Madrid he was a paid agent of the British government. If he traveled to Paris, or anywhere else, for either government, he usually managed to find a mission he could do for the other at the same time, and, in addition to money received for services rendered and information delivered, he drew expense accounts for the same trip from both Britain and Spain.

In London Father Hussey met a popular playwright, Richard Cumberland. In addition to writing plays, Cumberland held a minor government post, and he was a friend of Lord George Germain. In late 1779, with Spain at war with England, Hussey arranged for Germain to send both him and Cumberland to Spain to feel out possibilities of peace between the two countries.

In line with George III's immovable stand on the matter, Cumberland and Hussey were not to consider independence for the colonies. They were given equally firm instructions on Gibraltar—in fact, it was not even to be discussed, and Cumberland, the senior envoy, was not to enter Spain until Hussey had ascertained that the Spanish would not mention Gibraltar. Prospects for reaching a settlement were clearly nonexistent.

To the Spanish, however, since they were not fully aware of the rigidity of British intransigence, the time seemed good for exploring peace possibilities. The massive Franco-Spanish armada that had been assembled for an invasion of England had just anticlimactically dispersed in the fall of 1779, and Spain's leaders, including the prime minister, the conde de Floridablanca, were not enthusiastic about continuing the war. They saw no reason why the British could not make peace by giving them Gibraltar and arranging some kind of feudal-overlordship arrangement with the errant colonies—a relationship that sounded reasonable to Spaniards but that would have been utterly unacceptable to both Britain and the United States. Floridablanca, the epitome of the suave, conniving diplomat of the era, cared almost as little for the Family Compact with France and loyalty to the French alliance as he did for the insurrectionists in America, whom Spain had not the least intention of recognizing as a nation. If Floridablanca could have gained

Gibraltar by making peace with England behind France's back, it is doubtful that he would have flicked an aristocratic eyelash over the ethics of the case.

While Cumberland waited in Portugal, Hussey went on to Spain and sounded out the Spanish leaders. Although he soon discovered that Gibraltar was the one term the Spanish cared about, he let Cumberland think there were no bars to negotiation, and Cumberland let himself be persuaded. He arrived in Madrid with his wife and two attractive daughters and began a social life as spectacular as his diplomatic work was futile. Diplomatic circles in the Spanish capital were treated to an entertaining paradox. Cumberland, the representative of an enemy country, was feted and flattered by the Spanish court, and his lovely daughters were the toast of court society. John Jay, who was also in the Spanish capital, and representing a country that was Spain's co-belligerent, was all but insulted and had to struggle for every interview with any significant Spanish official.

Nothing came of the Cumberland negotiations, and Cumberland himself ended up badly in debt at the end of the episode. But Vergennes read the reports from Madrid and worried— which did not upset Floridablanca at all.

Mediation of the Imperial Rulers

At the other end of the diplomatic scale from double agents like Hussey were the powerful sovereigns of neutral empires; they too worked to manipulate the war's outcome. Maria Theresa, mother of France's Queen Marie Antoinette, first offered mediation in the spring of 1779, but France was not then receptive. Spain had just entered the war at France's side, plans were afoot for the great invasion of Britain, and no amount of pressure by the old empress on her daughter could spark French interest. The offer went unaccepted by either side throughout 1779 and 1780. Maria Theresa died in November 1780, and the Austrian mediation was left in the hands of her son Joseph II and the powerful chancellor, Prince von Kaunitz.

Catherine II of Russia also offered mediation, both before and after her establishment of the League of Armed Neutrality. In late summer of 1780 Nikita Panin suggested to a French envoy that there be an immediate armistice and that each of the thirteen states declare separately which way it wanted to go—for independence or for England. This local option, Panin pointed out, could satisfy the honor of France, so far as its promise in the alliance treaty not to make peace without American independence was concerned. As American military fortunes were not then good—Charleston had fallen in May, one of the war's lowest points for the allies—Vergennes was receptive. He had held out firmly for American independence not only to honor the alliance but because this weakening of Britain was the chief purpose of France's entry into the war. Now France seemed to be approaching bankruptcy, though no one could be sure just how closely, and compromise seemed like a good idea. Vergennes indicated that he was willing to accept Catherine as mediator.

Early the next year the British government proposed that both Austria and Russia serve as mediators; the British felt Austria would tend to favor them at the expense of France. The French and Spanish were hesitant, preferring Catherine alone. To their dismay, Catherine undercut them dramatically by accepting joint mediation with Austria, and, much worse, accepting Vienna as the site of a congress on the matter. Joseph II hated the French, and von Kaunitz was obviously eager to take them down a peg or two. Vergennes was horrified.

He was not too stunned, however, to begin preparing the way with the United States for a settlement that did not come up to the terms of the two countries' alliance. Vergennes wrote Luzerne in Philadelphia that he should let Congress know that, in case any crisis should arise, France would take charge of the U.S. side of peace negotiations, with or without U.S. approval. Vergennes also called John Adams from The Hague to Paris to prepare him for the mediation, which would probably involve some compromise on American independence—some states independent, others British. Adams refused to be prepared. He made it clear that U.S. ministers plenipotentiary must be recognized and treated as equals, and that unless the two mediating powers made U.S. independence and sovereignty an indispensable condition for peace and invited a U.S. representative to their peace meetings the United States would not cooperate with the mediation. This firmness is one reason for Adams's still-growing historical reputation as a diplomat.

Fortunately for the allies—and for the United States, which might have been carved up with no regard to its government's wishes—George III's obstinacy ruled out any agreement. Lord Stormont, the British Secretary of State, made it clear that there could be no truce until all the colonies had "returned to their allegiance." He also committed the folly of attempting to bribe both mediators with offers of territory in return for favorable terms.

The Battle of Yorktown put a conclusive end to the mediation. King George's attitude made it a vain effort in any case, but the willingness of France to yield on the issue of American independence showed the extent to which American aspirations were pawns in the world power politics of Europe.

The View from America

The Continental Congress had meanwhile come up with some peace terms of its own; yet even these were heavily influenced by European needs. A report on what the United States should demand at the peace table came out of a Congressional committee in February 1779. It called for these as minimum demands: independence; boundaries that were roughly those of the country to the Mississippi today, including the Northwest Territory that Britain had given to Canada under the Quebec Act, but not including East or West Florida; complete British evacuation of U.S. territory; rights to use the fisheries off Newfoundland and Nova Scotia; and free U.S. navigation of the Mississippi River. The committee's terms were debated by Congress for six months, and French Minister Gérard was an active lobbyist throughout the debate for the interests of France and Spain. France did not want U.S. fishing in the northern waters, and it supported Spain's demand for exclusive navigation of the Mississippi, a provision that would have left settlers moving into the western lands with no way to market their products. Congress finally voted to take the fisheries claim off the U.S. minimum demands list, but left the right to use the Mississippi. Britain's cession of Canada and Nova Scotia to the United States, a demand many congressmen felt should also be made, was to be considered "of utmost importance," but was not made a minimum demand. The U.S. negotiator was not to enter formal talks on peace unless Britain agreed to regard the United States as free, sovereign, and independent. John Adams was chosen to negotiate the peace treaty with British representatives and was instructed to work for Congress's peace terms.

Adams sailed to France, but he met little encouragement

there. Franklin was already established near Paris as the envoy of the United States, and Vergennes was a little impatient at being asked to deal with a peace commissioner in addition to the popular Franklin. He also had John Adams confused with John's cousin Samuel, whose reputation as a hot-headed radical Vergennes knew and whom Gérard's dispatches had identified as a leader in the anti-Deane, and thus by inference anti-French, faction in Congress. John Adams was treated in Paris no more graciously than John Jay was in Madrid. He eventually moved on to the Netherlands, feeling there was nothing much he could accomplish at Paris, and hoping to get a Dutch loan and Dutch recognition for the United States.

Then in June of 1781 Congress came up with new instructions and a new peace commission—five men, including Franklin and Adams, with Henry Laurens (who was in prison in England), John Jay (who was in Spain), and Thomas Jefferson (who did not leave America in time to serve) added. The instructions reduced the demands of 1779. Only U.S. independence and sovereignty were to be essential. The commissioners were to use their discretion in all other matters, including boundaries, fisheries, and Mississippi navigation. A new proviso called for nothing to be done without the "knowledge and concurrence" of the French ministry; the commissioners were to "ultimately govern yourselves by [the ministry's] advice and opinion."

This lowering of demands was the work of the French minister to the United States, the chevalier de la Luzerne. As zealous for French interests as Gérard had been, and far better liked and more skillful in cultivating congressmen, he had persuaded Congress that almost everything should be left open for negotiation and that the French government should make the decisions. Considering that the French government was then cheerfully contemplating slicing the United States into separate provinces and distributing some of them to Great Britain, the instructions could have been disastrous.

British-American Peace Talks

No one paid much attention to American peace efforts until after the Battle of Yorktown. Then things moved fast. Cornwallis surrendered on October 19, 1781. The prevailing westerlies carried the ships bearing the news to Europe quickly. Lord

North heard it on November 25 and exclaimed, "O God! It is all over!" The king and Lord North made groping, desperate efforts to save the North ministry and also sent out some peace feelers based on dealing separately with the several "provinces" of North America, an idea Franklin and Adams were hardly likely to listen to in the hour of victory. George III was miserable; he considered abdicating and even drafted an instrument of abdication. To live out his days as Elector of Hanover must have seemed a peaceful and tempting prospect.

The House of Commons put an end to the matter by voting on February 27, 1782, to stop fighting the war against the former colonies, and on March 20 Lord North resigned.

Lord Shelburne was the king's choice to replace North, but George was not able to appoint him immediately. Shelburne, although conciliatory to the colonies since the crisis of the 1760s, was very reluctant to recognize independence, which was what especially endeared him to the king. He did not have adequate support in Parliament, however, and George was forced to choose Lord Rockingham, popular leader of the opposition to the war. Lord Shelburne became powerful in the new government, even though he did not head it. Rockingham, immediately upon his appointment, made arrangements for discussions with the American commissioners in Paris.

Only one commissioner, Benjamin Franklin, was actually in Paris then, and the Englishman he first met with was Richard Oswald, the picked envoy of Lord Shelburne. Oswald was an elderly Scottish merchant who had long been sympathetic to the American position; he got along well with Franklin. His first probe was on the possibility of a separate peace. Would the North American states accept independence and leave the war, allowing Britain to concentrate on its European enemies? Franklin answered by taking Oswald to Versailles, where Vergennes and Franklin, in each other's presence, affirmed to Oswald that the treaty of alliance would be held to; there would be no separate peace.

Before Oswald returned to England, Franklin made a personal suggestion that Britain offer to cede Canada to the United States, thus building good will and providing resources with which the new country could compensate Patriots who had suffered property damage and Loyalists whose estates had been confiscated. Franklin soon regretted ever bringing up the possibility of compensating Loyalists. Canada was a prize, however, that much of Congress wanted, despite French opposition; it had also been dear to Franklin since the end of the Seven Years' War, when he had vigorously argued for Britain's taking Canada into the empire at the price of relinquishing rich sugar islands in the Caribbean.

Oswald returned to Paris in May, still without definite peace terms, and soon after his reappearance another British envoy arrived. He was Thomas Grenville, son of the man responsible for the Stamp Act. Grenville was the agent of the powerful parliamentary leader Charles James Fox, and the presence of both Oswald and Grenville in Paris gave evidence of the rivalry within the Rockingham ministry between Shelburne and Fox. Rockingham himself, a sick man, was not exerting much leadership. In any case, both the British representatives in Paris were offering basically the same terms. The colonies would be independent; however unhappy George III might be about it, the ministry had realized that independence was inevitable. However, independence would be a provision of the treaty and would not go into effect until the treaty was signed and ratified; independence would not be recognized during the negotiations, and the U.S. negotiators would not be considered representatives of an independent country. As for territorial demands, everything would go back to the way it was at the end of the Seven Years' War. This last provision was something many Frenchmen would not accept, having fought the Revolutionary War in large part to undo the humiliation and territorial losses suffered in the earlier war. And the United States would not make peace without France. The United States also would not open formal negotiations until its independence had been recognized.

Franklin, who found Oswald much easier to deal with than Grenville, was at his best in subtly displacing Fox's man. By July Grenville had resigned and gone back to England. The competent and legally trained John Jay had also arrived from his gruelling, highly educational tour of duty in Spain to back up Franklin. And Lord Rockingham had died. King George made Shelburne the new leader of the Cabinet.

Oswald still received no instructions to deal with the Americans as representatives of an independent nation, and Jay and Franklin stood firm on this issue. They could see, however, that on this they would get little support from France, and none from Spain. Spain, which had never had any alliance with the United

States, still had not recognized American independence; even Yorktown had not shaken the Spanish court. For Spain the war was an ordinary European war, Gibraltar was the peace term that really mattered, and an increasing uneasiness was being felt over potential U.S. power on the borders of Florida and Louisiana. Jay had negotiated long and tenaciously in Madrid for U.S. rights to navigate the Mississippi, but had finally been instructed from Philadelphia to yield the point. He had then offered Spain exclusive navigation of the lower Mississippi and a U.S. guarantee of all Spanish territory in America in return for a Spanish guarantee of U.S. territory, but, even with these concessions, Floridablanca had turned him down.

Now, in Paris, as Jay talked with the Spanish ambassador, the conde de Aranda, he learned that Spain not only wanted control of the lower Mississippi but also wanted to hem the United States in by a line running from north to south roughly five hundred miles east of the Mississippi. Spain was afraid to have the vigorous new country pushing against its Mississippi barrier and was using the Spanish raid of February 1781 on St. Joseph, two hundred miles east of the Mississippi, as justification for its extraordinary claims. And France seemed willing to support Spain. The basic self-interest of the European powers showed up again and again. Yet the Americans were bound by instructions to do nothing without the French ministry's knowledge and concurrence, and to be governed by the ministry's advice and opinion. After meeting with Vergennes on August 10, Jay went back to his lodgings and told Franklin, according to Jay family legend, that if the instructions interfered with America's honor and dignity, he would break them "like this"—as he threw his fragile clay pipe full force into the fireplace.*

It is not clear whether it was on this evening or somewhat later that the American commissioners decided to disregard their instructions about consulting and deferring to France. But the resolution expressed by the shattered pipe became the policy of the negotiators. The problem of the treaty obligation to make no separate peace without France was to be handled by including a provision in the peace treaty that it would not go into effect until Britain had also signed a treaty with France. Ignoring the unease of the French court and ministry, the Americans thereafter acted on their own.

*Morris, *Peacemakers*, p. 310.

The momentum toward agreement increased. Lafayette, back in France, was sent scurrying back and forth between Vergennes and the American commissioners, as the shrewd foreign minister tried to use this American hero for French interests. On September 7, 1782, Vergennes's undersecretary, Rayneval, left incognito for England, where he made contact with Lord Shelburne and spent several days with him at Shelburne's country estate in Wiltshire. Once the Americans knew Rayneval had gone, and where, there were fears that France was trying to make a separate peace. Apparently this was not really the case. The French and British governments just wanted to iron out some problems informally and face-to-face. They did, however, discuss matters—such as the offshore fishery rights—that vitally concerned the United States and should not have been discussed without American representatives present.

At this point Franklin fell ill in Paris, and Jay took command there. He turned to Benjamin Vaughan, a young man from the West Indies, who had a Bostonian mother, was pro-American, and had been sent by Shelburne to deal with the American commissioners. Jay asked Vaughan to go to England and counteract Rayneval's work with Shelburne. He was to work to make Shelburne understand that there could be no peace negotiations without Britain's first acknowledging U.S. independence, that no peace could be made that excluded Americans from sharing in the fisheries, that the boundaries must give the United States the Northwest Territory and land westward to the Mississippi, and that free navigation of the Mississippi was important to the Americans. Vaughan was a wise choice, an effective spokesman for the Americans. Shelburne heard him and was influenced. He was speaking, actually, only for Jay, who had kept the news of Vaughan's mission not only from Vergennes and Lafayette but from Franklin, who he was afraid would veto it.

Another master stroke of Jay's was a compromise on the immediate recognition of independence. He came up with the formula "the Thirteen United States" as the entity whose independence Britain could recognize. This was not the correct official name of the United States of America, a name that stuck in King George's throat, but it was more than recognition of the nation only after the treaty was signed, and more than the "thirteen united provinces" whose recognition Oswald felt might be acceptable to his government. On the nineteenth of September 1782, the die was cast: Oswald's new commission authorized him to treat with commissioners of the Thirteen United States.

On the thirteenth of the month, the great and final Franco-Spanish attack on Gibraltar had failed disastrously. If Shelburne had known, he might not have agreed to the new commission. But by the time the news came, it was too late. Formal negotiations began on September 27.

In little more than a week, Jay had a draft treaty ready. Franklin, who was still ill and had left the drafting and negotiations to Jay, approved it. Oswald readily signed it and sent it off to London with a strong endorsement.

The terms were favorable indeed for the United States. The claim to Canada, which had never been considered essential and which Britain was obviously unlikely to yield after the great Gibraltar victory, was abandoned. Everything else the Americans wanted was there.

In approving the draft Oswald had not violated his instructions, which had been written before the British success at Gibraltar and were aimed at separating the United States from France and reaching a quick settlement. When the draft got to London, however, things looked very different. Gibraltar and Rayneval's visit had changed the atmosphere. Cabinet members were horrorstruck when Jay's draft treaty was read. Oswald was instructed to go back and get the Northwest Territory (the draft treaty had a U.S. border with Canada well to the north of the present Canadian border). The right to dry fish on land near the offshore fisheries was to be denied. The Americans must pay their prewar debts and compensate the Loyalists for their property losses. And so forth. Independence, however, the Cabinet could not quarrel with; that had in effect already been recognized. Oswald was scolded. Another commissioner, Henry Strachey, who was expected to be much less sympathetic to the Americans, was sent along to keep him in line.

American reinforcements arrived at the same time from the Hague in the form of John Adams. Adams supported Jay firmly, and Franklin, who had earlier been a bit influenced by and involved with the French court, soon joined them in a united, decisive stance.

While the Americans were standing firm and keeping their distance from the French ministry, the French, led by Vergennes, were in almost constant consultation with the British. They were also trying to influence Congress in Philadelphia, through French Minister Luzerne, to give up fisheries and land in the Northwest Territory and to compensate the Loyalists so as to get a quick peace.

Time, however, was on the side of the Americans. Since Shelburne led the government of a constitutional monarchy, he had to consider his Parliament, which was due to meet in late November. He delayed the meeting until December. He felt he must have a treaty before then, or every detail of the negotiations would be questioned and attacked by one side or the other in Parliament, his narrowly based support would crumble, and his government would fall. Jay, Adams, Franklin, and Henry Laurens—released from British prison and finally present—held to their position. The preliminary treaty that was signed on the last day of November was a good one for the United States.

It affirmed independence. It drew between the United States and Canada the "line-of-the-Lakes" boundary that has basically lasted, a boundary that gave the United States considerably less than Jay's draft had, but did include the Northwest Territory. It gave the new country the land right up to the Mississippi. Navigation of the Mississippi was to be free to Great Britain and the United States from its source to the Gulf of Mexico. The disputed fisheries were to be open to Americans, and so were areas for drying and curing fish—although some subtle compromise language in this article left room for disputes later. All legitimate debts were to be paid. The problem of the Loyalists was handled by requiring Congress to urge the individual states to restore the property of genuine British subjects and peaceful Loyalists, a moral obligation which saved British pride.

The Bourbon Powers

What were France and Spain to make of this quick and favorable outcome of the American diplomats' efforts? Vergennes was upset. Although the treaty would not be final until France and Spain had negotiated their own, their bargaining chips were few indeed, what with American independence, boundaries, and fisheries already settled. Vergennes wrote harshly to Franklin. That master diplomat answered graciously, making apologies for the Americans' indiscretion in not consulting Vergennes and hoping the British would not have grounds for believing that such a small matter had caused trouble between the French and Americans. Vergennes subsided.

The Conde de Aranda, Spain's ambassador to France, also was angry. He had been negotiating with British representatives in Paris, and with Jay, over the western boundaries of the United States and the navigation of the Mississippi. Now the British had taken it upon themselves to give the Americans all the land as far as the Mississippi, and the two countries had agreed to share navigation of the Mississippi without an apparent thought to Spain's claims.

Vergennes and Aranda would have been even more upset if they had known the contents of a separate and secret article in the British-American treaty. It provided that the boundary between Florida and the United States would be shifted significantly northward if Britain, rather than Spain, held Florida as a result of the fortunes of war and the peace treaty between Spain and Britain. The truth was that the English-speaking peoples of the old British Empire were coming closer in trust, looking forward to mutually beneficial trade, and generally freezing out the Bourbons; the Americans felt more comfortable with Britain nudging their southernmost state than with Spain there.

The peace negotiations between France, Spain, and Great Britain were extraordinarily intricate, and Vergennes's job was probably the central one. He knew and held most of the many threads that had to be brought together to make an agreement. In most cases, however, he held only one end of the thread, and frenetic tugging was going on at the other end.

Gibraltar was the most difficult problem. Spain would not make peace without it; Floridablanca had to have it. The difficulty of getting it was not a constant factor, but varied with the shifts in the war and with the success the British negotiators had in keeping members of Parliament and writers of letters to the newspapers from finding out that Gibraltar, "the brightest jewel of the Crown," as the duke of Richmond called it, might be bartered away. Before the Franco-Spanish fleet was burned in attacking it, there was a good chance that Gibraltar could have gone to Spain for a moderately valuable base somewhere else. After the naval assault failed, and especially after Admiral Howe's British relief force reached the Rock, there was less chance. Once the preliminary treaty between the British and Americans had been signed, the Franco-Spanish bargaining position was still weaker. And when the news leaked out that

George III and the Shelburne ministry were willing to give up Gibraltar in return for a productive sugar island or two in the Caribbean, an outcry arose that threatened to bring down the ministry. In the end, the British had to refuse to give up Gibraltar, and the Spanish had to try to be content instead with the Floridas, which Gálvez had won by force of arms.

Ironically, George III, who had been so insistent that Gibraltar not even be discussed during the Hussey-Cumberland negotiations, had come around to the view that Puerto Rico, or two smaller islands, would be well worth trading off for the fortress. He continued to hope for such a trade after all his ministers had given up on the idea.

It was the Conde de Aranda who made the decision to let Gibraltar stay British in return for a speedy peace. In perspective, this was a statesmanlike decision, but it upset Charles III and infuriated Floridablanca when they learned of it. Since Floridablanca had long slighted, ignored, and jibed at Aranda, whom he saw as a political rival, the ambassador was probably not greatly disturbed by the principal minister's pique. He did have reason, in an absolute monarchy, to fear the king's wrath, but he was able to defend his actions convincingly. It was clear, he pointed out, that the Parliamentary opposition in England would never allow the British to give up Gibraltar. Spain's crucial interests were its American empire, which had been enlarged and strengthened by the agreement on Gibraltar. "How long can a rock disturb three empires, Your Excellency?" he asked. Charles III and Floridablanca decided to make the best of it.

What the Powers Gained

The Americans in Paris, by disregarding the shackling instructions of Congress, and Aranda, by stretching his authority to its limits and a bit beyond, had achieved a surprisingly speedy settlement of the tangled issues at stake in the war. A peace treaty was signed by representatives of Britain, France, and Spain at Versailles on January 20, 1783. There was relief in the ministries of all three nations, and rejoicing in France.

France apparently had achieved its primary war aim of weakening Britain, for the North American colonies had become independent, and the British Empire seemed shattered. France won some small additional territories in India, with small

additional revenues from trade. The French had wanted both
Gorée and Senegal. They got Senegal, and Britain kept rocky
Gorée; this meant that France and Britain could control their
respective slave-trading operations. The French were given back
the little fishing islands of St. Pierre and Miquelon, granted
them in 1763 but taken by Britain during the Revolution, and
were granted nonexclusive rights to certain Newfoundland fishing areas they wanted. A swap that could be considered mutually
beneficial was made in the Caribbean—formerly British Tobago
for formerly French Dominica. Thus territorial changes were
small. The French Empire was not regained. The damage to the
British Empire seemed considerable, but only the future could
show whether France would gain from it. The critical item, one
that did not appear in the peace treaty, was the state of French
government finances. France had in fact bankrupted itself in
this long world war. The Bourbon regime would never recover.

Spain had not gained Gibraltar, and if the Spanish king and
his ministers were honest with themselves, the war had not been
worth it to them. True, the Floridas, which had been settled by
Spain and had been lost in the Seven Years' War, had been won
back, and this was of great value. Since West Florida stretched to
the Mississippi, and since Spain kept New Orleans, the Gulf of
Mexico was virtually a Spanish lake, a major goal of Spanish
policy. Also, whatever agreements Britain and the United States
might have made about navigation of the Mississippi, both banks
of its last miles were firmly in Spanish hands, and those were the
miles that led to the rest of the world. Whether the Floridas were
worth the blood and money Spain had poured out might be
doubted, but the Spanish effort did make gains. Hurt pride over
Gibraltar made it hard for the Spanish court to count them.

The Netherlands, a loser from the beginning, had caused
Vergennes considerable trouble by having a government that
was intransigent in direct proportion to its maritime disasters.
The Dutch wanted the British to recognize the principle of
freedom of the seas even before they sat down at a negotiating
table. They also wanted the return of all the Dutch territories in
India and the West Indies that the British had captured, plus
compensation payment for property damage. None of this could
be accomplished. The Dutch gave in, but the treaty between
Britain and the Netherlands was not ready for signing at the
January ceremony in which the other European belligerents
made peace.

Britain, which appeared to have lost the war, and which certainly had to wipe a sizable part of its empire off its maps, oddly came out of the war in a quite creditable strategic situation. The British still had a healthy trade with the former colonies, while being liberated from the problems of governing and defending them. British money and energies were released for other adventures. Worldwide, little was lost. British power in India was stronger. Britain still ruled the waves. In relation to their European rivals, the English had somehow come out on top.

Appendix

Fighting at Sea in the Revolutionary War

The American Revolution in its global aspects was to a very large extent a naval war. Control of the seas and of the vital ports of the world was the key to victory, and none saw this more clearly than General Washington as he requested help from de Grasse in support of his operation ashore at Yorktown in 1781. Off the shores of India, as they did off the Breton coast and the Virginia capes, fleets of tall ships—most of them French and British—with their huge square sails filled with wind, played out a pattern of naval combat that had been set for more than a hundred years. From the perspective of two hundred years it is hard to imagine the ships themselves, let alone the actions in which they engaged. Since some of the terms used to describe these actions may be unfamiliar to some readers, a few comments may be helpful.

There were many types of ships in the navies of the several participants in the Revolutionary War. Most of these fought by ones or twos or threes; the biggest, heaviest, and most heavily armed, which were capable of standing up to hostile fleets in line of battle, were called ships of the line.

Although big in comparison with other vessels of their time, the ships of the line were only about two hundred feet long, about two thirds the length of the World War II submarine. They usually had about a fifty-foot beam, that is to say they were fifty feet wide. And they drew about twenty-two feet of water, or required a depth of twenty-two feet in order not to run aground. This very deep draft was necessary to keep the ship upright, offsetting the tremendous pressure of wind on the lofty sails.

These ships were magnificent architectural structures, hand-crafted by master artisans, and sometimes lavishly decorated, although the flamboyance of earlier periods had yielded to the practical limitations of expense by the 1770s. The cost of a ship might run as high as $1,500,000 in modern dollars, and each one consumed an estimated two thousand trees. Because of the expense and the long time required to build one, the Continental Congress authorized construction of only one ship of the line, late in the war. And before her designated skipper, John Paul Jones, could take her to sea, the Congress made a gift of her to the French king.

The hard wood of the English oak was preferred by British shipwrights, and by the 1770s whole forests of these ancient trees had perished to carry the British flag. Not only did these spreading giants provide the straight planking; their curves were easily cut into the knees that supported the decks where they joined the sides, or were shaped to the graceful lines of the ships' hulls. The planks on the sides of the hulls were four inches thick, and they could take considerable punishment from eighteenth-century cannonballs. The sea worms that tunneled voraciously into wooden hulls had resulted by the 1770s in the use of thin plates of copper as sheathing on ships' bottoms, which also discouraged the growth of seaweed and barnacles and so increased the speed of the ships that bore them. By the time of the Revolutionary War most of the British ships were sheathed, giving them an advantage in speed over the otherwise more maneuverable French ships. But when sheathed and unsheathed ships were combined in the same line of battle inevitably their different speeds made it impossible to maintain an even line.

The tall pines that grew in abundance in the American colonies had been an important source for masts and spars, and Britain was forced in 1776 to turn to Russia and the other nations bordering on the Baltic Sea as major providers of tall, straight timber. Few trees could be found for the lower masts of the largest ships, however, masts that measured a yard or more in diameter. These were usually pieced from several timbers held together by hoops, like a barrel.

The size of a ship depended on the number of guns she was to carry; the largest carrying a hundred guns or more on three gun decks, the 74s or smaller requiring only two gun decks. There were also the top deck, whose open, central portion was the quarterdeck; the orlop deck below the gun decks; and the hold, which served for storage of provisions, ammunition, spare sails, replacement parts, the anchor cable, and the numerous other items necessary to maintain a ship and her crew at sea for months or half a year. Every inch had a use, and the crew, which numbered about six hundred and fifty on a 74-gun ship, slung their hammocks close together in various areas of the dark and foul-smelling decks, where headroom barely sufficed for the short eighteenth-century men. Only the captain, and perhaps a few senior officers, had anything resembling privacy.

The ship of the line was ship-rigged; i.e., had three masts: foremast (pronounced fore′-m'st), mainmast, and mizzenmast (similarly pronounced). The spars, with their great square canvas sails, could be pivoted on the masts by lines attached to the spars and to the lower corners of the sails, in order to use the force of the wind on the course desired. Changing the positions of a full suit of sails required the coordinated efforts of a large crew, and ships in battle normally used only jib (the fore-and-aft sail at the bow of the vessel) and topsails (pronounced top′-s'ls) in order to simplify the work of shiphandling and free more men for the work of fighting.

Dependent entirely upon the wind for movement, the ship of the line might hope to make six knots directly before the wind and hardly more than one sailing against it. Of course no sailing vessel can sail directly against the wind, and a square rigger could sail no closer than 67.5 degrees on either side of the direction from which the wind was blowing. Like any sailing vessel, she had to sail a zigzagging course, making a series of tacks, if her objective was upwind from her position.

Tacking a square-rigged ship, that is, changing from one tack to the other (port, with the wind over the ship's left side, to starboard [star′-b'd], with the wind over the right side, for example) by heading into the eye of the wind, was a complicated maneuver and one that was well avoided during a battle. Not only did it involve all the business of shifting lines and sails, it meant that for a period while headed directly into the wind the forward movement of the ship was entirely halted. Worse, there was always the risk of "getting in irons," or "missing stays," with the ship sliding backward and unable to catch the wind on either tack. It was considerably easier to change course by wearing (or jibing, as it is generally called today), that is, by heading directly downwind so that the wind blew over the stern and the sails were easily shifted to catch it on the other side. In a strong wind and a heavy sea wearing was dangerous, since the ship would be broadside to the wind twice, but it was quicker than tacking, and it was commonly used when a commander wanted to change the direction of his line during a battle. His ships might wear together or wear in succession, each as she reached the point where the first ship had turned.

The forward progress of a square rigger could be halted entirely by swinging her foresails (fore'-s'ls) so that they filled from the front. This maneuver, heaving to, was frequently used in order to maintain approximately the same position while waiting for other ships, or otherwise to assist in getting into position to attack the enemy.

Tactics

The naval battles of the Revolutionary War were fought generally in conformance with rules that had been evolved a hundred years or so earlier. For the British navy these were contained in a book known as *Fighting Instructions*. Every commander was expected to know the rules and to fight in accordance with them to the extent the circumstances would permit. Every flagship was equipped with a set of colored signal flags to indicate which of the *Instructions* was in effect. Both their design and the position on the ship in which they were flown had meaning that the captains of all the other ships were supposed to read and act on. The problems of distinguishing and interpreting the flags at a distance, through the smoke of battle, rain, fog, or haze, through an eighteenth-century telescope on a heaving deck, are easy to understand. Signals were often misread, not seen at all, or intentionally ignored.

Controlling a dozen or so full-rigged ships in battle was a formidable challenge. The easiest way to do it was to sail in a single line, or line ahead, with the commander's flagship in the center. This system was common to all navies of the period, and the normal practice was for the contending fleets to sail in two lines on parallel courses, firing at each other with the guns on the facing sides.

The attacking fleet normally was to windward of the defender, on the side from which the wind was blowing, where its commander could control both the time and the place of contact. Holding this windward position was known as having the weather gauge. Having sighted the enemy, the attacking commander would maneuver to a favorable position and then form his ships in line ahead. To bring the line into range of the enemy vessels—that is, to "close" with the enemy—the commander would order his ships to proceed in line abreast, that is, to turn at once toward the enemy line and proceed until close enough to fire. Then, luffing or luffing up (sailing closer to the direction from which the wind was blowing), the ships would resume the line ahead formation, parallel to the enemy lines. They would thus bring their guns into position to fire, which was called bringing their broadsides (the fire of all their guns) to bear. The disadvantage while closing was on the attacker, for only his smaller guns were mounted so that they could fire over the bow. But the enemy's guns, mounted to fire at right angles to the ship, could rake the attackers from stem to stern as they approached and frequently damaged their rigging before they had gotten into line to fight. Once the line was formed again, the usual procedure was to concentrate on the ship directly opposite one's own in the line, exchanging broadsides as long as the two were within range, and this might be for several hours.

British captains generally preferred the windward position, which gave them control of when and where the battle would be joined and also had the advantage that the smoke from the guns of both ships would be blown into the faces of the gunners of the ships of the leeward (pronounced loo'-w'd) line. A third advantage was that the wind caused the ships of the other line to heel (or lean) away from his ships, so that a large area of their bottoms was out of water, presenting a vulnerable target. British ships scored well on hitting their enemies' hulls.

The French, less confident in their ability, usually preferred to fight from the leeward position, and it had its advantages. In the first place, although the French ships could not readily head upwind to close with their opponents, they could always head away from the wind and sail out of range of the attacking vessels, breaking off the action when they had had enough. Since their sides were presented to the enemy as his ships closed, they could fire when his ships came within range, raking them as they approached line abreast, or anticipating their fire if they approached from another angle. The ships of the leeward line had less opportunity to damage the enemy's hulls below the water line, since his ships were heeled toward them, but they could more readily damage the rigging and seriously interfere with his ability to sail.

Of the other types of ships that traveled with the ships of the line or operated independently or in small squadrons, most important were the frigates. These smaller square-rigged, three-masted vessels carried lighter guns on one or two gun decks. They were faster and more nimble than the big ships, and they were often used as scouts or messengers. On their own they had a good record of capturing small warships and lightly armed merchant vessels. They usually were rated between twenty and forty-four guns. Next smaller were the sloops of war. John Paul Jones's *Ranger* was one of these. She had three masts and was square-rigged. About a hundred and ten feet in total length (overall), she was designed to carry twenty 9-pounder guns. Smaller still were the single-masted sloops, like Jones's *Providence*. She was about seventy feet long and carried a huge, gaff-rigged fore-and-aft mainsail (that is, a rectangular sail with a spar or boom at the top and bottom, rigged parallel with the keel rather than at right angles to it), and a square topsail, plus a number of jibs. Brigs, brigantines, snows, ketches, and numerous variations also fought under naval ensigns or in the lucrative role of privateer.

Guns

Ships' guns were rated by the weight of the shot they fired, usually 9, 12, 18, or 24 pounds. There were also 32- and 42-pounders, and the short carronade that was introduced in British ships in 1779 could fire a shot as heavy as 68 pounds. Grape, canister, bar, chain, and other types of shot were fired on occasion, but the most common broadside was a hail of round cannonballs.

The heaviest of a ship's guns were normally mounted on the lowest gun deck for reasons of ballast. Guns were divided evenly between the two sides of a vessel and securely fastened in place when not in use. Doors covered the gun ports to keep out spray and rain when the ship was not engaged. The guns were mounted on carriages with small, solid wheels so that they could be run out through the ports to fire and run back in for loading or when the ship was under way. They could be shifted slightly to right or left and raised or depressed, but there was no aiming device, except occasionally a notch in the muzzle. The gun captain aimed his gun as best he could by peering through the smoke and trying to time the firing with the roll or pitch of BUthe ship. Accuracy was not an outstanding feature of naval gunfire; when achieved, it conferred a distinct advantage.

The first broadside, that is, the firing of the guns on the side of the ship that faced the enemy, was generally fired by all guns in unison on command. Thereafter guns were loaded and fired as fast as their crews could sponge out the barrels to remove any sparks or debris left from the previous round, ram down the muzzle a cartridge of powder wrapped in cloth, the shot, and a wad of rope yarn to hold it all in place, insert a priming iron and a quill filled with fine powder mixed with wine (or simply a bit of loose powder) in the touchhole on the top of the gun, then light it with a bit of cotton wick soaked in some flammable substance such as lye. Despite the inaccuracy, at close range the shots could be deadly and effective at splintering wood in rigging, deck, or hull.

While the bigger guns were firing broadsides, on the poop and quarter decks smaller guns were also firing. When the ships were in pistol range marines stationed on deck and in the rigging added to the firepower by shooting their muskets at whoever might be visible on the enemy deck and by lobbing grenades when opportunity offered.

The Men

Life on a ship in the eighteenth century, whether a merchant ship or a warship, was rough and often miserable. Some compensation was provided by the chance to travel to foreign shores and to win some of the prize money parceled out to the crew that was lucky enough to participate in the capture of an enemy vessel. But few volunteered for life in the navy, probably only 15 percent of the seamen on British ships. The remainder of the crew was not obtained through regular conscription in Britain but through a practice known as impressment, used by merchantmen as well as the British navy. Press gangs roamed the waterfront, seizing men to serve the British crown. Seamen much preferred the slightly better living conditions aboard commercial vessels, with the less brutal discipline and higher pay. Since men trained in the merchant fleet were most useful aboard a naval vessel they were a prime target for the naval press gangs.

The French had a system of conscription that provided men as required, but not necessarily much more willingly. BUOtherwise there was not much to choose among the various navies. All ships were crowded because of the necessity of maintaining crews to handle both ships and guns. Food was generally bad and deteriorated as weeks and months went by without replenishment. Discipline was often maintained by the generous use of the cat-o'-nine-tails on the laggard's back.

Common enemy to all the navies was disease—particularly smallpox, scurvy, and yellow fever. Sanitation was universally poor to nonexistent. In the crowded, dark, damp interiors of the ships, little could be done to prevent the spread of contagious diseases once they appeared. Few crews suffered as badly, however, as those of the Spanish fleet that arrived in the West Indies in 1780 with thousands sick and thousands more dead before they reached port.

The importance of fresh fruits and vegetables to ward off the menace of scurvy had not yet been universally recognized by the 1770s. Although there were exceptional captains who believed in it and provided fresh goods whenever possible, the daily ration of lime juice had not yet made "limeys" of the British seamen.

Bibliography

Adams, John. *The Works of John Adams, with a Life of the Author.* Edited by Charles Francis Adams. 10 vols. Boston: Little, Brown, 1856. Volume 7 has papers for the period covered by this book.

Alden, John R. *A History of the American Revolution.* New York: Alfred A. Knopf (Borzoi), 1969. A highly regarded, relatively recent general history of the Revolution.

Allen, Gardner W. *A Naval History of the American Revolution.* 2 vols. 1913. Reprint. New York: Russell & Russell, 1962.

Arendt, Hannah. *On Revolution.* New York: Viking Press (Viking Compass edition), 1965. A brilliant book, some of whose ideas are reflected in Chapter 2 of this book, although Arendt's view that the American Revolution was basically a "turning back," or restoration, is rejected.

Augur, Helen. *The Secret War of Independence.* New York: Duell, Sloan and Pearce, 1955. An excellent work concentrating on the procurement of supplies by the American patriots. Based on manuscript sources, it presents much new material and provocative interpretation.

Bailyn, Bernard, ed. *Pamphlets of the American Revolution, 1750-1776.* Vol. 1, 1750-1765. Cambridge, Mass.: Harvard University Press (Belknap Press), 1965. The heart of the book is the brilliant "General Introduction," which presents a fresh view of the development of the Revolution synthesized from concepts that emerged from Bailyn's study of the pamphlets.

Balch, Thomas. *The French in America during the War of Independence of the United States, 1777-1783.* Translated by Edwin Swift Balch and Elise Willing Balch. Vol. 2. Philadelphia: Porter & Coates, 1895. Gives lists of French regiments that served in America, with officer rosters and other detailed information.

Barrow, Thomas C. *Trade and Empire: The British Customs Service in Colonial America, 1660-1775.* Cambridge, Mass.: Harvard University Press, 1967. Presents the British imperial point of view on customs reform efforts—some of which were seen as "taxation without representation" by colonial leaders.

Beaumarchais, Pierre-Augustin Caron de. *The Barber of Seville, or the Useless Precaution*. Translated and edited by Brobury Pearce BUEllis. New York: Appleton-Century-Crofts, 1966.

Bemis, Samuel Flagg. *The Diplomacy of the American Revolution*. New York: D. Appleton-Century, 1935. A dated, moralistic tone does not detract from this book's fine scholarship, documented detail, and clear explanations of complex matters.

Bonsal, Stephen. *When the French Were Here: A Narrative of the Sojourn of the French Forces in America, and of Their Contribution to the Yorktown Campaign*. Garden City, N.Y.: Doubleday, Doran and Company, 1945. Deals only with Rochambeau's forces. Lively book by a journalist, with some documentation, no bibliography.

Boxer, C. R. *The Dutch Seaborne Empire: 1600-1800*. The History of Human Society, edited by J. H. Plumb. New York: Alfred A. Knopf, 1965.

Brown, Wallace. *The King's Friends: The Composition and Motives of the American Loyalist Claimants*. Providence, R. I.: Brown University Press, 1965.

Caughey, John Walton. *Bernardo de Gálvez in Louisiana, 1776-1783*. Berkeley: University of California Press, 1934. A very useful study based on Spanish primary sources.

Clowes, William Laird. *The Royal Navy: A History, from the Earliest Times to the Present*. 7 vols. London, 1897-1903. Reprint. New York: AMS Press, 1966. Ch. 31, Vol. 3, on the major naval operations of the Revolutionary War, is by A. T. Mahan and includes the fullest and most authoritative treatment available of naval actions involving European nations only. Ch. 32, Vol. 4, by H. W. Wilson, covers minor naval operations.

Coggins, Jack. *Ships and Seamen of the American Revolution*. Harrisburg, Pa.: Stackpole Books, 1969. Well-researched, clearly presented material with very helpful illustrations and diagrams.

Cox, Cynthia. *The Real Figaro: The Extraordinary Career of Caron de Beaumarchais*. London: Longmans, Green, 1962.

Crary, Catherine S., ed. *The Price of Loyalty: Tory Writings from the Revolutionary Era*. New York: McGraw-Hill, 1973.

Dodwell, H. H. *The Cambridge History of India*. Vol. 5, *British India, 1497-1858*. Cambridge: Cambridge University Press, 1968.

Dupuy, R. Ernest, and Trevor N. Dupuy. *The Compact History of the Revolutionary War*. New York: Hawthorn, 1963.

———. *Encyclopedia of Military History, from 3500 B.C. to the Present*. New York: Harper & Row, 1970.

———. *An Outline History of the American Revolution*. New York: Harper & Row, 1975. Includes summaries of all major engagements and, especially useful for this volume, brief descriptions of the various forces engaged, with statistics where these are available.

Dupuy, Trevor Nevitt. *The Military Life of Frederick the Great of Prussia*.

New York: Franklin Watts, 1969. Contains a succinct BUdescription and analysis of the Prussian organizational and tactical principles von Steuben brought to the Continental Army.

Dupuy, Trevor N., and Gay M. Hammerman. *People and Events of the American Revolution*. New York: R. R. Bowker; and Dunn Loring, Va.: T. N. Dupuy Associates, 1974.

Dupuy, Trevor N., and Grace P. Hayes. *The Military History of Revolutionary War Naval Battles*. New York: Franklin Watts, 1970.

Edler, Friedrich. *The Dutch Republic and the American Revolution*. Baltimore, 1911 Reprint. New York: A.M.S. Press, 1971.

Edwardes, Michael. *A History of India*. New York: Farrar, Straus and Cudahy, 1961.

Freeman, Douglas Southall. *George Washington: A Biography*. Vol. 4, *Leader of the Revolution*. Vol. 5, *Victory with the Help of France*. New York: Charles Scribner's Sons, 1951, 1952. Detailed, authoritative, indispensable.

Gardner, Brian. *The East India Company*. New York: McCall, 1971. A very readable account of the complicated operations of this immensely powerful institution.

Gay, Peter. *The Enlightenment*. Vol. 1, *The Rise of Modern Paganism*. New York: Alfred A. Knopf, 1966. The eighteenth-century intellectual background from a fresh and convincing point of view, in great richness of masterfully researched

Gipson, Lawrence Henry. *The British Empire before the American Revolution*. 15 vols. New York: Alfred A. Knopf, 1936-1970. Gipson first used the phrase "the Great War for the Empire" for the Seven Years' War.

Gottschalk, Louis. *Lafayette Comes to America*. 2nd impression, with corrections. Chicago: University of Chicago Press, 1965. This and the following two volumes are thorough scholarly works, with all the problems explored, and are carefully documented.

————. *Lafayette Joins the American Army*. 2nd impression with corrections. Chicago: University of Chicago Press, 1965.

————. *Lafayette and the Close of the American Revolution*. 2nd impression with corrections. Chicago: University of Chicago Press, 1965.

Gray, L. C. "The Market Surplus Problems of Colonial Tobacco." *Essays in American Colonial History*. Edited by Paul Goodman. New York: Holt, Rinehart and Winston, 1967.

Hayavadana, Rao C. *History of Mysore, 1399-1799*. 3 vols. Bangalore, India: Government Press, 1945-1946. Volume 2 covers the period 1704-1766; Volume 3, 1766-1799.

James, W. M. *The British Navy in Adversity: A Study of the War of American Independence*. 1926. Reprint. New York: Russell & Russell, 1970. Well written; useful.

Jameson, J. Franklin. "St. Eustatius in the American Revolution." *American Historical Review*. Vol. 8 (1903), pp. 683-708. Based on

material in Dutch archives, this paper is packed with
information.

Jensen, Merrill. *The Founding of a Nation: A History of the American
Revolution, 1763-1776.* London: Oxford University Press, 1968.
Very solid, invaluable guide to these years of the real
Revolution.

Koven, Mrs. Reginald de. *The Life and Letters of John Paul Jones.* 2 vols.
New York: Scribner's, 1913.

Lacour-Gayet, Georges. *La Marine militaire de la France sous le règne de
Louis XVI.* Paris: H. Champion, 1905.

Larrabee, Harold A. *Decision on the Chesapeake.* New York: Clarkson N.
Potter, 1964.

Lewis, Michael. *The Navy of Britain: A Historical Portrait.* London:
George Allen and Unwin, 1948.

Lindsay, J. O., ed. *The Old Regime, 1713-63.* Vol. 7 of *The New Cambridge Modern History.* Cambridge: Cambridge University Press,
1957.

Lowell, Edward J. *The Hessians and the Other German Auxiliaries of Great
Britain in the Revolutionary War.* 1884. Reprint. Williamstown,
Mass.: Corner House Publishers, 1970. A scholarly, gracefully
written, very useful book.

Mahan, Alfred Thayer. *The Influence of Sea Power upon History, 1660-
1783.* 5th ed. Boston: Little, Brown, and Company, 1894. This
book has influenced generations of naval officers since its first
appearance. Mahan also contributed the chapter for this period
to Clowes, *The Royal Navy,* q.v.

Majumdar, R. C.; H. C. Raychaudhuri; and Kalikinkar Datta. *An
Advanced History of India.* 2nd ed., reprinted, with corrections.
New York: St. Martin's Press, 1965.

Marcus. G. J. *A Naval History of England.* Vol. 1, *The Formative
Centuries.* Boston: Little, Brown (Atlantic Monthly Press),
1961.

Masselman, George. *The Cradle of Colonialism.* New Haven, Conn.:
Yale University Press, 1963. Deals with Dutch colonialism in
Southeast Asia.

Miller, Nathan. *Sea of Glory: The Continental Navy Fights for Independence.* New York: David McKay, 1974. Chapter 19, "Revolution
Becomes World War," gives some helpful background.

Morgan, Edmund S., ed. *The American Revolution: Two Centuries of
Interpretation.* Englewood Cliffs, N. J.: Prentice-Hall (Spec-
trum), 1965. Reasons for the coming of the Revolution as seen
by historians ever since it occurred.

Morison, Samuel Eliot. *John Paul Jones: A Sailor's Biography.* Boston:
Little, Brown (Atlantic Monthly Press), 1959. A scholarly yarn
by a great storyteller.

Morris, Richard B. *The Peacemakers: The Great Powers and American
Independence.* New York: Harper & Row (Harper Torchbooks),

1965. Solid but lively, this is an exhaustively researched BUbook on the peace negotiations.

FMunro, Innes. *A Narrative of the Military Operations on the Coromandel Coast against the Combined Forces of the French, Dutch, and Hyder Ally Cawn from the year 1780 to the Peace in 1784 in a Series of Letters*. London, T. Bensley and G. Nicol, 1789. The author was a captain in the 73rd Regiment of Highlanders.

Parkman, Francis. *Montcalm and Wolfe*. 1884. Reprint. New York: Crowell-Collier (Collier Books), 1962.

Patterson, A. Temple. *The Other Armada: The Franco-Spanish Attempt to Invade Britain in 1779*: Manchester University Press, 1960.

Paullin, Charles Oscar. *The Navy of the American Revolution: Its Administration, Its Policy, and Its Achievements*. 1906. Reprint. New York: Haskell House Publishers, 1971.

Perkins, James Breck. *France in the American Revolution*. 1906. Reprint. Williamstown, Mass.: Corner House Publishers, 1970.

Peterson, Harold L. *Arms and Armor in Colonial America*, 1526-1783. New York: Bramhall House, 1956.

Potter, E. B. *The United States and World Sea Power*. Englewood Cliffs, N. J.: Prentice-Hall, 1955.

Pratt, Fletcher. *The Compact History of the United States Navy*. 3rd edition, revised by Cdr. Hartley E. Howe. New York: Hawthorn Books, 1967.

Reynolds, Clark G. *Command of the Sea: The History and Strategy of Maritime Empires*. New York: William Morrow, 1974.

Rice, Howard C., Jr., and Anne S. K. Brown, translators and editors. *The American Campaigns of Rochambeau's Army, 1780, 1781, 1782, 1783*. 2 vols. Princeton, N. J.: Princeton University Press, and Providence, R. I.: Brown University Press, 1972. Makes available three journals of the campaigns, plus Berthier's exquisite maps of the march to Yorktown, reproduced in color.

Rodney, George, Lord. *Letter-Books and Order-Book of George, Lord Rodney, Admiral of the White Squadron*. Volume 1 includes letter books for July 6, 1780 to February 4, 1781, and December 10, 1781 to September 21, 1782. Printed for the Naval Historical Society by the New York Historical Society. New York, 1932.

Sachs, William S., and Ari Hoogenboom. *The Enterprising Colonials: Society on the Eve of the Revolution*. Chicago: Argonaut, 1965. An economic history, with the emphasis on colonial business.

Schlesinger, Arthur M. *The Colonial Merchants and the American Revolution, 1763-1776*. 1917. Reprint. New York: Frederick Ungar, 1957. Thorough and comprehensive. Its basic thesis, that the colonial merchants initiated the protest movement against taxation measures and then withdrew as the radicals took over, has come under thoughtful criticism, notably from Merrill Jensen.

Sheppard, E. W. *Coote Bahadur: A Life of Lieutenant-General Sir Eyre Coote, K. B.* London, W. Lavie, 1956.

Sheridan, Richard. "The Molasses Act and the Market Strategy of the British Planters." *Essays in American Colonial History*. Edited by Paul Goodman. New York: Holt, Rinehart and Winston, 1967.

Sosin, Jack M. *The Revolutionary Frontier, 1763-1783*. New York: Holt, Rinehart and Winston, 1967. A fine study on its subject, with brief mention of Spanish raids and conquests, and some useful bibliography.

Stinchcombe, William C. *The American Revolution and the French Alliance*. Syracuse, N. Y.: Syracuse University Press, 1969. Stresses diplomatic and public opinion aspects of alliance. Excellent material on press and clergy attitudes.

Stourzh, Gerald. *Benjamin Franklin and American Foreign Policy*. 2nd ed. Chicago: University of Chicago Press, 1969.

Thomson, Buchanan Parker. *La Ayuda española en la guerra de la independencia norteamericana*. Madrid: Ediciones Cultura Hispanica, 1967.

Troude, U. *Batailles navales de la France*. Paris, Challanel ainé, 1867.

U.S. Senate. *Rochambeau: A Commemoration by the Congress of the United States of America of the Services of the French Auxiliary Forces in the War of Independence*. Prepared by DeB. Randolph Keim. 59th Congress, 1st session, 1907. Detailed information on French units in the Revolutionary War.

Whitridge, Arnold. *Rochambeau*. New York: Macmillan, 1958.

Wilkinson, Spencer. *From Cromwell to Wellington: Twelve Soldiers*. London, 1899. Pages 213-250 deal with Sir Eyre Coote.

Wilks, Lt. Col. Mark. *Historical Sketches of the South of India*. 2 vols. 1810. Reprint. Mysore Government Branch Press, 1932. Volumes of over 800 pages each. Detailed maps. Author was political resident at Mysore.

Index

INVENTORY 1983